TIDES
of WAR

TIDES of WAR

A NOVEL OF THE AMERICAN CIVIL WAR
BY LEBRON MATTHEWS

Deeds Publishing, Atlanta

Copyright © 2014 - E. LeBron Matthews

ALL RIGHTS RESERVED - No part of this book may be reproduced in any form or by any electronic or mechanical means, including information storage and retrieval systems, without permission in writing from the author, except by a reviewer who may quote brief passages in a review.

Published by Deeds Publishing
Marietta, GA
www.deedspublishing.com

Printed in The United States of America

Library of Congress Cataloging-in-Publications Data is available upon request.

ISBN 978-1-941165-21-8

Books are available in quantity for promotional or premium use. For information, write Deeds Publishing, PO Box 682212, Marietta, GA 30068 or info@deedspublishing.com.

First Edition, 2014

10 9 8 7 6 5 4 3 2 1

For my wonderful wife, Pamela
Sharing life with her is true joy (Prov. 5:18)

AUTHOR'S NOTE

Tides of War IS A WORK OF FICTION. WHILE THE PRIMARY characters and some locations are products of the author's imagination, the story is integrated into actual events that occurred during the American Civil War. Consequently, many secondary characters, locations, and publications represent historical figures, places, and documents, respectively. Misspellings and mistakes in punctuation and grammar from quoted material have been retained for authenticity. Similarly, misspellings, mistakes in punctuation, and poor grammar have been incorporated into fictitious letters in order to maintain nineteenth-century style and flavor. Dialogue of actual people is based upon historical records of the particular individual and information about his or her geographic and social background. Except for the introduction of fictitious characters, the Battles of Sharpsburg (Antietam), Gettysburg, Chickamauga, Griswoldville, and Columbus are described as they actually transpired. Medicine, transportation, sexual mores, and religious ideology are true to the period.

PROLOGUE

WAR DESTROYS HUMAN CONTENTMENT LIKE OCEAN waves wash away sandcastles on a beach. The lives of individuals caught in its shifting tides cannot persist unaltered. Some are hit by its full ferocity and swept away as the tide recedes. Others are submerged in rising water, but when the tide ebbs, a misshapen pile of sand remains. All of those who feel its fury are forever changed by the experience. In 1861, a tsunami hit the United States. Although the exact number remains undetermined, as many as four million men took up arms to fight in the Civil War. They never would be the same. Nor would the families they left behind.

CHAPTER ONE
"Georgia Free!"

THE SILENCE WAS PUZZLING. FOR TWO DAYS, THE terrible roar of battle along Chickamauga Creek had pounded in Father's eardrums. Then all was inaudible. Blackness engulfed the panorama, and he slumped to the ground. The vanquished light slowly returned in a swirling palette of indistinct shapes. Strange humming sounds penetrated the quietness. Father gradually focused his eyes. He gazed up into the forest canopy. Rays of sunlight peeked through the leaves. Questions raced through his mind. *What happened? Stupid, you were shot. Did they kill me? No, I must be alive…but I don't feel anything. Where was I hit? Oh Lord, please don't let it be in the belly.* The notion of being shot in the abdomen terrified him. Stomach wounds typically were fatal. Death came slowly, and unbearable pain tortured the victim during his final hours. Father had witnessed too many soldiers die in agony to ignore the prospect of this gruesome fate. Fear prompted action. He ripped open his jacket and pants. His hands rapidly explored his abdomen. When he found no wound, hope surged through his numb body.

A warm liquid burned Father's left eye. His right hand instinctively reached up and wiped it away. The fluid stuck to his thumb and the palm of his hand. Its deep red color disclosed a head wound. He felt his scalp and discovered a gash on his forehead just above the hairline. Father had no idea how long he had been unconscious, but he gradually became aware that the line of battle had disappeared, and with it, his comrades in the Columbus Guards. Suddenly Father felt intense loneliness. *I must find them,* he decided. He tried to figure out what day it was and calculated that it must be September 20, 1863. How ironic, he thought, to be fighting on a Sunday, God's day of rest. He rolled over and struggled to get up. He collapsed after raising his torso only a few inches.

Exhausted by this feeble effort, Father lay still and stared into the trampled underbrush. Someone was looking back at him! The stranger wore a faded blue woolen jacket…a Federal soldier. Concentrating on the pale face, Father realized the man was dead. *Somebody's darling.* All enmity vanished. Then another horrifying possibility occurred to Father. *What if the regiment retreated? I had rather die than be taken prisoner. I must get out of here.* Confederate soldiers had heard horror tales about the Yankees' treatment of prisoners. Most preferred dying on the battlefield to freezing at Chicago's Camp Douglas or starving to death in Elmira, New York.

Father's real name was Edwin Anderson. "Father" was a nickname his younger comrades had bestowed upon him. At thirty-six, he was at least ten years older than most of the men in his company. Many of them had never been away from home until the war. In the army camps of northern Virginia, Edwin had instinctively become a surrogate parent for these boys.

Now, lying helpless in the underbrush, the shifting tides of war rolled in and carried "Father" Edwin Anderson's mind back to recollections of home. It had been less than three years, but it seemed like an eternity. Memories of a more naïve time replaced the thoughts about his uncertain future.

*　*　*

The news spread like wildfire. Georgia had seceded! The people of Columbus were not surprised by the decision. South Carolina, Florida, Alabama, and Mississippi had seceded before the members of Georgia's secession convention gathered in Milledgeville, the state capital. A total of 208 delegates voted in favor of leaving the Union. Only eighty-nine cast a nay vote. Most of the city's population had lived their entire lives as citizens of the United States of America. In this single act, 208 men—including Columbus's favorite son, Henry L. Benning—terminated their citizenship. This radical break with past history had long been anticipated by some Georgians. Now it had become reality for every Georgian. Georgia was an independent country. Excitement in the streets reached a fever pitch and exploded! Church bells pealed out the glorious news. Intoxicated with the significance of the tidings, militia companies fired volley after volley in salute. The familiar stars and stripes vanished from sight, replaced by blue flags emblazoned with a single white star. Citizens of the new republic gathered intuitively to celebrate. People did not fully understand the implications of the convention's decision, but everyone knew it was historically momentous.

Conversations on every street corner compared the action to that which an earlier generation had taken on July 4, 1776. The present generation impulsively insisted that today was a second Independence Day. Edwin Anderson stared at a copy of the *Daily Times*. The newspaper had been the voice of the secession movement in Columbus. Below the date, January 19, 1861, the headline expressed the editors' satisfaction. "Ordinance Passed! Georgia Free! The Empire State Itself Again!" The *Times*'s rival, the *Daily Enquirer*, had opposed secession, but now it too encouraged its readers to participate in the festivities. Although popular opinion within the state previously had been divided somewhat equally on the issue, secessionist candidates for delegates to the convention had won the vast majority of local elections. The electorate having spoken, the time for discord was over. Henceforth, except for a few individuals such as Colonel Randolph L. Mott in Columbus, the people of Georgia speedily united under the new circumstance.

The political opinions of the two local papers reflected emotions within Edwin's family. He had taken a cooperationist stance and opposed secession in the recent debates. His father-in-law, James Lewis, owned a small plantation outside of town and was a staunch secessionist. Edwin was a Baptist minister, but unlike most of his peers, had never been able to reconcile slavery with his Christian beliefs. As a boy, he had witnessed the removal of the Cherokee Indians from the north Georgia hills where he had grown up. The sight of neighbors being evicted from their houses simply because of their race still haunted him. He was deeply troubled by the biblical arguments his peers used to justify slavery.

Southern preachers self-righteously claimed that God was punishing the black race. They would read from Genesis 9:25 and boldly declare that slaves were cursed descendants of Ham. *People who spout scripture verses ought to read them first*, Edwin thought. *The text of Genesis 9:25—"And he said, 'Cursed be Canaan; a servant of servants shall he be unto his brethren'"—meant that Noah cursed Canaan, not his father Ham. The biblical genealogy in Genesis 10 implied the Africans were descendants of Cush, not Canaan. And even if they were, most folks seemed to overlook the word 'brethren' in the verse. It sure didn't fit the popular notion that black people were less human than white people. Too many preachers were building a reputation by telling people what they wanted to hear instead of what the Bible actually said.* Edwin shuddered at what the consequences of such behavior might be. But the day's news suggested he might soon find out.

Edwin mounted his chestnut-colored mare and rode toward his father-in-law's plantation to tell him the news. He could see the Wynns Hill section of town with its white-columned houses when he turned left on Mercer. The dirt road curved sharply to the east and skirted the city cemetery. The landscape turned rural as the road snaked its way toward Macon. The ride gave Edwin ample time to reflect. The more he considered his interpretation of the verse in Genesis, the angrier he became. But those thoughts gave way to apprehension. He didn't agree with the politicians any more than he did with the preachers. Did they really imagine secession would not lead to war? If war did come, what was his duty? Enlist? He had a family and was pastor of a small church. So should he stay home? He had been to war once and the experience still haunted his dreams.

Later that evening, Edwin and his wife, Ann, rode back into town for the grand celebration. The couple seemed oblivious to the cold night air. The sense of experiencing a historic moment strangely warmed the soul. Due to its significance, they permitted their two small children to accompany them to the night's festivities. The city's entire populace was wild with enthusiasm. Even slaves were caught up in the mania. Earlier, when Edwin had left his father-in-law's house, Obadiah, an old black slave with several teeth missing asked, "Marse Anderson, it be true dat we free?"

The question was so bizarre that Edwin was too stunned to reply. *If anything*, he thought to himself, *you are further from freedom than ever.* Edwin stared inquisitively until finally he realized that Obadiah considered himself a Georgian, too. He had lived his entire life on that plantation and it was his home. "Yes, Obadiah, Georgia has declared her independence," he replied and then headed home to pick up Ann.

At precisely eight o'clock, five guns announced the start of festivities. Most of the town's clergy joined the mayor and city council as they paraded through the streets. Edwin declined their invitation to participate. Standing on the sidewalk, he wondered if he had made a mistake. A deep voice interrupted this introspection. Richard Brenton was calling Edwin's name. Richard and Polly Brenton were his and Ann's closest friends in Columbus.

Polite society shunned Polly. Her first husband had been a scoundrel. Ann said that he had beaten Polly. Most people only knew that she had left him. The so-called good Christian folk of Columbus could never forgive her for the separation. Edwin wondered what had really happened. He looked down into Polly's face. Two large green eyes punctuated the freckled complexion of its oval shape. The evening breeze gently blew a strand of Polly's curly red hair across her forehead. She reached up and instinctively pushed it behind her ear. She and Ann were so different and yet so much alike. Ann's family enjoyed the prestige of the cotton aristocracy, and she was the epitome of the genteel southern lady. Like many girls of her social class, she had lived a sequestered existence. Consequently, she often seemed rather naïve about life. Polly's past and the isolation society had imposed upon her had made her self-reliant and skeptical. Yet the two had become inseparable. During the bitter struggles after her divorce, Polly had turned to Ann for comfort and support. Ann, who was older than Polly, was compassionate and caring. So despite the rebukes of her peers, Ann welcomed Polly into her life. Their relationship formed the basis for Edwin and Richard's friendship.

Richard Brenton, a zealous secessionist, worked as a bank clerk in Columbus. In the early days of the impending crisis, Edwin and Richard had fiercely debated the merits of secession. However, these arguments had placed a strain on their relationship, so the two men had reached an armistice. Both acknowledged that, in the end, they would abide by whatever decision Georgia made. Therefore neither would need to compromise his principles. They agreed that maintaining their friendship was more important than scoring points over politics.

As the two couples peered down the street, the parade came into view. Richard could not resist commenting on the apparent success of his political position. "I told you that this would be a grand day!" he quipped. Edwin would never give Richard the satisfaction of knowing it, but the sight had stirred his patriotism for their native state. As the Columbus Guards passed by, emotion overwhelmed him. He had served in the elite militia company in Mexico. Although he no longer was an active member, his connection to the unit remained strong. During the last few years, Captain Paul Semmes had made the Columbus Guards the finest company in the South. Their discipline showed in their synchronized movements as they marched down Broad Street. Their new uniforms intensified their martial appearance. The jacket, bright red with buff trim, imitated the latest European military fashion. The trousers were dark blue with a single red stripe. As they passed out of sight, Edwin unexpectedly yearned to be with them once more. But what would Ann say? *No, it's just the excitement of the moment*, he thought. *It will go away. Besides I'm too old to be a soldier.*

* * *

By the end of January, the parade of southern states leaving the Union had reached seven. In February, a convention of seceded states met in Montgomery, Alabama. On February 8, they adopted a new constitution and created the Confederate States of America. That night, Mississippi's delegation went to work to get support for Jefferson Davis to become the new nation's first president. Georgia's delegation decided to nominate favorite son

Robert Augustus Toombs. Toombs had served in the state legislature, the United States House of Representatives, and the United States Senate. Toombs might have been elected if the Georgians had acted earlier, but now it was too late. Three state delegations already were committed to Davis. Desiring harmony, Toombs refused to allow his name to be placed in nomination unless every state delegation voted for him. Therefore his name was withdrawn from consideration and Jefferson Davis was elected unanimously. Toombs became Secretary of State, but his relationship with Davis quickly soured. He resigned the office and secured an appointment as a brigadier general in the army.

* * *

As the days passed, Edwin Anderson could not erase the sight of those splendid soldiers in the Columbus Guards from his mind. He knew many of them personally. Reverend DeVotie, the distinguished pastor of Columbus Baptist Church, was the unit's unofficial chaplain. His son marched in their ranks. Several other members were related to Reverend Slade, the previous pastor of the church. Edwin counted both pastors as personal friends.

During the second week in February, Edwin rode back into town to attend to some financial business. He tied his horse to a hitching post and went into the Bank of Columbus on Broad Street. Closing the door behind him, he rubbed his numb hands together. The trip had been cold and the heated room felt good. He started towards Richard's desk but saw John Lindsay seated there. The cocky Lindsay was a diminutive red-haired man who had married Reverend Slade's daughter. It was strange seeing him and Richard together. Lindsay's red hair always reminded Edwin of Polly. He paused to let Lindsay finish his transaction.

"Ed," Richard shouted. "Come over here. We've got fabulous news!"

The sound of his voice echoed off the plaster walls and embarrassed Edwin. He observed the bank president, William Young, glance curtly at Richard. Hoping to avoid any additional attention, Edwin rushed over to the two excited men.

"Good afternoon, Richard. John. What's the explanation for such noisy exhilaration today?"

"I joined the Columbus Guards!" answered Richard. "We're going to Montgomery to help swear in President Davis. Why don't you go with us?"

"Richard, be realistic. I have a wife and two children. Besides, what would Deacon Archibald say about his pastor joining the army?"

The picture of the sour-faced deacon's reaction to such a possibility brought an unrestrained chuckle to both men. The deacon frequently chided Edwin over his friendship with Richard. He insisted that it was improper for a minister of the gospel to associate with a man married to "that red-headed Jezebel." Richard would have challenged any other man to a duel for describing his wife in such offensive language, but the emaciated deacon's frustration over Edwin's refusal to listen provided both men a mischievous object of delight, so Richard ignored the deacon's insults.

"Yeah, might shock the old geezer so much he couldn't talk. Then who would tell you what a preacher is supposed to do?"

"Now Richard, the deacon is only trying to…"

"Run the church," interrupted Richard.

"No, he means well. He loves the Lord and wants everything to be just right. He just doesn't always understand what the right thing really is. I guess that is why God made me pastor of our church. So I guess the deacon needs me more than the army."

The humor of all this was not lost on John Lindsay. He grinned and added, "Ed, that might change. The Yankees may not let us go without a fight."

"You don't honestly think that there will be a war, do you, John?" asked Richard.

"Not when they hear that they will have to fight the two of you," Edwin answered. "I need to get back home. Ann has been feeling poorly and she needs me to care for Charlotte and James. Enjoy the trip to Montgomery."

Edwin turned to leave. He almost was out the door when he suddenly realized that in his embarrassment over Richard and Lindsay's hullabaloo, he had failed to transact his banking business. Quickly he turned back and said, "Mr. Brenton," in an official voice. President Young looked up warily. "I almost forgot. I also have a deposit for my personal account."

"I'll be happy to be of service, Reverend Anderson," replied Richard in an equally professional tone. "Come, have a seat."

Lindsay excused himself and headed for the door. He grinned sheepishly as he and Edwin passed each other. Satisfied that Richard was engaged in bank affairs, Young went back to his paperwork.

The sun had disappeared by the time Edwin rode up to his modest wood frame house a few miles outside of town. An eerie red glow silhouetted him against the western sky as he came over the hill. Ann breathed a sigh of relief. A severe headache made activity difficult. Charlotte was nine years old. She tried to assist her mother by watching her baby brother. James was only four. He sensed that his sister was trying to keep him away from his mother and was more determined than ever to gain Mommy's attention. His efforts escalated into noisy confrontations between the two children. Consequently, Ann's head felt as if it would burst. Edwin had only been gone a couple of hours according to the clock on the mantle, but Ann's headache made the time feel closer to a century.

The sound of Edwin's heels on the back porch diverted James's attention, and the little boy scampered down the hallway staircase. He had only progressed halfway down the stairs when Edwin opened the back door. As Edwin removed his hat and coat, the frisky child screamed, "Daddy," and leaped from the stairs. His tiny arms locked around his father's neck. Edwin, with one arm still in his coat sleeve, reacted and caught the boy in midair.

"How's Daddy's little man?"

"Sharlee won't let me see Mommy," James complained in his squeaky voice.

"Aren't you glad to see Daddy?" Edwin asked as he squeezed his young son. "I love my little man."

"Daddy!" screamed Charlotte as she vaulted down the stairs. Edwin shifted James to one arm and lifted his daughter with the other. He kissed her soft cheek affectionately.

Edwin looked up the stairs and caught Ann grinning at her husband and children. Their exhibition of affection seemed to lessen her pain. She deeply loved Edwin. They had married shortly after he returned from the Mexican War. His decision to become a minister only strengthened the relationship. Her own personal commitment to Christ was the only thing in her life more profound than her love for her husband. Looking at the three figures at the bottom of the stairs, she thought, *I am truly blessed. God has given me the perfect family.*

Edwin's turmoil about enlisting equaled Ann's fear that he might join the army. The couple had not yet discussed the matter, but Ann knew her husband. She had seen him staring admiringly at the Columbus Guards on the night Georgia had seceded, and since then, she had often caught him gazing into space. At first she believed he was thinking about Mexico. He never talked about his experiences there, but she knew its ghosts frequently visited him at night. She also sensed the rising tide of patriotism in the area. She prayed that her darling husband would not be swept up in it. Militia units were recruiting new members with a sense of urgency. They were finding no shortage of volunteers. In her mind it all was a formula for her worst nightmare.

Speculation about war with the North punctuated most conversations at church meetings. The consensus of opinion asserted that war was desirable. It would be the only way to teach the North a lesson. Ann thought all of the talk of glory was ridiculous. It was not glory that haunted her husband after Mexico. *Didn't people think about the families that the soldiers left behind?* She hardly could stand Edwin's periodic absences when he traveled to preach a weeklong revival meeting. The prolonged absence that war might bring was unimaginable. Everyone said that any war would be over in less than six months, but she wondered about such rash predictions. *Didn't the Bible say in Ecclesiastes 9:11*, "I returned, and saw under the sun, that the race *is* not to the swift, nor the battle to the strong"? In her heart, Ann knew that a war's outcome could differ from people's predictions.

She felt Edwin's arms reach around and press her against his chest. The security of his embrace chased away her fears. She lifted herself on her toes and kissed him tenderly. "I missed you."

* * *

On February 16, the Columbus Guards left town for the president-elect's inauguration. They had volunteered to be his personal bodyguard. Because of the South's limited rail system, Davis traveled a circuitous route from Mississippi through Tennessee to Atlanta. He went from Atlanta to Opelika, Alabama, and then to Montgomery. The Columbus Guards planned to meet him in Opelika and escort him to the capital. Edwin and Ann came to South Commons to see the company off. A crowd of at least 150 well-wishers already had assembled by the time they arrived. Ann lacked the enthusiasm of those around her. She remembered the agony she felt when Edwin was in Mexico. Despite the rapture all around her, she could not escape the premonition that today's occasion was letting loose a catastrophe.

Richard looked magnificent in his uniform. The tightly fitted jacket accentuated his muscular frame. Polly peered into his deep blue eyes and quivered. She loved him more than life itself. After the failure of her first marriage, most men treated her as if she belonged in a brothel. Not Richard. He made her feel like the Queen of England. He escorted her to the most prestigious social galas. He seemed oblivious to the gossip and stares she elicited. She knew he wasn't. On more than one occasion, he had returned home with cuts and bruises. He always claimed they were from some insignificant accident. She wasn't dumb. No man was that clumsy, especially an athletic man such as Richard.

Amid the martial spectacle of the company's departure, Richard reached out and embraced Polly. He held her tightly and kissed her as if they were alone in their bedroom at night. Such public expressions of affection were scandalous. But then everything about their relationship was considered scandalous. The authoritative voice of Sergeant Allen abruptly terminated their intimate display.

"Columbus Guards! Fall in!"

The soldiers grabbed their rifles and accouterments and formed ranks. Civilians watched with approval as the dispersed soldiers instantly transformed into two straight ranks of military power. Polly's eyes never left Richard. Tears quietly flowed down her cheeks. Ann reached out and slid her hand into Polly's. "He'll be back soon," she whispered.

Captain Semmes swung into his saddle and barked, "Company, right face."

In unison, the entire company pivoted on their heels. The formation transformed itself once more. The two lines suddenly turned into a column, four-men wide, facing Broad Street, Columbus's main street.

"Forward," shouted Semmes.

Non-commissioned officers quickly repeated the command, "Forward!"

"March."

"March!" the sergeants echoed.

In unison, every man lifted his left foot, and the company moved down the street. At St. Clair Street, the column turned right and marched toward the depot. There they boarded the train that would carry them to Opelika.

The sharpness of the company mysteriously reminded Edwin of the camaraderie in Mexico. Over a decade later, he fondly recalled the friendship it fostered. Roswell Ellis was now a lieutenant in the company. Wesley Hodges had been there, too. Suddenly he was peculiarly jealous. He wanted desperately to go with Richard, Roswell, Wesley, and the feisty John Lindsay now. *I belong in the Columbus Guards*, he thought. *Why didn't I listen to Richard that day in the bank?*

"Edwin." Ann's soft voice summoned him back to reality. "Can Polly stay with us until Richard gets back from Montgomery?"

"Of course, dear. You know she can."

The city welcomed home the Columbus Guards with exuberance on February 27, a Wednesday. In Montgomery, the famed militia company had won accolades as the president's bodyguards. Their precision drills had thrilled the crowds in the capital. Praises from Montgomery were published in all the city papers. Edwin had been unable to shake his envy of Richard. He still had not talked to Ann about the possibility of enlisting. Yet deep within him a yearning to participate in the events taking place continued to grow. The ensuing internal strife between this craving and his responsibilities to his family and church dominated his thoughts more and more. Inspirational sermons no longer seemed to matter. He wondered if he was becoming one of those superficial preachers he condemned so strongly in his mind. And although he knew Ann disapproved, he rationalized that enlistment would be caring for his family by defending their freedom.

Later that Wednesday afternoon, the mood in town became more somber. A train arrived in Columbus carrying the body of Reverend N. L. DeVotie. DeVotie was the oldest son of the local Baptist pastor. He had been serving as chaplain of an Alabama company stationed at Fort Morgan in Mobile Bay. The previous Tuesday, DeVotie had slipped on some rocks near a steamboat wharf. The tidal current had pulled him out into the bay where he drowned. His body had not been recovered until Saturday. As the brightly colored locomotive pulled into the station, its whistle's shrill note punctuated the dramatic shift in the atmosphere. The side door on a baggage car directly behind the locomotive slid open and several soldiers piled out. They wore West Point-style shakos with a white feather plume tipped in light blue. Their dark blue frock coats were trimmed in light blue and fastened with a single row of brass buttons in the front. Light blue epaulettes crowned both shoulders. The trousers were cadet gray. These uniforms reminded some folks in Columbus of the United States Army, but the black armbands gave visible proof of their true identity. They silently stood in two lines facing each other.

The Columbus Guards and other militia units from the city had the sorrowful duty of meeting the body. A lieutenant with the Alabamians escorting the body approached Captain Semmes and the elder Reverend DeVotie. He spoke softly to the grieving minister. Then he turned and faced Semmes. The two exchanged military salutes and brief words. The lieutenant returned to the car, and a flag-draped coffin was passed to the waiting soldiers on the ground. The flag was blue and bore the words "INDEPENDENT NOW AND FOREVER" above the goddess Liberty. The soldiers carried the coffin to the DeVotie residence at the corner of St. Clair and Forsyth Streets. Except for the muffled cadence of the drums and the shuffle of soldiers' feet, everything was silent. Business leaders removed their tall beaver hats. Ladies in hoop dresses and slaves in homespun bowed their heads as the procession passed.

Edwin, Ann, and Polly met the funeral procession at the DeVotie house. Polly strained to spot Richard among the red uniforms. Edwin looked at his fellow Baptist pastor and tried to imagine the grief he was feeling. Anguish overwhelmed him as thoughts of losing his own children flashed through his mind. Edwin fluctuated between grief over the hypothetical death of his children and ecstasy from the knowledge they were alive. Ann was even more somber. She wondered how many more flag-draped coffins the future might bring. Visions of Edwin's corpse in one terrified her thereafter. Peace still reigned. But growing militia companies drilled daily on South Commons. People openly talked of war as if it were a scheduled event. In this bellicose atmosphere, could the United States and the new Confederacy avoid a shooting war?

In the weeks that followed the funeral, Ann and Polly confided in each other. Ann discovered that Polly shared similar fears about the future. Ann sensed that Polly's past magnified her worries. Richard had delivered Polly from a bitter existence. Ann had her beloved children if something happened to Edwin. Richard and Polly were childless. Polly had nothing…nothing. Realizing Polly's torment, Ann was more determined than ever to be her friend.

Eventually, Edwin revealed to Ann that in the event of war, he intended to enlist. He was seeking her blessing, but her words of approval were forced. Inside, Ann was angry with her husband. His decision had been reached without consulting her. Yet she and her children would be affected every bit as much as Edwin. While he was gone, she would have to rear the children alone. And the consequences if he were killed were more than she could endure. Normally the two of them discussed decisions of this magnitude before they were finalized. Ann loved Edwin too much to want him to leave. But she respected him too much to insist he stay. Instead, she simply said, "Whatever you think is right." Once the silence on the matter was broken, Ann needed Polly's support as much as Polly needed hers. The strange bond between the two women grew stronger than ever.

Almost two and half months after the younger Reverend DeVotie had been buried, the Andersons rode into town on a Friday morning. The children were spending the day with their grandfather, so the couple looked forward to a day without distraction. Ann wanted to do some shopping, and Edwin had a nine o'clock appointment with Mr. Young at the bank. The ride into town was delightful. The early morning air was crisp and cool, promising to be a typical, beautiful spring day. As the sun rose higher, the air grew warmer. The brilliant aura highlighted the new life that was on display everywhere. Fresh green leaves clothed gnarled oak and stately maple trees. Dogwood limbs flaunted fresh white blooms. Songbirds serenaded each other, oblivious to the shiny black buggy rolling along the dirt road. Edwin and Ann stopped once to admire a doe and her spotted fawns crossing the road. The sight was surely a good omen. Deer were indigenous to the region, but agriculture, especially for raising lucrative cotton, had cleared most of their natural wooded habitat and made them scarce.

Edwin and Ann met Richard and Polly Brenton at Frederick Wilhelm's restaurant on the corner of Randolph and Oglethorpe Streets for breakfast. The two couples chatted about their plans over a hot breakfast of ham and eggs, homemade biscuits, and grits. Ann intended to check on the dress Mrs. Dessau was making for her. Polly suggested they also go to Brands and Korner to check out the latest sheet music.

Ann smiled and added, "Then let's visit Dillingham and Denson. James Denson told my father that they just got in some new Persian rugs."

Edwin knew Ann missed the lifestyle she once lived. Her family was not the wealthiest in Muscogee County, but life at Stillwater, her father's plantation, remained far more luxurious than a rural Baptist pastor could offer. Still, Ann never complained. Whenever Edwin mentioned the subject, she always insisted his love was all the riches she ever needed. Even so, Edwin yearned to provide her with some of the finer things in life.

The bank was only a short walk away. After the meal, Edwin and Richard ambled west on Randolph. Broad Street was only a block from the restaurant. At the corner of Randolph and Broad, they paused to look at the new flag flying above the Eagle Mills near the river. The newly adopted flag of the Confederate States of America was gigantic, measuring fifteen by twenty-five feet. The banner rippled defiantly from its sixty-foot high flagpole. Nevertheless, the three alternating stripes of red, white, and red supported by a blue field with a circle of seven stars curiously reminded both men of the United States flag. Still, against a background of the early morning sky, the banner represented their new nation's hopes well. The harsh tone of Deacon Archibald's shrill voice unexpectedly shattered their patriotic musings.

"Preacher, I must talk with you." The deacon obviously was upset about something.

"Sure, Deacon Archibald. What is on your mind?"

Archibald glanced at Richard with contempt, and then said, "I need to talk with you privately…now!"

Richard smirked at the deacon's demeanor and politely excused himself. He wondered how Edwin tolerated the cranky old man. He suspected that the undisclosed source of the deacon's irritation was Polly again. The idea provided him inexplicable satisfaction.

After Richard departed, the deacon growled, "Your wife is with that red-headed Jezebel again. I swear she spends more time with her than she does at church. Preacher, it ain't right. It just ain't fittin'."

"Calm down, Deacon. Let's discuss this rationally. We only have church once a week, so I guess she does spend more time with Polly than in church."

Before Edwin could say more, the deacon launched into another tirade. He lifted his bony arm and shook his finger in his pastor's face. "I tell you, preacher, it ain't fittin' for our pastor's wife to associate with that Jezebel. Did you know that her first husband used to smuggle slaves into the country?"

Edwin only knew that Polly was divorced. He knew very little about the details. The deacon's revelation that her ex-husband was involved illegally in the slave trade made Edwin even more sympathetic towards her. He also found Archibald's logic incongruous; less than forty-eight hours earlier, in their regular Wednesday night prayer meeting, the deacon had stood and prayed, "Almighty Father, in Your righteous wrath, deliver us from these Philistine infidels who scorn our liberty and wrongly seek to meddle in our affairs." The deacon certainly had a way with words. Everyone knew that he was petitioning God to stop the Northern states from ending what he, like many other Southerners, called "our peculiar institution," a euphemism for slavery. An outsider might consider the deacon hypocritical, but Edwin recognized his contradictions arose more from cultural conformity than from overt hypocrisy.

"So, Deacon, do you think Ann should be more like Jesus?"

The question caught the antagonistic deacon off guard. He mechanically answered, "Yes, we all need to be more like Jesus."

Edwin reached into his pocket and pulled out a leather-bound New Testament. He opened it and read, "'And when the scribes and Pharisees saw him eat with publicans and sinners, they said unto his disciples, *How is it that he eateth and drinketh with publicans and sinners?* When Jesus heard *it*, he saith unto them, *They that are whole have no need of the physician, but they that are sick: I came not to call the righteous, but sinners to repentance.*' Mark 2:16-17." Before the deacon could reply, Edwin said meekly, "I'll tell Ann that you said she needed to spend more time with Polly." He grinned and added, "So that she can be more like Jesus."

The Deacon's face turned blood red. He futilely sought some way to rebut his pastor, but Edwin's aggressive move had checkmated him for the moment. Before he could formulate an alternative strategy of attack, church bells started to ring. The street was filled with commotion. People darted to and fro. Edwin stopped Thomas Barnard and asked, "Tom, what's going on?"

"War, preacher. We fired on Fort Sumter in Charleston Harbor this morning! We are at war with the Yankees."

Barnard's words brought a smile to Deacon Archibald's face. He had never been silent about his desire for secession. He hated northerners more than he detested Polly. He routinely called them

Philistine infidels or Canaanite heathens. *Strange how those who don't fight wars are their most vocal supporters*, thought Edwin as he looked at the sudden change in the deacon's comportment.

"Pastor Anderson," Archibald said, "we'll speak more about this later. I don't find your attitude a bit amusing. But in light of this meaningful news from South Carolina, I must see to other more pressing matters. Good day, sir."

"Good day, Deacon."

Although he had been watching events in Charleston closely, the news that a shooting war had commenced stunned Edwin. Part of him really had never seceded from the United States, and now Georgia was at war with the United States. Ironic name he mused, *United States…nothing united about them now*. He headed off to find Roswell Ellis, proprietor of the *Daily Times* newspaper. The paper's office was located at the corner of Randolph and Oglethorpe Streets, opposite the post office. Roswell and Edwin had fought together in Mexico, so he knew Roswell could get him back into the Columbus Guards. He hesitated. *What will Ann say? Should I tell her first? No, we've talked about it enough during the last few weeks. The time for talking is over. She will have to understand.*

When he arrived at the *Times* office, Edwin learned Ellis now commanded the Columbus Guards. He was not surprised. Ellis had assumed temporary command weeks earlier. Semmes had been tapped by Governor Brown for higher command. Ellis refused to swear Edwin into service at that moment. Instead, Ellis told him to go home and talk with Ann and to the church. Then, if he still wanted to enlist, he should report on Monday morning. Nevertheless, after leaving Ellis, Edwin stopped by the Redd and Johnson store to purchase fabric for the prescribed uniform. Mr. Reich, the tailor, measured him for the jacket and trousers. Holding the tape measure along the side of Edwin's leg, Reich said, "I've got a pair of pants already sewn up. They're for Mr. Hodges. He already has one pair and said he won't pick these up until next Friday. I suspect you need these more than he does. I'll still have his ready on time. I'm not sure how long the jacket will take. I'll send you word if it's ready before you leave for the coast. Otherwise, I'll send it to you there."

As Edwin stepped out of the store, he was startled to see Ann and Polly coming out of the dry goods store next door. He had forgotten that she had planned to buy some new clothes for the children. Both of them had outgrown the outfits they had worn last spring. Edwin knew Ann's father had given her some money. He no longer argued with Mr. Lewis about this. He was the children's grandfather and they were his pride and joy. He insisted spoiling them was his right. Still, the money rankled Edwin's pride.

Spotting her husband, Ann felt a sinking feeling in her chest. Before he could speak, she blurted out, "You've joined the army!" She had sensed his decision as soon as she had heard the news about Fort Sumter. She and Polly were headed for the bank in search of their husbands when they encountered Edwin.

"Yes…"

Edwin paused. Tears rolled down Ann's face. He suddenly regretted his haste to enlist. He glanced at Polly. She was crying also. He looked into Ann's glistening eyes. Instantly, his guilt began to fade. Without saying a word, she had let him know that she understood. Intuitively, he embraced her. As his lips met hers, he realized he was kissing his wife on the streets of Columbus. *I don't care.* At that moment, showing her that he loved her was more important than what people might think.

The couple's passion was interrupted by Richard's voice. "What will Deacon Archibald say when he learns about this blatant peccadillo? Kissing a woman, even if she is a man's wife, well that, sir, is a deliberate transgression of church propriety!"

That red-headed Jezebel has corrupted the preacher's wife, thought Edwin gleefully. He didn't dare say that in front of Polly. Nevertheless, the indecorous kiss had been strangely stimulating. He had not felt this way since he was a teenage boy. The exhilaration compounded his awareness of his deep love for Ann. He continued to embrace her as he studied the milky white skin of her round face. Blonde ringlets hung down both sides. Her cheeks were tinted pink, and her lips were full and moist. Her love for him was evident in her countenance. He gazed into her eyes. They were a pale blue like the sky. He felt as if he could drown in them. "I love you," he whispered softly.

Three days later, on April 15, Ann and her father drove Edwin to South Commons. He stepped out of the carriage and started toward the rows of white tents pitched in the grass. Ann watched Edwin as he walked away. Dressed in a burgundy plaid civilian shirt, the dark blue trousers he had purchased on Friday, and a pair of tan suspenders, his appearance was comical. Instead of the prescribed kepi, he wore a brown slouch hat. The only indication of a uniform was the red stripe down the seam of his trousers.

Unexpectedly, the reality of what he was doing stunned Edwin. He turned and raced back to Ann. Her straw-colored hair peeked out from beneath her deep maroon bonnet, its stiff hood shading her creamy skin. She continued looking at Edwin as he came closer. He was about six feet tall with a lean physique. His mahogany-brown hair, which had turned gray around the temples, and his receding hairline gave him a distinguished look. His mustache was neatly trimmed, and a wisp of hair grew under his lower lip.

When Edwin reached the carriage, Ann looked deep into his brown eyes. They telegraphed his love. He reached up, grabbed her petite waist, and swung her down to the ground. He pulled her tightly against his body and they kissed passionately. They continued their passion oblivious to the world around them. Now both regretted Edwin's decision to enlist. Finally Mr. Lewis interrupted, "Edwin, putting it off will not make it any easier." Edwin knew he was right. Slowly, he lifted Ann back to her seat, turned, and walked towards the tents. She watched him until her father drove away.

As Edwin walked into the company's camp, he met Captain Semmes. Instinctively, the pastor lifted his right hand in a crisp military salute. Semmes smiled, somewhat amused at his soldier's appearance. Edwin's hat covered his balding head, but his graying temples and facial hair were especially noticeable. Although years of eating fried chicken at church dinners had added a few pounds, Edwin was in good physical condition for a man his age.

"Father Anderson?" Semmes asked. Semmes was Roman Catholic and Edwin was Southern Baptist. Southern Baptists had earned a reputation for considering Catholics as evil as the red

Indians on the frontier, but in small communities like Columbus, the two groups had a live-and-let-live attitude, avoiding theological discussions with each other. Nevertheless, everyone knew the prejudice each side held inside. Semmes had once heard Edwin express an unexpected compassion for the Cherokee Indians. At the time, he commented, "Anderson, you sound more like a Jesuit priest than a Bible-thumping Baptist preacher." Ever since that occasion, he good-naturedly jested with Edwin, calling him Father, as if he were addressing a Catholic priest. Edwin took no offense, and Semmes, like other members of the esteemed Columbus Guards, held its former combat veterans in high regard.

"Reporting for duty, sir!" replied Edwin.

"Anderson, didn't you get enough of war in Mexico?"

"Yes sir, I did. Truth is, that's what led me into the ministry. But I reckon the Lord has some mysterious purpose in this madness. I can't explain why I'm here. But I just couldn't stay at home now. Besides, I figure the boys need some spiritual guidance. My wife thinks this war might be a lot longer than the politicians are saying."

Semmes laughed. The word *politicians* sparked remembrance of Governor Brown. Although Brown had appointed Semmes to secure arms for the state, the captain knew that he was not in the governor's favor. He returned Edwin's salute and strode away still laughing inside.

"Reverend Anderson?"

Edwin recognized John Lindsay's voice. He turned and saw Lindsay and two other members of the Columbus Guards staring at the red-striped trousers.

"Preacher, did you enlist?"

Before he could respond, one of the other soldiers, a slim man with a dark complexion and a dark brown mustache, interrupted. "I'm William Croft. Did the captain call you Father? You don't look like any priest I ever seen."

Lindsay snapped his elbow into the man's gut, prompting Croft to double over as he bellowed, "Ohh!"

"Respect your betters," Lindsay retorted, grinning impishly. "The captin' calls hem that because he is old enough to be your father. Why the judge probably sent hem here to keep you out of trouble."

"Are you Judge Croft's son?" Edwin asked.

"Yes," answered the soldier. He chuckled and glanced at Lindsay. "John, one of these days your arrogance is going to get you into serious trouble." He reached out his hand to Edwin and continued, "As I said, I'm Bill Croft. Richard said that you had rejoined the company. Welcome back..." Croft paused, uncertain how to address the older minister. Then he sheepishly uttered one word, "Father."

From then on Edwin Anderson was known as Father to the men in the Columbus Guards. For some of them, he really would become a stand-in father figure. He knew many of their parents. At first, the young men expected Edwin to fail at handling the rigors of military life. Some even hoped he would. They feared he might tattle to their parents if they misbehaved. But in the weeks that followed, Edwin would quickly demonstrate his physical endurance and prudent tolerance of their youthful conduct and soon be considered one of the boys.

Edwin awoke with stiffness in his joints. The first day of drills and exercises had been tough. Sleeping in a bedroll on the ground didn't help matters, and he craved the warmth of Ann's body by his side at night.

That morning, the unit had received an order from Governor Brown instructing them to report to General Lawton at Savannah. They were scheduled to leave at four o'clock that afternoon. A formal ceremony marked the occasion. Doctor Higgins, pastor of the Presbyterian Church, delivered a stirring address to the corps before departure. Reverend DeVotie responded, and Doctor Hawks, the Methodist pastor, pronounced the benediction.

After its enlistment campaign, the Columbus Guards now mustered nearly 120 members, thirty more than the governor had authorized for companies going into Confederate service. Therefore, only those members of the company who had been in the unit prior to the outbreak of hostilities made the train trip to Savannah on this occasion. The new members, including Edwin

Anderson, remained in Columbus until they could arrange for individual transportation. Since the company had broken camp, he was free to return home for a brief visit. Reverend DeVotie offered to drive him there in his royal green buggy, and Edwin gladly accepted the gracious offer.

As the carriage rumbled along the road, Edwin had trouble staying focused on the conversation. All he could think about was Ann, even though he had been away from her less than twenty-four hours. Reverend DeVotie suspected the nature of Edwin's distraction. He was compassionate enough not to press him, and eventually their conversation turned to silence.

The church was allowing Edwin's family to remain in the parsonage until another pastor was called. Ann said that she probably would move back in with her father before then. The sun was touching the western horizon when DeVotie's buggy pulled up to the parsonage's white picket fence. Edwin could see the warm glow of oil lanterns through the window curtains. His spine tingled in anticipation of the surprised look on Ann's face when he opened the door.

Instead, the surprise was on his face. As he swung open the front door, he sighted Polly. She stood barefoot on a wooden chair in the long hallway that ran down the center of the house. Her right hand withdrew a burning match from the wick of an oil lamp on the wall. A pastel blue cotton house dress highlighted her petite feminine form as she stretched to set the crystal globe back in place. Long red curls draped carelessly across her shoulders. Bright green eyes looked to see who had disturbed her. For an instant, Polly and Edwin exchanged a surreal glance. He knew she was staying with Ann. She had been there since Richard had set up camp with the rest of the Columbus Guards on South Commons. The momentary thoughts that she aroused troubled Edwin. He had never felt so attracted to her before. Then Polly called out, "Ann, your husband is home!" Edwin's guilt mysteriously eased.

* * *

Edwin finally arrived in Savannah a week after the first group of Columbus Guards. The unit had moved to nearby Tybee Island, so Edwin had to delay joining them until the steamer left the next morning. He found accommodations in an unpretentious hotel near the wharf. He shared his room with a greasy man named Mansfield who hailed from a small farm near Athens and was on his way to Tybee Island as well. Despite his roommate's obnoxious snoring, Edwin managed to fall asleep quickly. However, he awakened before daylight. He had been gone one day and again, he already missed Ann. Picturing her milk-white skin, he remembered the sweet taste of her soft lips and the pressure of her breasts against his chest when they kissed. *What was I thinking?* Lying in bed and staring at the dark ceiling, Edwin vowed that if he survived this war he would never leave Ann again.

After breakfast, the two men walked down to the wharf and boarded a small white steamboat for the six-hour trip. As the vessel approached the Tybee wharf, the recruits on board lined the railing to glimpse their new quarters. The island was ten miles long and three miles wide. One third of the land was covered in pine, palmetto, water oak, and other trees. Along the coast these were stunted, but inland the vegetation grew full height. The camp was visible in the distance. It resembled a planned city of hundreds of white tents. In the nearby field, several companies of militia drilled under the afternoon sun. Several groups of men frolicked in the surf like schoolchildren. A detail waiting to unload supplies from the steamer's hull stood in their shirtsleeves on the dock.

As he gazed at the tropical scene, memories of Vera Cruz flashed through Edwin's mind. The Columbus Guards had been part of General Winfield Scott's invasion of Mexico in 1847. Capturing the port city was the first step in the United States Army's campaign against Mexico City. The American siege had lasted twenty days. Edwin recalled digging trenches in the hot tropical sun. The labor was more arduous because of insufficient food. They had been limited to half rations. The final bombardment lasted eighty-eight hours. The continuous rumble of artillery and the terrified screams of the town's civilian population remained etched in his mind. So too was the sight of widespread looting by the American army after the town's fall. Devastating tropical storms and the epidemic of yellow fever added to the nightmare. For a second, he visualized these horrors in the panorama before him, but his confidence that their present cause was just and that God would be with them quickly vanquished such fears. Surely Georgia was safe from the distress of invasion.

Three men in the work detail on the dock wore blue trousers with the distinctive red stripe of the Columbus Guards. Edwin surveyed the party for familiar faces. His heart beat faster as he recognized his close friend, Richard Brenton. It only had been a week, but Richard looked different. The strong coastal sun had turned his skin dark, and the stubble on his chin had not seen a razor since he left Columbus. His linen shirtsleeves were rolled up around iron-hard biceps. He looked more like a field hand than a bank clerk.

"Richard!" yelled Edwin as he raced down the gangplank.

"About time you showed up. I was going to report you as a deserter. Give us a hand," replied Richard, "and we'll give you a ride to camp."

Edwin joined the detail flinging bags of flour into an old farm wagon. When all the bags were loaded, the small group of soldiers piled on top. The teamster clicked his mouth and with a flick of his wrist, sent an undulating wave down the reins to the brass bits on a pair of coffee-colored mules. The sudden jolt as they responded tossed about the wagon's human cargo like wind blowing tall grass.

"Father," teased Richard, "you joined this elite outfit to fight the Yankees. Instead you find yourself loading wagons like a black slave." He turned to the two other soldiers and introduced Edwin. "Gentlemen, this is Father. His real name is Reverend Edwin Anderson, but Captain Semmes calls him Father."

"Geez, he's old enough to be my father," remarked one of the strangers, a scrawny kid with freckles on his face. Edwin looked at him and smiled. Inside he knew the boy was right.

"Ed, this here is Willie Cobb. Willie lied about his age. He's only sixteen, so his papa sent one of his servants to tuck him in at night. Truth is, we tolerate the boy cause Jim, his nigra', is a darn good cook." Pointing to the other man in the wagon, Richard said, "This here is Tom King. The three of us have formed our mess together. We left a place for you in it. We had a number of inquiries because of Jim's cooking, but we turned them all down, didn't we boys?"

The two forced a smile and a nod, and Edwin knew Richard had used his physical strength to intimidate the two smaller men. Nevertheless, he was glad he and Richard would be together.

CHAPTER TWO
"Good day, Mrs. Anderson"

ANN KNEW THE BANGING AT THE FRONT DOOR WAS DEAcon Archibald. She had been expecting his visit for weeks. The Andersons had lived in this parsonage almost six years. It was the only home the children knew. Charlotte was three when they came to the church. James was born in their bedroom upstairs.

The house originally had been built in 1830 by the late Charles Colquitt when he moved into Muscogee County from Savannah. The Creek Indians were still in the area then, and the house was a typical frontier plan. At that time, it was a two-room log cabin, or more accurately two one-room log cabins that shared a single roof. The two cabins were separated by an eight-foot space known as a dog run. This dog run provided residents with a cool exterior shaded area. The walls were constructed of large hand-hewn logs.

During the decade after the dwelling was built, the federal government removed the Creeks from the region. Colquitt prospered and made dramatic renovations to his home. The dog run was enclosed to make a hallway. The logs were covered with clapboard. A second story was added, doubling the number of rooms to four. The family stopped cooking in the fireplace and built a kitchen behind the house. A few years later, a one-story addition was built on the back, along with a porch, and the kitchen was connected to the main structure with a covered walkway.

In 1848, Colquitt built a large classic Greek Revival plantation house a few miles northeast of the old homestead. He donated his old farmhouse to the church for use as a parsonage. Edwin's predecessor owned his own residence in Harris County. During the eighteen months he had been the pastor, the house stood empty and fell into disrepair. Edwin and Ann had worked hard refurbishing the residence. Every room held cherished memories. The old wood house was their home.

But Edwin had been gone over five weeks now. Deacon Archibald's bony fist continued pounding the front door. His shrill voice was shouting, "Mrs. Anderson, Mrs. Anderson!"

How rude, Ann thought, as she answered, "Coming." She opened the wooden door, forced a smile, and politely said, "Won't you come in, Deacon?"

"Thank you," the old man replied. "I want you to know that this is as unpleasant a task as I ever had. Mrs. Anderson, Reverend Anderson is away in the army. I don't think this war will last another six months, but I have a responsibility to the congregation. I met last night after church with Brother Newman and Brother Douglas. We agreed that we need to begin searching for a new pastor soon. The people just can't go that long without a spiritual shepherd…"

The people just can't go that long without a spiritual shepherd, thought Ann sarcastically. *What you mean is the war has given you an opportunity to take over running the church again*. Edwin was well loved and therefore too influential for the good deacon. She had seen the deacon and his two comrades whispering before church the previous day. In Edwin's absence, Archibald spoke. His message was more like a patriotic speech than a sermon. After the service, the three once again huddled together. She could see Archibald sticking his finger in Douglas's face. When she, Polly, and the children passed, the trio courteously tipped their hats but made no effort to engage her in conversation.

"Mrs. Anderson, are you listening to me?"

"Yes, Deacon, please continue."

"As I was saying, the people just can't go another six months without a spiritual shepherd. We love your husband. He has been the best pastor we've ever had. But we simply can't wait until he gets back. You are welcome to remain in the house for six more weeks…unless of course we call a new pastor. If we don't find a pastor by the end of the six weeks, we can look at extending you on a weekly basis after that."

"Thank you, Deacon, for your generosity," Ann replied, almost gagging at her answer. "I'll write Edwin and get his advice. I'd like to discuss this with my father also."

"Of course, Mrs. Anderson. We're not pressuring you to do anything. I just wanted you to be aware of what is going on. That way you can make the necessary plans. As always, it's been a pleasure to speak with you. I hope to see you in prayer meeting Wednesday evening."

Archibald started to turn and leave, but young James ran into the hallway screaming, "De-CAN Are-she-bold!"

"Well, good morning, Master James."

Charlotte entered the hall behind James. At the same time, Polly came in the back door holding a plate of biscuits. She said, "Ann, I took the biscuits out of the oven, just like you said." When she saw the deacon, she became silent.

"Miss Charlotte, how are you this fine morning?" Archibald asked.

"Fine, sir."

"Good day, Mrs. Anderson," said Archibald again.

"Deacon, aren't you going to speak to Mrs. Brenton?" asked Ann.

She knew he deliberately avoided addressing her friend. He and his wife blatantly shunned Polly on every occasion possible. Since she had moved in with Ann, the opportunities had multiplied. Before Richard's departure, he and Polly had boarded in the Planter's Hotel in Columbus. When Edwin left to join the Columbus Guards on the Georgia coast, Ann and Polly resolved to continue living together so they could share their mutual anguish over their husbands' absences. Because of the children, they decided to live in Ann's house.

In her anguish over her separation from her husband, Ann had failed to consider the reality that her home belonged to the church. She continued to attend church just as she previously had. Once Polly moved in, she did likewise. Deacon Archibald usually managed to avoid Polly. On the other hand, Mrs. Archibald repeatedly embarrassed Ann. Whenever she was near Polly, Mrs. Archibald cocked her head back, looking disdainfully down her nose at Ann's housemate. As soon as Mrs. Archibald made eye contact, she deliberately turned her head away. She would gossip about Polly to the other women in the church, often intending for Polly to overhear what was said.

Polly's composure amazed Ann. She could never have held her temper so handily. She continued going to the church because technically, Edwin still was its pastor. When he tried to resign, the congregation had insisted he take a leave of absence instead.

"Mrs. Brenton, sorry, I didn't see you standing there," Archibald said grudgingly. Once more he said, "Good day, Mrs. Anderson." He then spun swiftly and walked out. He didn't quite slam the door, but the noise it made when it hit the frame clearly sounded his displeasure.

"Well, good day to you, too," said Ann mockingly.

"Ann Anderson!" Polly chided.

Instantly both women burst into laughter. The sarcasm was lost on the two small children. But the ladies' mirth was contagious, and their high-pitched giggles added to the frivolity of the moment. Composing herself, Ann finally spoke. "Children, run along and play. Mommy will call you as soon as Mommy and Mrs. Polly get breakfast on the table."

The children scampered up the stairs to their room. The two adults watched until they were out of sight. The ladies stood there silently until they heard the children playing with their toys.

Polly was the first to speak. "What was that all about?"

"Deacon Archibald said the church was going to look for a new pastor."

"Short leave of absence they gave Ed," Polly smirked.

"Deacon said that he believed the war would be over in six months. But he said that the people just can't go another six months without a spiritual shepherd. So…"

"So," interrupted Polly, "he will be their spiritual shepherd."

"That's not exactly what he said."

"But that's what he meant," insisted Polly. "You know as well as me, getting a new pastor these days simply ain't going to happen. All the preachers joined the army. Even Reverend DeVotie has gone to be with the Columbus Guards at Tybee Island. The good deacon plans to become the church's spiritual potentate and keep everybody on his straight and narrow. He'll use that pulpit to drum up enthusiasm for the cause rather than to tell folks what the Bible has to say about living to please God."

Ann knew Polly was right. Her blunt honesty was one of the characteristics Ann enjoyed most about Polly. Edwin always tried to see the best in people. Sometimes she thought he was too trusting. In contrast, Polly's harsh experience had hardened her skeptical expectations of human behavior. She also had an analytical mind that seemed to reach accurate conclusions instantaneously. Both women enjoyed their chats. After Polly moved in with Ann, the two women spent hours talking. Finding genuine support in each other, they soon shared some of their most private thoughts.

Ann learned new details about Polly's first marriage during these intimate conversations. Polly was barely sixteen when she married Jacob Prescott. He was a rich man who had acquired much of his wealth through dubious means. Polly's family was what most Southerners called "poor white trash." Her parents, Tait and Annabel Cullen, had migrated to America from Scotland before Polly was born. They settled in Montgomery, Alabama. Their mercantile business initially was successful. Then Annabel died while giving birth to Polly. Without his wife's strong guidance, her slothful father lost the business.

Tait's misfortunes plummeted even lower due to risky investments and get-rich-quick schemes. Thereafter, he found odd jobs working in a local slave market where he met Prescott. Tait Cullen still had aspirations of grandeur. He fancied marrying off his only daughter to Prescott so her affluence could then convert his poverty into negotiable prestige. In Prescott, Tait found a like mind. Together, and without Polly's knowledge at the time, they hatched a con scheme in which Tait masqueraded as an affluent Scottish businessman. Consequently they relocated to Mobile. Underwritten with Prescott's money, Cullen's charade introduced Polly to the city's society. Polly and Prescott were married soon after the move to Mobile.

But Prescott was just as much scorned by Mobile society as Polly's father had been in Montgomery. By the time Tait Cullen recognized this reality, Polly was pregnant. The strained relationship between her father and her husband ruptured. One of them challenged the other—Polly did not know which—to a duel. Prescott killed her father in the gunfight. Her father's death traumatized Polly, which in turn infuriated her husband. Hoping that it would improve their marriage, Prescott sold his house in Mobile and bought a small plantation in Russell County, Alabama.

One evening in a drunken fit, he beat Polly unconscious. She lost the baby and was bedridden for several weeks thereafter. Polly vowed to run away. Georgia was only ten miles from Prescott's plantation. She hoped the nearby state would offer her some sanctuary from Prescott's abuse.

As soon as she recovered sufficient strength, she left, taking some gold coins from Prescott's roll-top desk. When the stable slave refused to hitch up a buggy, Polly grabbed a nearby horse's mane and somehow managed to mount the steed. Kicking her heels into its flanks, the horse bolted and raced away. She swore that an angel guided the horse on that ride. "I just hung onto that animal for dear life," she said later. The horse was still racing when it reached the Chattahoochee River at Girard.

Richard was walking down Front Street in Columbus when he heard the clatter of hoofs on the planks of the City Bridge. Polly's runaway horse galloped out of the darkness of the covered bridge at full speed. Surprised pedestrians did not have time to react. The horse struck Richard hard, knocking him into the muddy street. The collision startled the horse, and it bucked, dumping Polly on top of Richard.

Richard cursed and struggled to remove the thrown rider from his chest. As they thrashed about on the ground, Richard realized his assailant was a woman. His cursing ended the moment he looked into Polly's face. She was beautiful, even though she still bore traces of two black eyes. In his twenty-seven years, Richard had never been so smitten. He quickly introduced himself. Polly stood and nodded but did not reveal her identity. She didn't trust men. Richard had been bruised badly in the accident and arose with some difficulty. Nevertheless, he retrieved Polly's steed from the edge of the river. He coaxed the horse back to the street and led it to a nearby livery stable.

As they walked, Richard invited the runaway wife to dine with him at Fredrick Wilhelm's restaurant. She hesitated, but her benefactor looked so pitiful that Polly gently acquiesced. The couple attracted more than one inquisitive stare. Richard had not taken time to change his mud-splattered suit, and Polly acted uneasily. All of her life, Polly had been dominated by cruel, abusive men. Her harrowing dash had enabled her to escape her private purgatory, but she felt lonely and afraid. Still, she intuitively sensed this disheveled stranger was different. Richard's demeanor and compassion gradually calmed her. She told him everything. As she revealed her sordid tale, Richard raged inside. He wanted to exact revenge on her estranged husband, but he maintained his composure. Instead of retribution, he obtained a room for Polly at the spacious Planter's Hotel on Broad Street. The room was directly across the hall from his.

Polly immediately set out to divorce Jacob Prescott. Unfortunately, she encountered numerous difficulties. Georgia recently had passed a new divorce law and attorneys were unfamiliar with its provisions, so they advised her to wait. Some were unsure she could legally divorce in Georgia since she and her husband were residents of Alabama. Polly was afraid to return to that state. Her estranged husband had too many felonious associates from his illegal slave trading. They could return a fugitive wife as easily as they could smuggle other human cargo. She knew he had criminal connections in Georgia, too, but with Richard hovering nearby all the time, she felt safe in Columbus, so Polly temporarily abandoned all thoughts of divorce.

Richard continued functioning as her benefactor. He had fallen in love and wanted a more intimate relationship. However, because of her marital status, Polly refused all of his advances. Serendipitously though, six months later they learned Prescott had divorced her on the grounds of abandonment and adultery. He falsely accused her of living with Richard. He also accused her of theft because of the gold coins, but the circuit judge threw out the criminal charges. Freed by her new status, the young divorcee reciprocated Richard's love. Three months, later the two were married in a private civil ceremony.

By that time, Polly's reputation was destroyed. Gossip based on her ex-husband's accusations and the proximity of her room to Richard's in the hotel stuck. The absence of a religious ceremony illegitimatized her marriage to Richard in many people's opinions. She remained isolated until she met Ann one day in a dressmaker's shop. The encounter must have been providential, for the two seemed to have nothing in common. Yet they became instant friends, much to the chagrin of the members of Edwin's church.

In her conversations with Polly, Ann talked incessantly about Edwin. Polly was beginning to feel that she knew Ed as well as she knew Richard. Previously, Edwin had always seemed aloof to her. She always assumed that since he was a Baptist preacher, he surely considered her to be undesirable company for his wife. But now Ann made him seem very human. Polly regretted not getting to know him better. Both Richard and Ann really cared about him. Perhaps she had been wrong in her assumptions.

CHAPTER THREE
"With distinguished gallantry"

FATHER EDWIN ANDERSON AND THE OTHER MEMBERS of the Columbus Guards had become Company G of the Second Georgia Volunteer Infantry Regiment. They were assigned to a Georgia brigade commanded by the frustrated politician, Robert Toombs. Sixteen months had passed since they had left Columbus for the war. Willie Cobb had come down with measles and died two months after Edwin had met him on the dock at Tybee Island. Tom King had lost his leg at Malvern Hill.

The survivors in the Columbus Guards were hardened veterans now. They had perfected their combat skills in battles at Williamsburg, Garnett's Farm, Malvern Hill, Thoroughfare Gap, and Second Manassas. Victory, and an end to the war, seemed close as they splashed across the Potomac River and entered Maryland. Excitement filled the air. An army band struck up the popular tune "Maryland, My Maryland." The men of the Columbus Guards splashed through the water amid jokes about their obvious need for bathing. Unfortunately, it was only waist high and the crossing took very little time.

On Monday, September 15, 1862, the Second and Twentieth Georgia occupied the heights west of the Rohrbach Bridge, the lower of three bridges that spanned Antietam Creek near Sharpsburg, Maryland. The position was a high wooded bluff that dropped sharply down to the creek bank. A sturdy stone wall and an old quarry provided natural breastworks at the top of the hill. The numerous oak trees that dotted the slope afforded additional protection for defenders.

A Texas company already held the high ground north of the bridge. Therefore, General Toombs placed the Twentieth Georgia on the right of the Texans. He then extended his line downstream by forming the Second on the right of the Twentieth. The ground provided a strong tactical position. Whether it was sufficiently strong to compensate for the two regiments' numerical weakness remained to be seen. Army regulations authorized a single regiment to consist of one thousand men. The combat effective strength of these two Georgia regiments combined was less than four hundred rifles. Many soldiers carried antiquated .69 caliber smoothbore muskets. These would be of little use until after the enemy crossed the bridge. Toombs had assumed temporary division command, so he placed Colonel Henry Benning in tactical command of the defense at the bridge.

Henry Benning had been a prominent Columbus politician before the war. He had served as an associate justice on the Georgia Supreme Court. Benning was a strong proponent of secession and represented Muscogee County in the Georgia secession convention. Unlike many political generals in this war, Benning was a capable field commander. His actions before this bridge, when coupled with his record as commander of the Seventeenth Georgia, would earn him the nickname "Old Rock."

The formal battle line of two ranks was dispersed to take advantage of the natural defenses available along the sloping hill. Father clutched his Enfield and carefully moved toward an old oak tree. The leather soles of his brogans made the descent on the steep slope treacherous. If he was not careful, he might slip and tumble into the creek. A tremendous roar of laughter rose from Company D when one of its members splashed into the water. *Need to watch my step*, thought Father. Reaching the selected tree, he noticed that Richard was behind a slightly smaller oak a few yards below him.

Richard turned and grinned. "I'm not the sharpshooter, you are. I need to get closer to hit my target," he joked.

"You be careful and don't get yourself shot," replied Father. "I don't want to look for another messmate."

Father turned his attention to preparing his own position. To his left front, a triple-arched stone bridge spanned the creek. Father estimated it to be about 125 feet long and 10 or 12 feet wide.

The swift water of Antietam Creek was at least four to five feet deep here. On the far side, low open ground gradually climbed to rolling farmland. Some fields were newly plowed. Others were planted in corn. A small wooded area crowned the crest of the far ridge while a stone wall ran north from the mouth of the bridge. A dirt road ran parallel to the creek directly in front of Father before making a sharp turn onto the bridge. It then climbed the hillside on which Father and Richard waited. From there it ran into the small town of Sharpsburg.

Once again casting his eyes across the creek, Father noted a rail-and-post fence between the road and the creek bank. The road wound across the eastern ridges and dipped into the valley downstream from the bridge. It hugged the creek bank for a quarter of a mile. Father guessed that any Yankee advance would come up this road. He figured the Federal troops would remain in a column of four. They would slow as they turned onto the bridge. Casualties on the bridge would slow the movement even more. He would have a continuous parade of targets for several minutes. He knew that he could manage at least three shots per minute, surely inflicting a lot of damage before…before?

Father realized that once the Federals were on the bridge, sheer numbers might force a crossing. At some point, he would need to shift his fire to the bridge. Its stone sides would protect the attacking soldiers. He would have a smaller target, so he needed to be accurate. At the same time, the urgency of stopping the attack called for increasing his rate of fire. The two needs worked against each other. For a moment Father thought, *How surreal…a minister of the gospel coolly calculating how to kill his fellow human beings.* Then he put it out of his mind. When the time came, he would do his duty. Strange as it might seem, once shooting commenced, he no longer thought about what he was doing. He just did what the months of drilling had trained him to do.

The rest of the day and most of Tuesday were spent waiting for the inevitable. The men of the Columbus Guards joked, ate hard tack crackers, read Bibles, and tried to forget what was certain to come. Late Tuesday afternoon, the distinct sound of artillery fire was heard from the ridge across the stream. "Oh, sh____!"

someone cried out, but the explosion drowned out his profanity. Father curled up and hugged the ground. There was nothing else he could do. His fate rested with a higher power. The guns fell silent with the setting sun over the western horizon. The shells had sprayed some men with dirt and broken a few tree limbs, but no one in the Columbus Guards had been injured. Captain Ellis calmly walked among the company making sure everyone was ready for morning. Father was coming back from filling his canteen in the creek when Ellis spotted him. Unlike most of the men in the ranks, Roswell Ellis never called Edwin Anderson "Father." The two had known each other too long to change.

"Ed, where have you been?" Ellis inquired.

"Refilling my canteen, and Richard's. Likely won't have time to do it in the morning. How's your water, Roswell?"

"I have a full canteen already. Do you and Private Brenton have sufficient ammunition?"

"Both of us have forty rounds in our cartridge boxes and another twenty stuffed into our pockets. I hope we don't need more than that."

"Colonel Benning posted pickets across the creek, so don't shoot unless you know what you are shooting at. Ed, I know you know that, but I'm a captain now and…"

Richard walked up and interrupted. "What the captain means is I am not as good of a soldier as you," he joked. "The captain knows I don't have the experience you two Mexican War soldiers possess. So he wants to be sure I don't shoot a good soldier by mistake."

"Brenton, what I want is for you to take care of yourself. You take too many chances. Don't expose yourself needlessly tomorrow," said Ellis. "Do you have sufficient cover?"

"Yes, sir," responded Richard.

"Ed, take care of yourself, too. Don't make me write a letter telling Ann you got yourself killed," said Ellis.

"You too, Roswell. We both survived Mexico. Let's get through this one as well."

"Amen," Ellis whispered.

"Amen," Edwin and Richard echoed softly.

Captain Ellis quietly moved on. He would check each and every member of the Columbus Guards before dawn. Edwin handed back Richard's canteen. Richard pulled out the cork stopper and swallowed a large gulp of water.

"Oh, that tastes good," he said.

"Better save some for tomorrow. We won't be able to refill once the Yanks open the ball," Edwin chided.

"I'll be fine. Ed…" Richard paused and looked directly into Edwin's eyes.

"Yes, Richard?"

"Ed, if I'm not fine. I mean, if something happens tomorrow…"

"You having one of them premonitions, Richard?"

"No, but one never knows, does he? Anyway, if I do get killed tomorrow, will you and Ann look after Polly?".

"Of course. I always assumed you knew we would. And if you survive and I am killed, I hope you and Polly will take care of Ann and the kids. I know her father will provide for her financial needs. But she'll need friends who care about her."

Neither man spoke another word. They grasped each other's hands and for a few seconds, looked into each other's eyes. They could see down into the other's soul and recognized the pain and fear each felt. Death had become too real on the battlefields of this war. Whenever their Army of Northern Virginia met the Union Army of the Potomac in battle, the casualty lists numbered in the thousands.

Edwin and Richard were finishing another piece of hardtack when they heard the alarm, "Here they come!" The cry was punctuated by musket fire as the brigade's pickets fell back towards the bridge and safety. Instantly, the drums added the steady cadence of the long roll. Edwin and Richard grabbed two Enfields leaning against a nearby tree. They bolted for their selected positions and wiggled to find just the right posture. Edwin slid into the spot he had hollowed out over the previous two days. Bracing his rifle against the tree trunk, he rested his finger on the trigger and began looking down the sights on the barrel.

Across Antietam Creek, heavy columns of Federal infantry came across the crest of the ridge. The Confederates watched with awe as the powerful force arrayed against them deployed into a line of battle. The large number of American flags indicated at least one corps confronted the small southern force. Then, to the amazement of the Confederate veterans, two companies moved forward. Two lone companies! The Yankees seemed to have idiots in command. All of that power, and their officers were only sending two rifle companies.

"Pick your targets, boys. Make every shot count," Roswell Ellis said coolly.

"Fire at will. Fire!" bellowed the familiar voice of Lieutenant Colonel William Holmes, commanding officer of the Second Georgia. The regiment responded with a crisp explosion as every rifle discharged simultaneously. A steady roar followed as the Georgians loaded and fired as quickly as each man's individual ability allowed. Pale gray smoke enveloped the heights. Edwin no longer could see the far side of the creek. Still, he bit off the end of cartridges, poured their powder down the hot barrel of his gun, and rammed a soft lead .58 caliber Minie ball against the powder. Reaching into the cap box on his belt, he pulled out a brass four-winged musket percussion cap and placed it on the nipple of the rifle. Taking aim at the spot where he guessed the Federal line might be, Father squeezed the trigger firmly. The butt of the gun recoiled into his shoulder. As he started to repeat the procedure, he heard Roswell Ellis shouting, "Cease fire! Cease fire!"

As the smoke dissipated, Edwin saw numerous blue bodies lying in the freshly plowed field across the creek. Closer to the crest of the hill, he could make out the survivors racing for safety. An hour later, a lone regiment emerged from the wood line and moved down the slope. They reached the rail fence directly in front of Edwin and Richard. Climbing over this small obstacle, they reformed into a line of battle. For the next ten minutes, a bloody firefight raged along Antietam Creek. During this fight, Father used the last round in the top of the tins in his cartridge box. He reached into his pockets, pulled out a cartridge, and continued firing. Once again the attacking Federals broke and the survivors ran for safety. Father sat down and relaxed against the tree as the fighting ended. He pulled the tins out of his leather cartridge box and restocked their top compartments with bullets from the bottom compartments. Then he gulped several swallows of water from his canteen. The powder on his lips fouled the drink with the taste of sulfur, but the liquid eased his parched throat.

Around eleven thirty, two more blue-clad regiments swept down the hill toward the bridge. Unexpectedly, a pig and her piglets scampered up the creek bank and darted into the blue line. The sow ran between the legs on an unfortunate Union soldier, carrying him astride her back. The pig continued up the hill with her panicked victim screaming for help. The Confederate line erupted in loud jeers and laughter. This third charge met with the same results as the previous two. By this time, the fields across the creek were covered in dead and wounded Union soldiers. Among the Confederates defending the bridge, casualties had been light.

"Richard, how are you doing down there?" shouted Father.

"I'm fine, Ed. Running low on ammunition. Have any to spare?"

"No, I was using rounds from the bottom of the tin in that last attack. I guess I have about fifteen rounds left."

Father reached into his pants pockets and retrieved the remaining cartridges. He carefully arranged them with those left in the leather cartridge box on his right hip. Only one of the two tins had the full ten rounds it was designed to carry. The other tin had four rounds.

"I've got fourteen rounds, fifteen if you count the one already loaded in my rifle," Father told Richard.

"That's two more than I have."

Pulling a single cartridge from the incomplete tin, Edwin tossed it to Richard.

"Here, now we are even."

Around one o'clock, the Federal army made one more attempt to force their way across the bridge. This time, three stands of colors indicated three Union regiments were advancing. The midday sunlight reflected off their fixed bayonets. Forward they came in an irresistible floodtide. Along the Confederate line officers barked out the command to fire. Sergeants and corporals repeated their commands, but they went unheard as the gray line unleashed a storm of lead balls. Large gaps appeared in the blue tide rolling down the hillside. But then the ferocity of the firing began to waver. Snipers in the treetops dropped to the ground and headed towards Sharpsburg. All along the line, men with empty cartridge boxes shouldered their weapons and moved back to the rear. By this time, Union soldiers were across the bridge. For the first time, those men in the Confederate regiments who were armed with ancient .69 caliber smoothbore muskets joined the fight. But the issue had been decided once the Yankees managed to get across the bridge. Now it was the Confederates' time to die.

Johnny Slade was struck as he reached into his cartridge box. He died the next day in a field hospital. Richard stepped out from behind his tree. Methodically he stepped backwards towards Father. More and more Union troops were fanning out on their side of the bridge.

"Ed, it's time for us to go," he stated emphatically.

"Sure is."

A loud thud startled both men as a lead ball slammed into the tree beside them.

"That's too close! Let's go!" screamed Richard.

The two friends turned to climb the hill. Father heard the sickening sound of lead smashing flesh and bone. He turned in time to see Richard spin around. A surprised expression exposed Richard's transformation. He hit the ground hard. Father stopped and knelt beside his friend. Richard attempted to speak. A glance at the hole in his chest divulged the fatality of the wound. Blood poured out of Richard's mouth. His eyes begged for help. Then his expression turned peaceful.

Father checked for signs of life. Nothing. Richard was dead. He reached inside Richard's jacket and pulled out his wallet and a tintype photograph of Polly. For a moment, he looked at the image and recalled the memory of her in the hallway at home. Again he felt an unwelcome attraction to her. A bullet hit the ground, spraying dust in Father's face. Polly's memory evaporated. Edwin Anderson clenched his Enfield and sprinted up the slope towards Sharpsburg. The blue wave surged up the hill in pursuit of the fleeing Rebels. The lifeless body of Edwin's closest friend now lay behind enemy lines. For a moment as he ran, Father contemplated its fate, probably burial in a shallow mass grave. He did not linger on such morbid thoughts. He was alive and he wanted to stay that way.

General Lee, in his official report on the battle, wrote, "General Toombs's small command repulsed five different assaults made by greatly superior force, and maintained its position with distinguished gallantry." The distinguished gallantry had cost Father his closest friend. As he raced for Sharpsburg, he again thought of Polly. Richard's death would hurt her far more than it did Father. Still, he was alive and could not help feeling joy. Then his thoughts turned to Ann. Oh how he loved her. The more he thought of Ann, the faster he ran. Surviving to get back home to her drove him forward even though his body was exhausted.

CHAPTER FOUR
"How firm a foundation"

POLLY'S HANDS TREMBLED AS SHE CLUTCHED THE ENvelope. She knew its contents without opening it. Edwin only would have written her if there was bad news.

September 28, 1862
Winchester, Virginia

Dear Polly,

This is my first opportunity to write since Sharpsburg. Richard was killed in the battle there on September 17. I was with him when God called him home. He died instantly and did not suffer. I know that nothing I can say will alleviate your suffering, but I am praying that our kind heavenly Father will comfort you in these sorrowful days ahead. I have lost my best friend and closest comrade in our struggle for independence. In the 16 months since we last saw you, he and I have shared everything (except your letters to him of course). I will send you his personal effects separately. Ann and I will gladly be of assistance to you.

Your obedient servant,
Edwin Anderson

The news of Richard's death wasn't a surprise to Polly. She had read it the in the casualty list of the Columbus *Daily Enquirer*. The paper had posted it on September 30, just two days after Edwin's letter had been written. That was a month ago. *Confederate mail stinks*, Polly thought. She could never entertain a return to the old country, especially since its soldiers had killed Richard. But she had to admit the Yankee mail service had been far more dependable.

Edwin's letter rekindled memories of the day she learned Richard had been killed at Sharpsburg. Rumors of a great battle in Maryland had begun circulating days earlier. She had ridden into town that Tuesday with Ann. Word of the fight along Antietam Creek near the small hamlet of Sharpsburg greeted the two women before they could exit their carriage. Like other families of men in the Columbus Guards, Ann and Polly gathered at the newspaper office after every battle to glean any word of their husbands, brothers, sons, or fathers. Regardless of class distinctions, on these occasions, the military families shared an intangible bond of trepidation. Whose names would appear on the increasingly longer lists of dead and wounded? A shriek might announce that a young mother had become a widow. Or that a mother had lost her only child.

The absence of a loved one's name brought temporary relief but never eased the fear that next time, the shriek might be one's own voice. This year, these occasions came with unrelenting fury. In April, John Lindsay had been wounded near Yorktown, Virginia. In June and July, the Columbus Guards had engaged in bloody battles near Richmond. In August, they had fought at Second Manassas. Then the invasion of Maryland came with new hope that a victory north of the Potomac River might end this evil war. Instead, the battle ended in a tactical stalemate. Robert E. Lee's Confederate Army of Northern Virginia retreated back into Virginia. The war would go on. More gatherings at the newspaper office were assured. But first the list from Maryland had to be read.

Ann's finger quivered as it slid down the column of names. She whispered each one softly to herself. Polly intently read her lips The enlisted casualties were posted in alphabetical order by last name. When Edwin Anderson's name did not appear, Ann let out a small sigh of relief. She glanced at Polly and continued down the list. "Brenton, Private Richard." She lifted her head and looked straight at Polly, whose face had turned pale.

"Richard?" Polly asked with a tone of disbelief.

Ann could only nod. She felt tears welling up in her eyes.

"Is he…"

Before Polly could complete the question, the word "dead" escaped Ann's lips. She hugged Polly as tears ran down both women's cheeks. Kinsfolk of other members of the Columbus Guards joined them in grieving. The common experience they shared with having family in the company created a bond greater than old social conventions. In that moment at the newspaper office, no one thought about Polly's past. The fear of potentially losing a loved one generated a distinctive empathy.

The war had drawn Ann and Polly closer than ever. They had lived in the same house since the men had left. First at the church parsonage and then at Mr. Lewis's plantation. When James Lewis learned of Deacon Archibald's visit, he insisted his only daughter move back home. Ann was fiercely independent and agreed to do so only with the stipulation that Polly could live there, too.

That winter, the cook, Delia, had gotten sick. During the slave's illness, Ann persuaded her father to let Polly and her prepare the family meals. Ann had become accustomed to cooking since marrying Edwin. The couple did not own slaves. Mr. Lewis had wanted Ann to take a handmaid, but her strong-willed husband refused to allow it. Later, Edwin divulged to Ann that he had misgivings about the South's peculiar institution, but he never expressed these publically for fear of being branded an abolitionist. Edwin was just as happy to let Mr. Lewis think that he valued self-sufficiency.

Ann had grown up with slavery and never questioned its morality. Her father was a good man and he owned slaves. If slavery was wrong, he surely would have renounced it. Still, after living with Edwin so long, she now found herself strangely uncomfortable around her father's slaves. However, she did find working in the kitchen again to be very rewarding. Polly, on the other hand, was no cook. While married to Prescott, a slave had cooked their meals, and Polly and Richard had always dined in Columbus's restaurants. When she was staying with Ann at the church parsonage, she only shared in the cooking duties when Ann gave precise instructions. After a few days of her getting under foot in Mr. Lewis's kitchen, Ann suggested that Polly check in on Delia.

Polly knocked on the door of the small room behind the kitchen. She cautiously opened it and peered meekly around. The wooden floor was unfinished. The hand-made brick walls were devoid of plaster. Large fireplaces were located on each side of an interior wall that separated the room from the kitchen. The one in the kitchen was used for cooking while the one in Delia's drafty room provided heat in winter. A small wooden table and chairs stood in front of the fireplace. In the far corner, Delia lay on a pallet on the floor.

Delia had blankets pulled up around her neck. Sweat covered her face. She looked at Ann's guest with suspicion. *What dis white woman want?* Delia asked herself. She had heard Mr. Lewis describe Polly as a fallen woman. *Maybe dis here white woman not be so bad. After all, de massa don't care berry much fo' her. Dems berry good recommendations fo' me*, Delia thought.

"Delia," Polly whispered, "how are you doing?"

"She be sickey-sickey, misses."

Polly had not noticed a young girl standing in the dark corner of the room. She looked to be about eight years of age. She was barefoot and wearing a tan homespun dress. Her black hair was covered with a faded red handkerchief. Defensively, she stepped between Polly and Delia.

"I be cold," Delia answered with great difficulty.

Polly reached down and touched Delia's forehead.

"Delia, you're burning up. You've got a bad fever. Is this your granddaughter?"

"Yes, ma'am. Her name be Sarah."

"Sarah, can you get me a bucket of water and a couple of clean towels?" Polly asked.

"We not got no towels, ma'am. We has some old rags we uses fo' washing on de wall over yonder," the young girl responded.

"Are they clean?"

"Yes, ma'am."

"Good, they will do. Bring them to me," Polly said, "and go get me a bucket of water."

The young girl hesitated. She peered at Delia for guidance.

Delia responded to her granddaughter's inquisitive glance, "Honey chile, does as dis white woman says."

"Yes, ma'am."

Polly took one of the rags and began wiping Delia's forehead. Over the next few days, Polly treated Delia, and slowly, the ailing woman recovered. A week later, when Polly knocked on the door, no one answered. She wondered if Delia had suddenly grown worse during the night. Surely if that had been the case, Sarah would have come to get her. She opened the door and looked inside. No one was there. Puzzled by Delia's absence, Polly headed to the kitchen to see if Ann knew something. To her surprise, Polly found Delia, not Ann, bending over an iron skillet in the fireplace. She was humming "Amazing Grace" as she cooked. When Delia turned around, Polly's presence startled her.

"Delia, are you okay?"

"Yes, ma'am, Miss Polly. I never feels finer. You da berry best nurse dat be."

Polly felt a previously unknown inner satisfaction. From that day on, whenever one of Mr. Lewis's slaves took ill, they sent for her. They started calling her Doctor Polly. Eventually some of the poorer white folks in the community came to her for help, too. She seemed to have a natural inclination for medicine. One day when she was in Mr. Lewis's library, Polly saw two volumes on a shelf: *A Treatise on the Practice of Medicine* by John Eberle. She reached up and grabbed volume one. She was so absorbed in reading that she failed to hear James Lewis enter the room.

"Mrs. Benton, feel free to take that book and read it if you want."

Those were the kindest words Lewis had spoken to her since she had moved into his home. Polly knew that he strongly disapproved of her and tolerated her presence only because he was afraid of alienating his precious daughter. Now, though, Polly's nursing skills had touched his pragmatic side. His slaves represented a significant financial investment. Therefore, to him their sickness threatened his economic situation. Blissfully ignorant of this crass logic, Polly appreciated Lewis's permission to study these medical books. She read both volumes...twice. Mr. Lewis occasionally borrowed medical books and journals from doctors he knew so she could read them.

After learning that Richard had been killed at Sharpsburg, Polly's unorthodox view of God solidified. Although she continued going to church with Ann, she no longer imagined that spiritual solace could be found in a house of worship. She always had believed in a higher power, but for her, the deity was distant and mysterious. He was even more so in the aftermath of her personal loss. She never had much confidence in the church. Church people had shunned her ever since she had divorced her first husband. Their attitude made her wonder if their talk about God's love was true. *Apparently*, she thought, *God loves everybody, unless they are divorced, or their ancestors were born in Africa, or they happened to be very poor.* People at church had issued the obligatory condolences when Richard died, but only a very few had shown Polly sincere sympathy. Whatever God might be like, she was becoming more skeptical than ever of organized religion.

Polly's scrutiny of slavery amplified the estrangement between her and the church. Southern Christians' defense of the South's peculiar institution baffled her. She did not understand how decent people could reconcile their creed of God's love with slavery. Folks treated the slaves as if they were not even human. She certainly was no abolitionist, but nursing Mr. Lewis's sick slaves had opened a new door into the lives of these people. She knew that they dared not disclose all of their opinions to any white person, but no matter what preachers and politicians said, Polly realized the slaves were not content living under the control of their owners. Their skin might be darker, but they had the same aspirations as other people to be free.

Ann alone prevented Polly from breaking completely from evangelical Christianity. She not only talked of God's love, she lived it. Something genuine in Ann's attitude made it impossible for Polly to refute Ann's statements about her God. Ann did not seem even to harbor any bitterness towards Deacon Archibald. Her comportment towards him amazed Polly. When they encountered him every Sunday at church, Ann always demonstrated sincere concern for his health and well-being. If Polly made an uncomplimentary remark about the deacon, Ann laughed and mentioned one of his positive attributes afterwards. Still, Polly could not embrace Ann's view of a loving God. *If God loves me, why am I so lonely?* she wondered. *Besides, how could a loving God let Richard die?* She concluded that God evidently had little interest in human affairs.

Despite her newfound fulfillment in medicine, Polly lapsed into a deep depression. Nights were torment for her. She burned lamps, and her weeping frequently disturbed the rest of the household. She barely ate enough to stay alive. Already a petite lady, Polly looked more emaciated daily. Her complexion lost its luster, and her eyes seemed permanently red.

One day, while Ann was in the parlor, she heard a loud thud in the hallway. Rushing into the hall, she saw Polly lying on the floor. Ann began screaming for Charlotte. Young James—he was named for his grandfather—responded instead.

"Where's your sister?"

"Upstairs, Mommy. What's Miss Polly doing on the floor?"

"Don't worry about Miss Polly," Ann answered. "Go get your sister."

James said, "Yes, ma'am," and raced up the stairs yelling, "Charlotte! Mommy wants you. Miss Polly is taking a nap in the hall on the floor!"

A few moments later his baffled sister warily descended the stairs, pausing periodically to absorb the sight of her mother kneeling beside the prone figure on the floor. Polly Brenton's recent behavior frightened the young girl, so she tried to stay away from her mother's friend as much as possible.

"Hurry, Charlotte, hurry!"

Charlotte knew by the tone in her mother's voice not to procrastinate, so down the stairs she flew. Ann reached out and grabbed both of her daughter's shoulders, forcing Charlotte to look directly into her mother's eyes. Then, in a slow deliberate voice, Ann said, "Obadiah is down at the barn. Run down to the barn and tell him to come here immediately. Then find Granddaddy and tell him that Miss Polly passed out. Do you understand me?"

"Yes, ma'am."

Ann continued to peer directly into her daughter's eyes and commanded, "Then repeat what I said."

"You said to go to the barn and get Obadiah. Then go tell Granddaddy that Miss Polly was out on the floor."

"That's right. Now go tell Obadiah to hurry."

Looking around, Ann saw her frightened son pressing himself against the wall and looking intently at the mystifying sight of his mother kneeling by her friend sleeping on the floor. He was so focused on the scene that he did not hear his mother call his name the first time.

"James! James!"

"Yes, ma'am."

"James, go out to the kitchen and tell Delia to come here to Mommy. Do you understand?"

"Yes, ma'am," he answered. Then he turned and ran out the back door.

Delia came racing into the room, but before she could reach Ann and Polly, the front door opened and a massive dark figure stood silhouetted against the sunlight. It was Obadiah. Despite his age and missing teeth, Obadiah, the plantation's blacksmith, was big and powerfully built. Since he spent most of his day laboring at the forge, he had torn the sleeves off his shirt. The chiseled muscles of his dark brown arms were apparent, and his clothing could not hide his obvious physical strength.

"Obadiah, pick Miss Polly up and move her to her bed."

The brawny slave reached down and lifted Polly's limp body in his arms. Gingerly he carried her up the steps. Ann and Delia followed. James tagged along behind his mother at a discreet distance. When they reached the bedroom, Delia turned down the covers, and Obadiah carefully placed Polly on her bed. Ann gave James some instructions and in a few minutes, the young boy returned holding a ceramic bowl in both arms. Inside of the bowl was a matching ceramic pitcher filled with water. A towel and washcloth were slung over the boy's left shoulder. His face was turning red from his load. Obadiah quickly relieved the child of his burden and placed the items on the dresser. Feeling ill at ease in a white woman's bedroom, Obadiah requested permission to return to his duties. Ann thanked him for his assistance as he departed. After pouring the water into the bowl, she wet the washcloth and tenderly wiped Polly's face. She heard her father's footsteps in the hallway downstairs and felt a flush of pride in her children. Charlotte and James had carried out her instructions judiciously. They had responded well in the crisis.

Polly opened her eyes. Looking up at Ann and Delia, she muttered, "More than I can bear. More than I can bear." Then she lost consciousness again. When she awoke, Ann was seated in a chair by the bed.

"What happened?" Polly asked.

"You fainted," answered Ann. "You don't have to be a doctor to know that you are half-starved and exhausted. Delia is making you a pot of chicken soup and you, my dear friend, are going to eat it. Do you understand?"

Polly nodded her head up and down slightly. The children had retreated to the back porch after all of the excitement. The two women were alone in the house, and it was peacefully quiet when they heard the back door open. Delia was singing as she came into the house. "Fear not, I am with thee; o be not dismayed, for I am thy God, and will still give thee aid; I'll strengthen thee, help thee, and cause thee to stand, upheld by My righteous, omnipotent hand."

Polly recognized the hymn from church, but the words of the second stanza seemed to be a message from God specifically for her today. For a moment her hope surged, only to retreat before her doubts. Delia's tender voice interrupted this inner struggle before either point of view could prevail.

"Miss Polly, I makes you some of my famed chicken soup. Dis soup cures most anything dat ills you."

I bet it won't mend a broken heart, Polly sarcastically thought.

It took both women's vast wiles, but Ann and Delia persuaded Polly to eat the entire bowl of soup. Remarkably, she felt a bit better and requested something to drink. Over the next few days, Polly's appetite improved. With more rest, her strength gradually returned. She stopped taking meals in bed and joined the family in the dining room. One afternoon after supper, Polly walked into the parlor, sat down in a plush, wing-back Queen Anne chair, and gazed briefly at a black leather-bound Bible on the adjacent table. On impulse, she picked the Bible up and opened it. Her eyes focused on a verse just above her thumb, Isaiah 41:10. "Fear thou not; for I *am* with thee: be not dismayed; for I *am* thy God: I will strengthen thee; yea, I will help thee; yea, I will uphold thee with the right hand of my righteousness." The words reminded her of the song Delia had sung the day she had passed out. The song and the Bible verse seemed to have identical words.

Polly could not get them out of her mind. She read them daily. "Fear thou not; for I *am* with thee: be not dismayed; for I *am* thy God: I will strengthen thee; yea, I will help thee; yea, I will uphold thee with the right hand of my righteousness." Three days later she walked into the kitchen to talk with Delia.

"Delia, do you remember the song you were singing the day I fainted?"

"No ma'am, I is always singin' hymns. I sings so many I is not sure what ones I sings when. Can you hums a few notes fo' me?"

"The words of this one went "Fear thou not, I am with thee...""

"Oh, not fear thou not, fear not," said Delia. Then she sang, "Fear not, I am with thee; o be not dismayed, for I am thy God, and will still give thee aid. I'll strengthen thee, help thee, and cause thee to stand, upheld by My righteous, omnipotent hand."

"Yes, that's it. What is that hymn? Can you sing the whole thing?" asked Polly.

"Yes, ma'am."

"Great! Sing."

"Right now?"

"Yes, now. Come on, sing it for me, please," begged Polly.

"How firm a foundation, ye saints of the Lord, is laid for your faith in His excellent Word! What more can He say than to you He hath said, to you who for refuge to Jesus have fled? Fear not, I am with thee; o be not dismayed, for I am thy God, and will still give thee aid; I'll strengthen thee, help thee, and cause thee to stand, upheld by My righteous, omnipotent hand."

Delia sang the rest of the old hymn, but Polly's reflections remained fixated upon the first two verses. Was God speaking to her? Assuming it to be only a coincidence seemed incredulous. First she had heard Delia singing just the second verse to the hymn. Then she had picked up a Bible and randomly turned to Isaiah 41:10. Finally, when she asked about the hymn, she learned it began, "How firm a foundation, ye saints of the Lord, is laid for your faith in His excellent Word!" Could she have been wrong to conclude God had no interest in human affairs? Was it possible that God might be interested in Polly Brenton? Did God's excellent Word have something to say to her?

Polly returned to her bedroom. Sitting on the side of her bed, she opened her Bible. This time she deliberately turned to Isaiah 41:10. Once again she read, "Fear thou not; for I *am* with thee: be not dismayed; for I *am* thy God: I will strengthen thee; yea, I will help thee; yea, I will uphold thee with the right hand of my righteousness."

She closed her Bible and prayed, "Lord, I don't really know what to say. But I'm going to give You a chance. I think You are speaking to me. I am not sure what exactly you are telling me. But I am going to trust you to figure everything out. I still hurt, and I still have lots of questions. Nevertheless, You are my God." She meditated upon this unexpected turn in her attitude. Nearly ten minutes later she finally said, "In Jesus name, Amen." God did care about Polly Brenton.

Her opinion about church folks remained hostile, but her view about the deity had dramatically shifted. Polly realized that her new assessment of God might change her attitudes about other things as well. If so, she would deal with the adjustments whenever they came. For the present, she recognized that the course of her life had taken a new direction. That alone was sufficient.

CHAPTER FIVE
"I'll never, no never forsake"

RAIN HAD BEEN FALLING STEADILY SINCE NOON. WATER ran off the brim of James Lewis's hat as he stepped onto his porch. He pulled off his wet overcoat and hung it on a peg by the back door. He placed his old slouch hat on top of it. Despite his best effort, his trousers still were dripping water as he stepped into the hallway.

"Daddy, you are getting the floor wet."

"Ann, my darling daughter, I'm sorry. I'm sure you will forgive me when I tell you the reason for my haste. I brought you some mail, three letters from Virginia."

Ann shrieked in glee. Mail delivery continued to be unreliable, so a single letter from Edwin was cause for rejoicing. Three letters called for unbridled celebration. Lewis sorted through several envelopes he withdrew from a pocket inside his black suit coat. He handed three of them to Ann. She opened each letter and read every word, oblivious to her children demanding she read them out loud. Her mind could hear Edwin's voice speaking each word. Her heart raced as she moved down each line on the page. Edwin was fine. The letters were written from camp seven miles south of Richmond. Hood's division had been detached from Lee's army all winter, serving as part of the capital's defense.

Edwin wrote about his messmates, regimental drills, and the weather. As a rule though, the bulk of his letters devoted most of their content to comments about missing his family. He always addressed each child individually. Occasionally he included a paragraph to Polly, although he never wrote her directly. Every now and then, Edwin would tease Ann about some unidentified pretty girl in Virginia. More often, though, his messages to his wife were very intimate. Edwin once wrote, "The next time I kiss you on Broad Street, I may not stop with a kiss. Brushing your soft lips only arouses my longing to carry out Solomon's instructions in Proverbs 5:19 and caress your firm breasts."

On more than one occasion, his words aroused her yearning for physical intimacy. Edwin frequently spoke that way to her when they were alone in their bedroom at night, but seeing such language in black ink on white paper embarrassed Ann. Still, she adored his suggestive references. His deep love for her saturated each remark.

Ann folded the last letter and looked around. Polly had heard the commotion and joined the family. The war was two years old and the same ritual surrounded the delivery of every letter. Ann read them first. Then the entire family gathered in the parlor to listen to her read the appropriate parts out loud for everyone to enjoy. After the assembled family digested the first two letters, Ann read in a clear, audible voice:

March 20, 1863
Dear Ann,

Two days ago Gen. Lee called for our division to return to the army. We marched to Ashland, a small town just north of Richmond. The weather had improved dramatically over the last week. Instead of cold winter wind and rain, it seemed like spring was just around the corner. But when we reached Ashland, a terrible winter storm hit without warning. We had 10 in. of snow. I've seen more snow in my two winters in Virginia than I had seen in all the rest of my life put together. I am ready for Georgia weather! Anyway, that afternoon we got orders to return to our old bivouac below Richmond. Just got everything squared away and thought I would drop you a line or two. I love you! I miss you and the children so much. I pray to God daily that this war ends soon so I can come home.

Charlotte, are you still Daddy's little girl? I bet you are a grown lady now. Be a good girl and help your Mommy. I love you and miss you. Hugs and kisses.

James, are you enjoying living with Granddaddy? He can teach you lots of important lessons about being a man. Be sure to learn your letters and ciphering. Pray for Daddy while I am in the army. When I get home we can hunt and fish and play ball. I miss you. I love you.

John Lindsay and I were frying some bacon when Gen'l. Benning...yes Old Rock...got promoted. He is a real general now. I know Mr. Lewis will be very happy for his old friend. Well anyway, he escorted a group of civilians around camp. Most of them were old men. However, one was a real pretty young lady with red hair. Some of the boys started kidding John, wanting to know if she was his sister. Said they wanted him to introduce her. She reminded me of Polly. How is Polly? Is she still living with you at Stillwater?

My dear wife, I miss you. I can't wait to touch your...

Ann blushed, stopped reading, and said, "I better not read the rest to you. It's between your Daddy and Mommy."

"No, no, Mommy we want to hear the whole letter," insisted Charlotte.

"Me too!" screamed James.

"Well I don't guess your Daddy will mind," responded Ann as she scanned the letter for an appropriate spot to resume reading. "Now where was I? Oh here we are."

...I miss you all so much. I hope I can get furlough this coming winter so I can come home for a few days. Kiss Charlotte and James for me.

Your loving husband,
Ed

P.S. I sent you some sheet music for Polly. Richard told me how much she liked J. R. Thomas's music. I came across "Annie of the Vale" in Richmond. I know Richard would have gotten it for her if he were still alive. Let me know when you receive it.

As Ann read these last few lines, Polly's anguish over Richard's death surged within her once more. Her newfound relationship to God did not assuage her grief. The pain was still there. Despite her deep love for Ann, Polly could not help feeling resentment toward her because Edwin was alive. These family celebrations that accompanied the arrival of Edwin's letters only aggravated her sorrow. Nevertheless, she had become so much a part of this family that she could not separate herself from them on these occasions. They had shared her misery when she was at her lowest. She must share their joy even though inside it only made her own heartache worse. After all, that is the nature of real families. She mused about this oddity she called her family now: an old man long set in traditional southern ways, a Baptist preacher's wife and her two small children, and a spurned divorcee. Polly smiled faintly as she thought about this bizarre twist wrought by the bloody struggle between the states.

The amusement did not linger. Ann's embarrassment heightened as her innocent children attempted to pull more of their father's words from her. As Ann's discomfort increased, Polly's sorrow swelled. So too did her annoying jealousy of Ann's serenity. Whenever such envious feelings invaded her mind, Polly usually tried to erase them by focusing upon her patients. Only this time she had no sick people to nurse. Everyone in the area seemed extremely healthy for the moment, so Polly endured her personal torment in silence. In their rapture over the letter, everyone else was utterly unaware of her ordeal. And for their ignorance, she was grateful.

Finally the celebration broke up. Everyone headed upstairs for the night. Polly closed the door to her room but could still hear the voices of the children resisting Ann's efforts to calm them down. As she listened to the eternal struggle between the excited children and their mother, Polly's eyes came to rest on the chest of drawers. The moment gave birth to an unexpected yearning within her. It was totally unwelcome.

Polly opened the drawer of the chest and pulled out Edwin's letter concerning Richard's death. Carefully she took it from the envelope and slowly read each line. Perhaps because of its close connection to Richard's last moments of life, the letter gave her some semblance of peace. Gradually her attention shifted to Edwin's name. Little by little Richard's image was fading. She was not forgetting him. Her love for him always would be there. However, her life with him was over. He was gone, lying in an unmarked grave in southern Maryland. She was beginning to realize that the old adage "life goes on" was true.

What troubled Polly was the strength that Edwin's persona was gaining in her memory. He was Ann's husband. Yet she could not deny that she now felt this hopeless attraction for Edwin. Other than Richard, he had been the only man who did not disparage her because of her past. She rationalized that now he was the only living man who still respected her as a human being. He even sent her sheet music. Surely this fascination with Edwin was nothing more than appreciation for his concern for her. Nevertheless, the presence of this perplexing lure tormented her. An undesirable sense of guilt overwhelmed Polly whenever Ann talked about Edwin.

I'll throw the letter away, she thought. *That will get rid of this confusion.*

Instead, she put the letter in its envelope and placed it back in the drawer. Despite all of her emotional conflict, she could not let go of it. Pushing the drawer into place, she looked at the photograph of Richard on top of the chest. He had sat for the picture before leaving Columbus. He was wearing the distinctive red jacket uniform of the Columbus Guards. Even with his martial expression, he looked so handsome. She picked up the photograph, clutched it tightly against her chest, and wept.

Downstairs, Ann could hear Polly sobbing. Without thinking, Ann climbed the stairs to comfort her. At the door of Polly's room, she could hear Polly repeating Richard's name. She placed her hand on the doorknob, but something stopped her. She hesitated momentarily and then went back downstairs.

The next morning, the children didn't come down as usual. Normally James bounded down the stairs hollering, "Grandpa! Grandpa! Let's play." Charlotte, now eleven, would follow, scolding her younger brother as if she were his mother. With breakfast already on the table, Ann stood at the foot of the staircase and called out their names. Charlotte came out of the children's room first. She was clutching the old doll she claimed she had outgrown. Ann recognized immediately something was wrong.

"Mommy, I don't feel good," Charlotte muttered.

"What's wrong darling?" asked Ann.

"I just don't feel good, Mommy."

By this time Ann was up the stairs, her hand intuitively feeling her daughter's forehead. Simultaneously her mind was adding James to the equation. She glimpsed him through the open bedroom door. He was still in bed.

"Darling, you may have a touch of fever. Does your tummy hurt?" Ann asked.

"Yes, ma'am, a little."

"Go back to bed. Let Mommy check on your brother. I think he may be sick, too."

"Yes, ma'am," replied Charlotte weakly as she trudged back to her bed, dragging her doll by its feet.

Inside the room, Ann tenderly tucked Charlotte into the covers. She leaned over and softly kissed her daughter on the forehead. *Yes, she's definitely got fever*, she thought. Promptly, she moved to James and sat on the edge of his bed. She bent over and kissed his forehead just as she had Charlotte's. She recognized instantly that he, too, had a fever. "Angel, what's wrong?" she asked.

"Mommy, my tummy hurts," whispered young James.

"I know, angel. Just lay still and Mommy will take care of you...both of you." Ann softly pressed her son's abdomen. He grimaced in response.

"Can I help?" It was Polly's voice. Aroused by Ann's disappearance and the failure of the two energetic children, she came upstairs to investigate. Standing in the doorway, she already was planning her treatment.

"Thank God you are here, Polly. Both of the children are running a fever. It's not bad, but I fear it's just beginning. Polly, I haven't said anything, but I feel weak myself."

"Ann, don't worry. We'll take care of Charlotte and James. And if you get sick, I'll take care of you, too," Polly assured her friend.

By late afternoon, the children's fevers were noticeably higher. Ann also was running a fever, but she refused to leave her children's side. Days passed, but the three sick Andersons showed no signs of improvement. Indeed, new and alarming symptoms appeared. James's nose bled periodically. Ann complained of headaches. None of them would eat. Each day, they grew weaker. Mr. Lewis seemed almost hysterical at times. Polly knew he felt helpless.

Ann and the children were the only family he had. Ann's mother and two brothers had died in a smallpox epidemic a decade earlier. He blamed the doctors for their death. Several doctors were personal friends of his, but since the death of his wife and two sons, he refused to employ any doctor professionally. Polly knew Ann and the children needed a doctor now, so she waited for the right moment to bring up the subject.

She had been up long before dawn that morning. Delia had just made a fresh pot of coffee when Mr. Lewis joined her at the table. Polly peeked over the rim of her cup as she sipped her coffee. Dark circles surrounded Lewis's eyes. He stared into the cup Delia set before him. He did not touch it. He just gazed at the brown liquid as if it were a looking glass. Finally, Polly set her cup back into the saucer on the table and spoke.

"Mr. Lewis, you need to send for Dr. Farley this morning," she said.

"Dr. Farley? He's not a doctor," Lewis snapped gruffly.

"Mr. Lewis, he is the finest physician in Columbus, Georgia," Polly replied.

"That may be, but it doesn't count for much. They're all book-learning doctors. I had just as soon send for a Creek Indian medicine man as one of these newfangled so-called doctors. Doctors used to learn their trade by apprenticeship to experienced doctors. Now they go to some school and read books. Then they hang out their shingle and read magazines to find out what was the latest experiment that did not kill some poor patient. They tout it as some great medical advance and then try it on their first unsuspecting victim. Can you imagine that some magazine published in Paris or London can cure a sick person in Georgia or Alabama?"

Polly let him rant. Interrupting him would be counterproductive. But his question presented an opportunity to restate her appeal. "No, Mr. Lewis, I don't think it can. That's why we need doctors. Send for Dr. Farley."

"I tell you, Farley is no doctor! Why he doesn't even believe in bleeding patients. He calls it an archaic holdover from medieval ignorance. In my day, doctors cupped and applied leeches liberally. Bleeding decreases the tissue's excitability."

"Mr. Lewis, bloodletting may have some useful purpose in a few cases, so let's give Dr. Farley an opportunity to prescribe the leeches if they are necessary." Polly knew Farley would not advocate the outdated practice, but she hoped her suggestion might persuade Lewis to send for the physician. Her slight deceit worked. After breakfast, Lewis sent Obadiah into town to fetch Dr. Farley.

By the time Dr. Farley arrived, Ann and the children had extremely high fevers and occasional episodes of delirium. When the doctor entered the children's bedroom, James was in an agitated state. The doctor examined Charlotte first. Turning to Polly, he said, "Mrs. Brenton, see if you can calm the child."

Upon completion of his preliminary examination of Charlotte, Mr. Lewis asked, "Do you know what is wrong?"

"I'll know more after I examine the boy and their mother, but I am concerned about your granddaughter's increased body heat, rapid pulse, and delirium," answered Farley. Lifting James's nightgown, the doctor muttered a single word, "Roses."

"Sir?" quizzed Polly.

"Roses, see," the doctor replied while pointing to the young boy's belly.

Polly looked at James's distended abdomen. It now was covered with a rash of rose-colored spots. She knew the doctor's diagnosis before he spoke.

"Typhoid fever…the child has typhoid fever," declared Dr. Farley. "Likely all three have it. They'll need mustard plasters and quinine. It's all in God's hands now." Dr. Farley motioned to Polly and Mr. Lewis. The trio stepped into the hall. Dr. Farley continued, "Mustard plasters, two to three times daily. Give them quinine twice a day. I'll be back tomorrow to check on them. I can see myself out, Mr. Lewis."

Though he knew he had to prepare himself for the worst, James Lewis bowed his head and begged God to spare his grandchildren. In his despair, he bargained with God, vowing to do numerous good deeds if He only would spare his daughter and grandchildren. Deep inside however, Lewis knew these promises were of no substantial value. God was sovereign and would do whatever fit His purposes. And those divine purposes were not necessarily in keeping with the desires of a Georgia planter.

Dr. Farley and Polly walked down the stairs together. They paused momentarily in the hallway. Dr. Farley did not say another word, but Polly could see he was clearly worried. As he opened the front door to leave, she sped toward the kitchen to gather the ingredients for making three mustard plasters.

Polly ground the black mustard seed and mixed it with flour and water. She placed the paste on the three requisite cloths and positioned one on each patient's abdomen. She checked the pocket watch Mr. Lewis provided her. The plaster needed to be removed in thirty minutes. She checked them periodically. After twenty minutes, the children's skin already was turning red, so she removed the plaster. Both were sleeping. The rest would do them good. Next she checked Ann's plaster. Her normally pale complexion was pink from the fever, but beneath the plaster, it was red. Polly removed the cloth, and Ann dozed off.

Polly did all she could to care for Ann, Charlotte, and James. They burned with high fevers. Their delirium worsened. All three developed acute diarrhea. Their stools were green and smelled like pea soup. Some contained blood. Polly assigned Sarah the endless task of emptying the chamber pots. Sarah gagged the first few times she took them out; slaves did not have the luxury of avoiding unpleasant assignments. She evaded looking into the pots and in time, she managed to suffer the foul stench.

Over three weeks had passed since Ann and the children had become sick. Polly was exhausted. She rarely slept more than an hour at a time. Even then, she slept in her clothes. Delia slept very little, too. Mr. Lewis had relieved her of her kitchen duties in order to assist Polly. The intimate nature of caring for the Anderson family drew the two women closer. Despite the vast divide that separated the two, one a slave, the other a social outcast, they were becoming close friends. Each began to understand the inward suffering of the other. Delia wanted to be free, but she dared not allow her stoicism to belie even the slightest hint of her wish. To everyone except Polly, Delia seemed content with her lot in life. Though never spoken, Polly could sense Delia's frustration. What Polly didn't know is that the kitchen slave tried to plot strategies to escape and run away to the Lincoln soldiers. So far, nothing feasible had materialized. While Delia hid her hopes of escaping, Polly's loneliness was obvious. Less apparent was her resentment towards a society that ostracized her because of her divorce from Jacob Prescott and enslaved Delia because of the color of her skin.

Ann started to show signs of improvement. The delirium occurred less frequently and her fever dropped slightly. James, on the other hand, grew weaker. It had been evident to Polly for several days that the illness would be fatal for him. James Lewis persisted in denial however. Young James was named after him and had become his primary joy in life since moving to Stillwater two years earlier. During these critical years of the boy's young life, Lewis had thrived as his primary male role model. He frequently set the child in front of him on his saddle as he inspected the plantation. The boy especially enjoyed fishing expeditions, and the two often were gone before the sun rose and did not return until after sunset.

Dr. Farley had indicated the typhoid fever would last about four weeks. If Ann and the children survived that long, they likely would live. Polly hung a calendar in her room and crossed off each day when she went to bed. Tonight she marked out Saturday, May 16. Four weeks were nearly past and everyone was still living.

She stretched out on her bed and passed out. The stress and labor had taken their toll on her physically. She no longer could resist nature's bidding. She settled into a deep sleep.

A loud pounding on her door roused Polly. At first her mind seemed unable to comprehend the sound, but the knocking persisted, and soon she heard Sarah's voice screaming her name. Polly had stationed Sarah in the hall where she could see both Ann and the children's rooms. Sarah had instructions to awaken Polly if there was the slightest change in her patients. Polly bolted out of bed and opened the door. Sarah stood there shaking.

"Misses Polly, it be Masa James. He jerkin' sumtin' fierce. I comes to git you. Buts before I can wakes you up, he done stops. So I goes back to de doe, but I can't hears him breathin'. I goes to de bed and stills can't hears him. So I comes to fetch you as fast as I can," Sarah reported rapidly.

An oil lamp was sitting on a table in the hallway. Polly picked it up and entered the children's bedroom. The warm golden light dispelled the darkness. Mr. Lewis had been awakened by the commotion in the hallway and followed her into the room. Polly could hear labored breathing, but it was Charlotte. She quickly thought, "Charlotte's breathing doesn't sound good. It's a bad sign." Polly reached down and touched James's forehead. She felt sick. He was cold. She turned to Mr. Lewis and said, "James is gone."

Mr. Lewis maintained some composure momentarily, but soon he was bawling uncontrollably. Polly encouraged him to go back to his room so that he did not disturb Charlotte. Sarah went and got Delia.

A few minutes later, Mr. Lewis returned. "I will stay here with Charlotte. How is she doing?" he said.

"Not good, I'm afraid," replied Polly. "Mr. Lewis, I think we need to get Dr. Farley. If you will stay here, I'll check on Ann and send Obadiah to fetch the doctor."

"Please do. I'm not going anywhere. Don't say anything to Ann about James. The news might devastate her. We don't want to do anything to slow her recovery."

"Yes sir," answered Polly. "I doubt she would comprehend it anyway."

Obadiah returned with Dr. Farley as the sun peeked over the eastern horizon. Delia had joined Polly and Mr. Lewis in the children's bedroom. Sarah had been too shaken by her night's ordeal to return. The physician examined both children. He confirmed James was dead. Mr. Lewis instructed Obadiah to build a coffin. Before the slave could leave the room, Dr. Farley motioned for him to stop. He asked everyone to step into the hallway. A dark cloud settled over everyone. The doctor's gesture foretold dreaded news.

As the group assembled, Dr. Farley said, "Mr. Lewis, there's no good way to say this, but the girl is not going to recover. She will join her brother before the day is over. Obadiah might as well make two coffins."

Everyone was in shock. They had known for weeks that this was a real possibility. Nevertheless, they were not prepared for the physician's announcement. Obadiah slowly descended the stairs and went outside. Dr. Farley went into Ann's chamber to examine her. James Lewis, surrounded by Delia and Polly Brenton, bowed his head and prayed. He begged God to spare his daughter and granddaughter. Periodically Delia punctuated her master's petition with a muffled "Amen" or "Yes, Jesus."

Dr. Farley reported Ann's condition was critical. He did not indicate she was dying, but he stopped short of predicting her recovery. Lewis and Polly divided their time between Ann and Charlotte. Obadiah removed James's body from the bedroom and placed it in the wooden coffin he had built. He moved a table into the downstairs hallway, draped it with black cloth, and set the small open casket upon it. Just before dark, Charlotte passed away. Obadiah placed her beside her brother.

The next morning, Obadiah and Sarah completed draping the front porch with black crepe. James Lewis sat by Ann's bed and held his daughter's hand. He did not speak, but countless memories wandered through his mind. Polly stood next to him with her hand on his shoulder. Delia stayed at the foot of the bed. Tears left wet tracks on her brown cheeks. It was apparent to everyone that Ann would join her children soon. Around midmorning, Ann awakened. She seemed startled and sighed. Shortly thereafter she whispered weakly, "I thought I would be in heaven with my sweet Jesus."

James Lewis cleared his throat and said quietly, "My dear daughter, it won't be long. Soon you will be with your..." He almost let "children" slip but quickly said "mother" instead. Ann was oblivious to her children's fate. She did not know they slumbered in wooden coffins downstairs. Ann only knew that she soon was going to a better place.

Ann smiled and went back to sleep for several hours. When the mantle clock downstairs in her father's study struck three, she once again opened her eyes, looked around the room at the somber faces watching her, and forced a smile. "Delia, will you sing for me?" Ann asked softly.

"Yes, ma'am," Delia answered. Her two hands clutched the footboard of Ann's bed. She looked up as if she could see into heaven itself. Then her pure voice reverberated through the house. Ann closed her eyes and listened serenely.

"How firm a foundation, ye saints of the Lord, is laid for your faith in His excellent Word! What more can He say than to you He hath said, to you who for refuge to Jesus have fled? Fear not, I am with thee; o be not dismayed, for I am thy God, and will still give thee aid; I'll strengthen thee, help thee, and cause thee to stand, upheld by My righteous, omnipotent hand…The soul that on Jesus hath leaned for repose I will not, I will not desert to his foes; that soul, though all hell should endeavor to shake, I'll never, no never, no never forsake."

As Delia's last note faded away, Ann's strength grew fainter. She knew it would not be long. Turning to Polly, Ann motioned for her to bend over. Mr. Lewis stood up to make room. Ann's voice was barely audible. Polly turned her head and put her ear close to Ann's mouth. Her speech trembled, but Ann's words were clear. "Polly, take care of James and Charlotte. Tell Edwin that God will never forsake him. Tell him that I'll see him when he gets to heaven. But tell him not to come too soon. Polly, please take care of him. He needs a woman's strong hand." Ann's expression changed. An eerie peace settled on her face. Her breathing grew shallow and a few minutes later stopped all together.

Ann's statement puzzled Polly. *What did Ann mean?* Her request for Polly to take care of the children was self-evident. But what did Ann expect her to do about Edwin? For now Polly could only imagine.

Obadiah fabricated another coffin. Ann's remains were placed in the hall with her children's. Her father cut a lock of hair from each one of the deceased. He wanted a post-mortem image of his grandchildren, so he sent Obadiah into Columbus to fetch a photographer. The three coffins remained in the hallway until they were interred.

After the funeral, James Lewis retired to his study. He pulled a sheet of paper out of a drawer, dipped his pen into the inkwell, and began writing.

Stillwater Plantation
May 19, 1863

Dear Edwin,

With great sorrow I take my pen in hand to write you of the tragic events of yesterday and Sunday. There is no good way to tell you of our great loss. On Sunday Charlotte and James died from typhoid fever. Ann was sick too but refused to leave the children's side until she collapsed. She died yesterday afternoon. I was with her when she passed. So was Polly Brenton. Ann, Charlotte, and James are all together now with our loving Lord, and with Ann's mother and brothers. We buried them side by side this afternoon in our family plot. Rev. DeVotie preached the funeral service. He spoke about God's inseparable love. His text was Romans 8:35-39. You would have been pleased. I find great comfort in knowing that one day I will be reunited with them and with my own dear wife & sons.

Edwin, I know that you and I have not always agreed, but I now realize that what we shared was greater than what divided us. We now must grieve over our loss. I hope that we can share this sorrow together. I hope that when you come home, you will stop by Stillwater and visit with me. We have so much to talk about.

Your obedient servant,
James

P.S. I would be remiss if I failed to share with you how wonderful Polly was. She nursed all three of our precious angels. Dr. Farley said that if she were a man, she would make a fine physician. I have asked her to live here at Stillwater.

James Lewis did not fold the letter immediately. He knew it must be mailed, but he also knew the pain it would bring. As he gazed at the correspondence, he remembered the death of his own wife and sons. At least when she had died, he still had Ann. Edwin had lost his entire family. Once more, the grieving planter wept uncontrollably.

Hearing Mr. Lewis crying, Polly opened the door and entered the room quietly. She placed her right hand on his left shoulder without speaking. Softly she cried with him. Neither knew how much time had passed, but they were still weeping when Delia entered the house to remove the supper dishes. Mr. Lewis was the first to regain his composure. He looked up at Polly and said, "I have written Edwin. I think he would appreciate a note from you. Here, sit at my desk. Take as much time as you need."

Mr. Lewis folded his letter and put it in an envelope. He took another sheet of paper from his drawer and placed it on the desk with another envelope. Rising from his chair, he looked at Polly, and said, "Thank you, Mrs. Brenton. You have been a wonderful comfort to me these last few weeks." He paused a moment and said, "Polly, I really do mean it."

She looked at his distraught face. His eyes betrayed a tenderness toward Polly that she had never seen. Then James Lewis left the room abruptly, closing the door behind him. When the door shut, Polly could hear him sobbing again. She wanted to go to him, but she felt compelled to follow his suggestion and write Edwin. She first pulled Edwin's letter from the pocket in the skirt of her dress. She had kept it in her clothing since the day Ann had died. Polly knew it by heart, but she read it quietly. Perhaps it could help her find the appropriate words to write him with similar sad tidings. Maybe it held the key to Ann's mysterious charge.

September 28, 1862
Winchester, Virginia

Dear Polly,

This is my first opportunity to write since Sharpsburg. Richard was killed in the battle there on September 17. I was with him when God called him home. He died instantly and did not suffer. I know that nothing I can say will alleviate your suffering, but I am praying that our kind heavenly Father will comfort you in these sorrowful days ahead. I have lost my best friend and closest comrade in our struggle for independence. In the 16 months since we last saw you, he and I have shared everything (except your letters to him of course). I will send you his personal effects separately. Ann and I will gladly be of assistance to you.

Your obedient servant,
Edwin Anderson

Polly returned Edwin's letter to its envelope and placed it back in her pocket. She picked up Mr. Lewis's pen and began writing.

May 19, 1863
Dear Ed,

Ann, Charlotte, and little James have gone to be with Richard in heaven. I know that nothing I can say will assuage your suffering in their absence. I am praying that our kind heavenly Father will comfort you in these sorrowful days. I was with Ann when she passed, and her last words were of you. She loved you deeply. She and I grew closer than ever during the last two years. We were the sister neither of us had. Perhaps one day God will grant you and me occasion to share our grief over the loss of our families. You will always have a special place in my heart. As you have opportunity, please write me and Mr. Lewis. Your letters have provided the rare occasions for genuine joy at Stillwater. May God watch over you.

Affectionately yours,
Polly Brenton

After sealing the envelope, Polly carefully wrote across the front, "Pvt. Edwin Anderson, Company G, 2nd Georgia Infantry, Army of Northern Virginia." She left it on the desk with Mr. Lewis's letter.

Polly knew her decision would hurt Mr. Lewis almost as much as Ann's death. Nearly two weeks had passed since Ann's funeral. Polly had remained at Stillwater. She and Mr. Lewis spent hours each day reminiscing about Ann. The time seemed to help both of them. Oddly enough, the tragedy had completely changed Mr. Lewis's relationship with Polly. Any traces of his disdain toward her had vanished. Although Polly realized that she never could replace Ann, Mr. Lewis now considered Polly his only family. He still thought of Edwin as family, but his son-in-law had been absent for two years now. In some ways, he was as much a memory as Ann. No end to the war was in sight. Edwin's return was a long time away…if he returned. Each week brought news of the war's new victims. The casualty list grew exponentially. Edwin's chances of surviving the war were growing slimmer every day. Polly was now the closest thing to family Mr. Lewis had.

Polly had not slept well the previous night. She kept waking up thinking about what she should do. She felt Mr. Lewis's pain, and a part of her felt obligated to stay at Stillwater. After all, he had opened his home to her even when he considered her undesirable. She had lived there since Deacon Archibald had evicted Ann from the church parsonage during the first year of the war.

The thought of Deacon Archibald infuriated Polly and swung the pendulum of her emotions in the other direction. She wanted to get as far away from Columbus as she could.

In the morning, Obadiah drove Mr. Lewis and Polly to church in the rockaway carriage. Delia rode on the driver's seat with Obadiah. Polly and Mr. Lewis sat together on the inside seat. The sweet fragrance of fresh flowers in bloom impregnated the early morning air. But even nature's rebirth could not hide the war's nasty shadow. The fighting was hundreds of miles away, in Tennessee and Virginia, but its specter was obvious. Neglected fences and houses in need of whitewash testified to the absence of the young men who normally performed those chores.

The impact was even more profound at the church. The structure showed similar neglect. Mr. Lewis and others had volunteered their slaves to work, but shortages of necessary supplies hampered their tasks. The bronze bell in the steeple had been donated to the war effort. It had been recast into a cannon tube by now. But the building wasn't where the war's cost really showed. The people in attendance reflected the greatest toll.

Polly gazed at the crowd standing outside the church. Men who had not volunteered for the Confederate army in '61 had been drafted in the following years, leaving only old men, women, and children to gather for Sunday services. Jesse Stewart was the only young man present. Jesse sat in his wheelchair. He had lost both legs in the fighting at Pittsburg Landing. Even teenage boys were few. Most of them were in the army, too. A significant number of women wore black dresses, a sign of mourning. Most of the other ladies were in homespun. Only two elderly women wore hoops and formal dresses, but the fabric looked old and worn.

The experiences of the war only solidified Polly's hostility toward organized religion, even though her faith was stronger than ever. She attended church to satisfy other people's dogma, first Ann's and today Mr. Lewis's. Polly knew God had sustained her through the perils of her rocky life, but in her mind, instead of making people better, the church only seemed to make an individual's flaws and hypocrisy more obvious to others. For now however, Polly felt obliged to maintain her role in this strange drama called life.

Obadiah drove the rockaway to an old oak tree. The tree's canopy shaded several vehicles parked beneath its branches. Mr. Lewis stepped out of the vehicle and turned to assist Polly. Delia remained seated while Obadiah secured the carriage. As Polly and Mr. Lewis walked towards the church, they heard Obadiah and some of the other slaves laughing. Church functions were one of the rare occasions slaves had to socialize with their peers from other plantations and farms.

"Obadiah, don't be late to services," chided Lewis.

"Yes su'ah, Marse Lewis," replied the slave.

Deacon Archibald greeted Mr. Lewis at the front door.

"Good morning, James."

"Good morning, Deacon."

"James, how are you doing?" The deacon sounded genuinely concerned.

"Deacon, it's hard. Losing Ann and the grandchildren so close together was almost more than I could handle. I am thankful that the Lord saw fit to give me Polly during these trying times."

At the mention of her name, Deacon Archibald turned and acknowledged her presence. He nodded his head and said coldly, "Madam." His gesture and tone made Polly feel isolated, but for Mr. Lewis's sake, she maintained a façade of civility. Inside she wanted to slap the deacon's face, turn around, and leave.

"Who's speaking this morning?" James Lewis asked.

Polly expected Deacon Archibald to answer "Me." Instead he said, "Reverend Josiah Moss, from Talbot County."

Polly entered the sanctuary with Mr. Lewis. He always sat up front. Today was no different. But the empty space where Ann and the children usually sat made Polly feel more conspicuous. She was certain every eye in the choir was looking at her. For the moment, she envied Obadiah and Delia. If her skin were black, she too would be relegated upstairs to the balcony. No one would pay any attention to her there. Most of the congregation ignored the presence of slaves in Sunday worship.

Josiah Moss was an old man. He crept up to the pulpit when the time came for him to deliver the sermon. As she watched him, Polly anticipated a boring lecture, but the preacher's deep, booming voice caught her attention. She quickly reexamined the speaker. His tall and lanky body was stooped. He wore a dark broadcloth suit. A black cravat decorated the standup collar of his white linen shirt. His thin face was obscured by a bushy white beard, but his blue eyes seemed so friendly. As she listened to him speak, Polly gradually forgot about the other people's animosity.

Reverend Moss's text came from Matthew 10:42: "And whosoever shall give to drink unto one of these little ones a cup of cold *water* only in the name of a disciple, verily I say unto you, he shall in no wise lose his reward." Moss declared it was a Christian obligation to help the less fortunate. A strange sense of responsibility burned within Polly as he spoke. For the second time in her life, she was convinced that God was speaking directly to her. For the first time, she entertained the possibility that the church might have a role in God's design. Perhaps people simply didn't listen to God, so they managed churches by human notions. Polly didn't dwell long on this new insight. She heard Moss describe the suffering of the wounded in Confederate hospitals. The remainder of the sermon occupied her full attention after that. She was more certain than ever that God was speaking to her through the message.

As Reverend Moss concluded his sermon, Polly bowed her head and silently prayed, "Dear Lord, I can't do much, but I am a good nurse if I do say so myself. If you can use me to help our suffering soldiers, here I am."

As Polly and Mr. Lewis rode home, she planned how she would tell him. It was best to wait until they returned to Stillwater, she concluded. Perhaps she would tell him at lunch. But inexplicably, Mr. Lewis looked at her and asked, "What's the matter, Polly?"

"I've volunteered to be a nurse," she blurted out.

"A nurse? Where?"

"Chattanooga."

"Chattanooga, Tennessee?"

"Yes, sir."

"Why so far away? Couldn't you be a nurse here?"

"I suppose. But our soldiers need nurses more than the folks here. I keep thinking about Edwin's letter, the one about Richard's death. If I can in some small way prevent just one wife from receiving a letter like that, well…you see. I just have to try. Do you understand?"

Mr. Lewis did not answer immediately. Polly could tell that he was in deep thought. Then he turned, put his arm around her shoulders, and said, "Yes, Polly, I think I do understand. We all need to do what we can to help our boys in the army. Perhaps separation from you can be considered as my own special contribution to the war effort."

Mr. Lewis's quick acceptance of her decision startled Polly. At first she didn't know exactly what to say, but she managed a sheepish, "Yes, sir." Then she began to cry.

Lewis smiled and responded, "Now, now, dear. It's all right. I understand. I'll admit I want you to stay here. But I won't be selfish. Are you sure about Chattanooga?"

"Yes, sir. I have a friend from Mobile, Kate Cumming…Kate is a nurse with the Army of Tennessee. She's at a hospital in Chattanooga. I wrote her before Ann got sick…to inquire about the possibility of becoming an army nurse. I got a letter from her. She talked to a Dr. Stout. He's in charge of all the hospitals in Chattanooga. He's given preliminary approval to my application, but when Ann got sick, I couldn't leave her. She needed me. Well, last Thursday, I received another letter from Kate wanting to know if I was coming. After Ann's death, I didn't know if I should leave you. The sermon today answered my doubts. I am more certain than ever that this is what I must do. I have an odd sense that I have some important rendezvous to keep up there."

Again there was silence as Mr. Lewis absorbed Polly's statement. As the entrance to Stillwater came into view, Mr. Lewis finally spoke again. "When will you be leaving?"

"I don't really know. As soon as possible I suppose."

"I'll tell you what. Let's say no more about it today. Tomorrow, we'll go into Columbus and make the preparations. You can take a train from Columbus to Atlanta and then on into Chattanooga. Well, it's not that simple. The railroad doesn't run directly from Columbus to Atlanta, but time enough for that later. It'll take a couple of days to get to Chattanooga. You will need to stay the night in Atlanta. I recommend that you to stay at the Trout House. It's Atlanta's finest hotel. Less than a block from the depot. You'll need cash for the room and for travel expenses. I can give you enough for the trip to Chattanooga."

"Mr. Lewis, I couldn't take your money," Polly answered.

"Polly, you have saved me a lot more money than this trip will cost."

Mr. Lewis's statement puzzled Polly. "How is that?" she asked.

"You are a good nurse," he said. "Without your skill, my people would have been out of work sick much longer than they were. Your nursing helped them do more work, so it's only fair for me to compensate you."

"Mr. Lewis, I couldn't take your money," Polly repeated. "I nursed your slaves because it was the right thing. I have saved enough from what the white folks around here paid me. It's not much, but it's enough for train fare. I can rest on the trains. Kate said I would be taken care of after I reach Chattanooga."

"Nonsense! I am taking care of this. Let's just say it's my way of helping those poor lads who have sacrificed so much for our country."

"Yes, sir," Polly responded.

Mr. Lewis leaned forward and said, "Delia, I am in the mood for some of your delicious skillet-fried chicken."

"Yes, suh, I cans fry up sum fo' dinnah tonight."

Another week and a half passed before Polly and Mr. Lewis could make all of the necessary arrangements. The South was under martial law, so Polly had to go to the provost marshal's office and obtain a passport to travel. Finally, everything was ready. They rode into town where Polly could catch the morning train to Opelika, Alabama, and then onto West Point, Georgia. At West Point, she could transfer to a train going to Atlanta.

As they stood on the station platform in Columbus, Mr. Lewis warned Polly, "Don't talk to strangers. If a man offers to help you in any way, just say, 'Thank you, sir, I don't need any assistance.' Remember that at every military post, you will need your passport countersigned. In some cases you may need an additional pass or voucher, so check with the railroad whenever you change trains. One last thing; and it's very important. We don't have standard railroad time in the Confederacy. Each railroad operates on its own local time. For example when it's eleven thirty in Atlanta, it's 11:43 in Augusta. I don't know about all the towns where you will change trains. But it could cause you to miss a train if you are not careful."

"Yes, sir. I'll try and remember everything."

"Here, take this new *Lloyd's Railroad Guide*. It's got most of the information you need. You can read it on the train."

"Thank you, Mr. Lewis," said Polly as she took the pamphlet from Lewis's hand.

Just before she got on the train, James Lewis hugged Polly and kissed her on her forehead. "Polly, thank you for everything. I can never repay you…"

"Repay me? No, Mr. Lewis, it is I who owe you."

"Polly, you can never know what you have meant to me these last couple of months. But I'll tell you what. Let's agree that we are indebted to each other."

"Yes, sir."

"When the war is over—or if you change your mind—remember, Stillwater is your home."

"Thank you, Mr. Lewis. I'll remember."

Polly followed Mr. Lewis's advice and spent the night in Atlanta at the Trout House. Elegant wallpaper adorned her room, and the bed was very comfortable, but Polly arose earlier than necessary. Even though she only needed to purchase her ticket and send Kate Cumming a telegraph with her arrival time in Chattanooga, Mr. Lewis's warning about variations in local times made her panicky. She did not want to miss the train. The city gas lamps marginally illuminated the sidewalk as she walked the short distance to the car shed, Atlanta's magnificent railroad depot.

Frightened by the dangers that might lurk in the darkness, Polly set a rapid stride. Her heart was pounding when she reached the station. Once inside the colossal structure, she crossed the twin tracks of the Western and Atlantic Railroad to reach the center platform. There she paused long enough to locate the ticket window. Most passengers purchased tickets from the conductor after they boarded the cars. However Polly's new *Lloyd's Railroad Guide* advised buying tickets before boarding the train. Besides, after her tense hike to the station, she just wanted some calming human contact. She handed the man at the window four Georgia twenty-five cent banknotes and a Confederate five-dollar bill and said, "One ticket to Chattanooga please." The man examined the bills and put them into a small tin box on the counter in front of him.

Handing Polly her ticket, he said, "Morning train leaves at six forty-five. You can wait in the room over yonder until Mr. Fuller calls for passengers."

Polly started toward the door that the ticket agent had indicated but paused to take stock of the moment. On the track adjacent to her was a polished locomotive. Its cab and tender were painted dark green. A bronze plate on its boiler identified the engine as the General. Behind it were a baggage car and two straw-colored passenger cars. They showed signs of wear. The paint was faded and flaking off. The glass in a few windows was broken. Smoke from the locomotive hovered low to the ground and burned Polly's eyes. She looked up at the curved trusses that secured the car shed's massive barrel roof. It spanned all four tracks that passed through the depot. Above the center platform, a clerestory skylight ran the entire length of the structure. Polly felt so small inside this immense space.

Her introspection was terminated by a voice yelling, "Morning passenger train to Chattanooga, all aboard." Polly joined the passengers loading into the straw-colored cars. She quickly located a window seat and sat down. The train was not full today, so no one sat beside her. Soon she felt the train lurch forward beneath her. Then her head fell against the car's small window and she was fast asleep. She did not awaken until she felt a gentle hand shaking her shoulder and a kind voice saying, "Ticket? Ma'am, do you have a ticket?" She handed him the ticket she had purchased in Atlanta.

"Thank you, ma'am," said the conductor. "We're at Big Shanty. It's the breakfast stop."

Polly looked up at the man and thought he looked too young to be so bald. Then she softy said, "Thank you, sir. I appreciate you letting me know."

The Lacy Hotel at Big Shanty was a large wood frame building. A white picket fence separated it from the railroad tracks. Between the fence and the track, a low spot was filled with water. Several ducks swam in this pool, paying scant attention to Polly and the other passengers.

Polly did not stop on the porch where the train crew was washing their hands in a basin. She went into a large dining room with a single table. Hot food already was set out. She handed Mr. Lacy a Georgia twenty-five cent banknote and sat down. Mrs. Lacy sat at the head of the table and said grace before the meal. Grits, ham with red gravy, eggs, hot biscuits, flapjacks with butter, sorghum, and coffee made from sweet potatoes were available, but Polly only ate flapjacks with butter and sorghum. She sipped her coffee and tried to remember what real coffee tasted like. Before she drained the last drop, the conductor called for the passengers to reload the train for Chattanooga.

Chattanooga was a small village on the Tennessee River. Its population had swelled to 10,000 because of the war. It produced some iron, but the city's importance grew from its railroads. The Memphis and Charleston Railroad connected this hub with the Mississippi River and the Trans Mississippi. The Nashville and Chattanooga Railroad connected it to the state capital and then into Kentucky. However, Federal occupation of Memphis and Nashville made both railroads vital supply lines for Confederate forces operating between Chattanooga and these cities. The East Tennessee and Georgia Railroad linked the city to southwest Virginia. The Western and Atlantic connected it with Atlanta and the railroad network of the deep South. These two railroads provided a direct connection between Robert E. Lee's Army of Northern Virginia above Richmond and Braxton Bragg's Army of Tennessee east of Nashville.

The train finally reached Chattanooga around six thirty that evening, slightly behind schedule. The Chattanooga depot was very similar to Atlanta's car shed but smaller, and the lower courses were made of stone rather than brick. Polly recognized Kate Cumming standing on the center platform as the train braked inside the depot. A single Confederate soldier stood beside her. After the two ladies greeted each other warmly, the soldier picked up Polly's bag. Outside they climbed into an army ambulance, and the three headed into town.

The canvas sides of the ambulance were rolled up, so Polly soaked in the sights as they pulled away from the depot. She was awed by the natural beauty of the place. Green mountains surrounded the city. The late afternoon sun silhouetted the formidable profile of Lookout Mountain against the western sky. Most of the wooden structures in town needed a coat of whitewash. Among the few brick buildings was a three-story hotel named the Crutchfield House. It stood a short distance from the depot and caught Polly's attention quickly.

Kate grinned and said, "Hotel de Crutchfield. I stayed there when I first arrived here. The rooms were too expensive and quite inferior. It's a hospital now, the Foard. Mrs. Newsom is in charge there."

The ambulance pulled up to a row of brick warehouses. A few stores also lined the street. A nice three-story frame house stood on the corner. Kate led Polly into a sparsely furnished room inside the house. A bed, a small desk with a single chair, and an upright dresser were the only furniture. Faded pink floral-patterned wallpaper dominated the room. On one wall, a window framed the picturesque Tennessee River and the mountain ranges on its far side, but a refreshing breeze from the river rippled the white lace curtains, obscuring Polly's view of the landscape.

Kate said, "Polly, I must apologize for bringing you here to talk. But you will discover that in a hospital, there is no privacy. I wanted to talk with you before introducing you to the staff."

"I understand, Kate," replied Polly. "You must have questions."

"Yes, Polly, I do. I have certain responsibilities here. Let's sit down where we can discuss everything without unsympathetic ears hearing what they may not understand."

The two friends sat on the bed. For a moment, the room was silent as they nervously eyeballed each other. Their wariness evaporated as both realized how much they had missed each other's friendship. Polly regretted not contacting Kate earlier. She had thought that Richard and the Andersons were the only people who really cared about her. Now she recognized she had been wrong. She had several friends. Richard and Ann were gone, but James Lewis and Delia had embraced her. Polly knew she could depend on them. She was confident about Edwin as well. Now she was ready to confide in Kate.

"Polly, what happened?" Kate finally asked. "You just disappeared. I heard gossip that your husband killed your father in a duel, but nothing ever came of the rumors. All I really know is that one day, your house was sold to Mr. Rowe and you were gone. You never wrote me until last spring. I thought something terrible had happened to you."

"Kate, 'terrible' does not do justice to my fate. Prescott was a cruel beast. You knew I was pregnant at the time, did you not?"

"Yes, almost everyone in Mobile was aware that you were expecting."

"He beat me and I lost the baby." Polly burst into tears. Ann had been the only person to whom she had spoken about her miscarriage. Now she was telling an old friend who had known her before she had lost the baby. Memories of the trauma and of Ann's death suddenly incapacitated her.

Kate reached over and patted the top of Polly's thigh. Kate's voice was reassuring. "It's okay, dear. But Dr. Stout has high standards for ladies in the hospitals. And I need to know a few things before I introduce you to him and the surgeons. What happened to Mr. Prescott? Your letter said your name was Brenton."

"I ran away from him after we lost the baby, so he divorced me. Said that I abandoned him. Well, I guess I did. If I had stayed with him, Kate, he would have killed me." Polly then related the entire episode, at least what she knew about it. As she spoke, a heavy burden seemed to lift from her shoulders. She had not talked to anyone so honestly since Ann's death.

When Polly finally ceased talking, Kate asked, "Do you know what has become of that scoundrel Prescott?"

"He's dead," answered Polly. "Not long after he divorced me, I heard that a jealous husband shot him over in Selma."

"Is that when you remarried?"

"It was about that time. Kate, I honestly can't remember if Richard and I were married before Prescott's death or after it. All I can say for certain is that it was after the divorce. Kate, Richard was so great. We had a wonderful marriage."

"Where's Mr. Brenton now?"

"Kate, I'm a widow. Richard was killed at Sharpsburg last fall. That's part of the reason I contacted you. I wanted to do whatever I can to prevent more widows."

As the two ladies continued to talk, they shared old memories and filled in the gaps about what they had done since last seeing each other in Mobile. The sun already was setting behind Lookout Mountain when Kate said, "Polly, if anyone asks about your family, just tell them that your husband was killed at Sharpsburg. That should satisfy their curiosity. No one needs to know anything else. Now come with me and I'll show you your quarters. Your room is just down the hall. Tomorrow we will take care of assignments and other matters. For now, welcome to Newsom Hospital and the glorious Confederate Army of Tennessee."

Newsom Hospital had capacity for 750 patients. Though her hours were long and often tiresome, Polly found her work at Newsom pleasing. She arose every morning at four o'clock and frequently did not get to bed until midnight. Yet the work acted like a tonic for her sadness. For the most part, her duties involved preparing meals for the ward, distributing clothing, and simply comforting the sick and wounded. The ward's brick walls were whitewashed with pure slaked lime mixed in water to deodorize the space. Unfortunately, foul human body odor and the putrid scent of decay overwhelmed any benefits the lime provided.

When she entered the ward a week after her arrival, the patient lying on a bunk in the corner of the room startled Polly. He wore a Federal uniform. His dark blue sack coat was stained with human sweat and mud. But it was not the color of the uniform that surprised Polly; there were other Yankees in the ward. What startled Polly was the color of the man's skin, dark chocolate. The sight of a black man in a Yankee uniform confused her. Because of her relationship with Delia, Polly had developed a strange compassion for most black people she encountered. But this one was wearing a Yankee uniform…and she still retained hostile feelings for the men who had killed Richard. The sight roused conflicting emotions. "Kate, is he one of those new colored soldiers I read about in the newspaper?" she asked.

"No, he's not a soldier. He's one of the Negro laborers the Yankees employ," answered Kate. "The Yankees treat them worse than we treat our slaves. Likely he is a runaway. Look at him. He's dying. I'm sure if he knew how his liberators were going to use him, he would have stayed home."

"I suppose," replied Polly half-heartedly.

"The Yankees call these poor wretches *contraband*," said Kate. "They lambaste us for referring to slaves as *property*, and they call them *illegitimate property*."

The recuperating Confederate soldiers who were serving as nurses during their convalescence were ignoring this black man in uniform. Their temporary assignments did not produce skilled nursing. Nor did their combat experience always engender compassion for the enemy. Most at least attempted to provide some care for prisoners, primarily because they were afraid word of mistreatment might be reciprocated in the future, at which time they might be the victim in a Yankee hospital. But they clearly showed their disdain for this runaway slave. One nurse had even proclaimed loudly that if he had his weapon, he would "gladly bayonet the nigra." Kate and Polly watched as one nurse checked the other patients in the room but simply skipped the suffering black man.

As they watched, Dr. Alexander Hunter, a surgeon at Newsom, joined them. Observing the nurses' indifference toward the Yankee contraband, he said to Kate, "Miss Cumming, would you or Mrs. Brenton mind caring for that poor Negro. He is dying."

"Sir, I don't mind," Polly said. Then she thought, *What did I just say? Yes, I do mind. But I already have opened my big mouth.*

"Are you sure?" asked Dr. Hunter.

"Yes, sir, I mean, no, sir, I don't mind. I used to doctor Mr. Lewis's slaves back in Georgia."

For the next few days, Polly gave the man special attention. His name was Esau. He claimed he was a freedman from Ohio, but his accent suggested southern Louisiana. Polly figured he most likely had been a slave on some sugar cane plantation. He died the following Tuesday, but not as a result of poor treatment. Polly's nursing skills had impressed both Kate and Dr. Hunter. Without any fanfare, her nursing duties increased and included changing bandages and assisting Dr. Hunter and the other surgeons treating wounds.

* * *

The first enemy troops reached Chattanooga on Wednesday, July 1. The din in the streets was louder than normal. Kate and Polly were too busy caring for patients to check out its cause. The army had sent its sick back to Chattanooga in anticipation of another battle, so the hospital was full. The two women failed to notice that Dr. Hunter had entered the ward.

"Miss Cumming. Mrs. Brenton."

"One moment, sir," Kate answered.

"No, wrap up whatever you are doing. I need to speak with you immediately," responded Dr. Hunter. Both women quickly finished and headed for the doctor. They were slowed by Confederate soldiers rushing to several windows that faced the river. These men carried folded yellow flags, which were soon hanging from the window sills.

"Ladies, Yankee cannons are posted across the river. They intend to shell the city soon. It's too late to evacuate you. We're hanging flags to mark this structure as a hospital. I suggest you stay in your quarters until the army can get us out of here."

"Dr. Hunter," said Kate. "The Yankees are just as likely to blow up our quarters as they are this hospital. I'm staying with these boys in here. They need me. If it is time for me to stand before my Maker, I had rather have been doing His work here than hiding in a closet there."

"Me, too," said Polly softly.

CHAPTER SIX
"Give them hell, boys, give them hell."

AT ROLL CALL ON THE MORNING OF JUNE 20, CAPTAIN Ellis handed Father two letters. Edwin had no time to read them as the army resumed its march down the Shenandoah Valley, so he stuck the letters in his pocket. That evening after the regiment had stacked arms, he dropped his bedroll and accouterments under a large oak. Other members of the Columbus Guards likewise placed their gear around this and other nearby trees. John Lindsay began digging a fire pit. Other comrades began gathering firewood. Father reached into his pocket and pulled out the two letters.

Both envelopes were the same. A patriotic cannon and flag design were printed in blue on one side. Ann's recent letters were all mailed in the same style envelope, so Father's casual glance that morning led him to assume both were from her. Sitting up against the trunk of the oak tree, Father held the letters in both hands and smiled in wonderful anticipation of his only connection with his family. Polly's letter was on top. Her handwriting and Ann's were so similar that Father did not discern its author. He checked the postmark. Then he shuffled the letters to check the postmark on the other letter, intending to read them in the order they were mailed. Mr. Lewis's handwriting jumped out. Father's stomach dropped. A letter from his father-in-law could only mean bad news.

Father's hands trembled as he tore open the envelope and unfolded its contents. *"With great sorrow I take my pen in hand to write you of the tragic events..."* Tears rolled down his cheeks as he continued reading. The envelope and Polly's letter slipped out of his hand as the hardened warrior bowed his head and wept.

Lindsay heard Father's crying. He stopped digging and approached Father slowly. "What's wrong old man?" he asked. His voice showed sincere concern, not course frivolity.

"Dead...they're all dead," Father sobbed without looking up. "Who's dead?"

Father now looked up at Lindsay and whispered, "Ann, the kids. My family is all dead." The news had knocked the life out of him. He simply no longer had the strength to speak.

Father handed Lindsay Mr. Lewis's letter. Lindsay read it and picked up its envelope along with Polly's letter. He put them in Father's pocket. He knew nothing he could do would ease Father's grief. He just squeezed Father's shoulder and said, "Sorry, pard."

Like Lindsay, the rest of the company did not know what to say. They empathized with him. They even grieved with him. But the war had hardened them against normal human emotions. For two years they had witnessed killing on an unprecedented scale. To preserve their sanity, they had developed a callousness to death that enabled them to cope in their world of brutal human butchery.

But Father could not escape the pain. He thought back to that cold February day two years earlier when Reverend DeVotie's drowned son was brought back to Columbus from Mobile. That day, he combated the grief of abstract death with the reality that his own children were alive. Now the deaths were real, and his thoughts could not bring them back to life. This reality was far more distressing than he had imagined. Ann was gone, too! Never again would he look into her light blue eyes. Never again would he embrace her slender figure. *Oh God!* How he hurt. The sorrow seemed too great for him to bear. Why did they die? He pleaded with God for answers, but he could find none. His anguish would not abate. A bitter sense of guilt overwhelmed him. Was it his fault for leaving them? If he had stayed home instead of joining the army, would they still be alive?

During the next few days, General James Longstreet's First Corps of the Army of Northern Virginia—including the Columbus Guards—continued moving down the Shenandoah towards Maryland. The almost mechanical habit of marching allowed Father's mind to wander and drift into despondency. The more depressed he became, the more he blamed God. The Baptist pastor-turned-soldier faced a spiritual crisis. He was abandoning his faith in God. His troubled emotional state was apparent to everyone in the company. John Lindsay, afraid Father might do something irrational, attempted to keep an eye on him.

The evening after the Columbus Guards crossed the Potomac River into Maryland, Father disappeared. After the company had stacked rifles, he dropped his equipment under a tree, as usual, and walked out of camp with others to gather firewood. But Father failed to return. Captain Ellis had assigned Lindsay to regimental headquarters as a runner, so he was not there to watch after Father. He learned of Father's absence when he rejoined the company later that night. Lindsay enlisted Sergeants Thomas Chaffin and Theodore Fogle as volunteers to help him. The three men then set out to find their missing comrade.

Approaching a small well-kept farm in the darkness, the trio heard Father singing the melancholy "All Quiet on the Potomac Tonight." Quickly, the three soldiers rushed to the sound. What they discovered was both amusing and distressing. Father was leaning against a barn. In his right hand was a small brown jug. His obvious intoxication left no mystery to its contents. A farmer held a pitchfork against Father's torso. Every time Father moved, the farmer pressed the metal points harder against his chest.

Father spotted Lindsay in the trio and hollered, "Johnny, my boy, this crazy farmer is trying to kill me dead." Then he burst into laughter. "Mister farmer man, you can't kill me with a big fork. You need a big gun!" His speech was slurred and mixed with laughter. "Johnny, my boy, give this here farmer your Enfield. He don't have no shotgun." Father continued, "Mister, if Johnny gives you his gun, can you kill me dead?"

The farmer lowered his pitchfork slightly as the three soldiers approached. Lindsay reached Father just as he collapsed into his arms. The jug fell to the ground and shattered. The little whiskey remaining inside soaked into the ground.

"Help me here," Lindsay said to his companions. The two sergeants grabbed Father under his shoulders. Both were smiling at the sight of a drunken preacher. Father lifted his head and nodded at his two benefactors.

"Father, where did you get that jug of busthead?" asked Sergeant Fogle.

"I was hankering for some genuine coffee. So went foraging at one of these big Dutch farmhouses up the road a piece. Couldn't find any coffee, but the old Dutchman sold me this here jug of apple cider."

"Sold you, did he?" quipped Chaffin.

Father grinned impishly and boasted, "Sure did, Sergeant. I plunked down two Confederate dollars." Father looked at Chaffin and winked. Then he twisted his head to look at Fogle. His grin faded and he whispered, "I think that good-for-nothin' Dutchman hornswoggled me. I'm beginning to suspect this here cider is a mite strong."

"Do tell," responded Chaffin.

Both sergeants erupted in uncontrollable laughter. They were quite certain Father knew what he was drinking, but the preacher's pretense at ignorance only added to their comedic consciousness.

The bewildered farmer lowered his pitchfork completely and addressed Lindsay. "Sir, this man was trying to steal my chickens. Every time you rebels come here, someone steals my chickens."

"Well, you stopped him, didn't you?"

"Yes, sir, I did. I've had him pinned against this wall for over an hour."

"What did you plan to do with him?"

"I wasn't rightly sure. He kept begging me to kill him, but I was just hoping the army would come by and I could turn him over to them."

"Well mister, here we are," responded Chaffin. "I guess you can turn him over to us."

"Yes, sir, I suppose I can. I was kind of hoping our boys might show up before you rebs did," answered the farmer.

"Mister, you sure are brave for an abolitionist," Fogle smirked, "talking that way to three armed Confederate soldiers."

"Fogle, simmer down," Chaffin said with a grin. "Mister, this here drunken reb is Private Edwin Anderson of the famed Columbus Guards. Why even drunk, a Guard can handle a half dozen Yankees."

"Maybe, but this one Maryland farmer seems to have done all right," asserted the farmer.

The three soldiers laughed.

"Mister, I reckon you are right," noted Lindsay. "Would you have a pot of coffee to share with your prisoner?"

The loyalist farmer invited the four Confederates into his house. His wife boiled a pot of coffee in the fireplace while her husband and his guests talked. The conversation avoided politics, but each side did their best to outdo the other in bragging about their respective home communities. It was almost dawn when the four returned to camp. Men already were stirring in preparation to march. Camp gossip said they would invade Pennsylvania by nightfall.

As the column moved out, Captain Ellis walked alongside Father and said, "Edwin Anderson, if you ever pull another stunt like you did last night, I will personally boot your inebriated carcass all the way back to Mexico."

Edwin did not say a word. He just hung his head in shame and continued putting one foot in front of the other. The lack of sleep the previous night made marching more difficult, but embarrassment fueled Father's determination to keep up with his company. That night he would have no problem dozing off. After supper he headed for his bedroll, which was already spread under a large chestnut tree. Confederate soldiers inevitably slept under trees, their heads at its base and their bodies radiating out like spokes in a wheel. Father removed his jacket and started folding it into a pillow. As he did, the two letters in his pocket fell onto his blanket.

Father reached down. He had not opened Polly's letter. Sweat had soaked his jacket as he marched in the hot June sun. It had smeared the ink so that Polly's script on the envelope no longer was legible. He hesitated for a moment. Then he tore the end of the envelope off and pulled out the letter. He took a candle out of his haversack and fixed it in the socket of his bayonet. Driving the point of the bayonet into the ground provided an excellent improvised lamp. He read Polly's letter. He was amazed at her newfound faith in God. *Perhaps she had not loved Richard as much as I loved Ann*, Father conjectured. He was not yet ready to make peace with God. His bitterness over Ann's death was too great.

Thinking that destroying the letter from Ann's father might take away some of his pain, Edwin walked back over to the campfire, read Mr. Lewis's letter for the last time, and then deliberately placed it in the flames. No one spoke. By their silence, each man at the fire extended his sympathy to Edwin. Two years of war had created an indescribable bond. Only those who shared in this brotherhood could comprehend it. Each man in his own way grieved with Father over his loss. No one questioned his ritual propitiation. They allowed him to deal with his grief as he saw fit…at least as long as it did not risk the lives of other members of the company. As the fire consumed the letter, Father extended his hand again to burn Polly's letter. However, he could not bring himself to destroy it. Instead, he returned it to his jacket pocket.

The invasion of Pennsylvania was going well. Benning's Brigade camped outside Chambersburg and remained there over a week. Father's depression deepened with the relative inactivity of camp life. At times, he was assigned duty with details destroying military targets in the area. Otherwise he stayed to himself, alternating between reading the letter from Polly and staring at the tintype of Ann he kept in his jacket pocket. The tintype was over two years old. Its paper folder had vanished long ago. The metal was bent in several places, but Ann's image was sharp and clear. His daily gazes at it previously initiated strong yearnings to hold her in his arms again. The yearnings were still present, but now they were being crushed by the realization he never would see Ann again. Thinking of her brought a sharp, continuous pain to his chest.

A late afternoon shower soaked the Columbus Guards' campsite on June 30. As the sun rose the next day, the wet ground glistened in the early morning light. Favorable aromas teased the men's appetites as they cooked the customary three days' rations, including salt pork, turkeys, chickens, ducks, and mutton, all purchased from the local farmers. Fresh loaves of bread, hams, cheese, butter, and jams also were on the menu. Much to the chagrin of the sellers, the cornucopia was all paid for with Confederate money. Large portions of Pennsylvania's bounty were consumed immediately. That which the soldiers did not eat was stuffed in soiled haversacks. Blankets were rolled up and accouterments readied. Despite an early morning reveille, no order for the brigade to march was given. Instead, an incessant stream of creaking wagons clogged the road.

Benning's Brigade was now part of General John Bell Hood's division. That morning, the division had held a dress parade and conducted inspections. However, after two years of war, these veterans required little oversight to keep equipment ready for combat. As the temperature climbed and the hours ticked by, the soldiers sought the usual diversions: playing cards, reading the Bible, and writing letters. The most popular activity was the steady conversation, most of which was jovial prattle.

Unable to leave the area, Father drifted from huddle to huddle where he feigned a smile and then moved to the next group of soldiers. Around noon, he sat up against an old oak tree. Pulling his slouch hat down over his eyes, he gave the appearance of sleep. In reality, good and evil clashed within his soul. Father's doubts about God's relevance persisted, but he finally prayed again. He asked God to let him be killed in the next battle. Death surely would bring relief from his suffering. He recalled how Job's wife, in Job 2:9, advised her husband to "curse God and die," so momentarily Father considered doing just that to ensure his demise. However, he could not bring himself to go quite that far. Instead, he contented himself with begging God to just let him die.

Late that afternoon, drums beating the long roll stirred the idle gathering. All around Chambersburg, men scurried to fall in with their companies. Father rushed to find his place in the ranks of the Columbus Guards. Quickly, the disarray transformed into two lengthy, orderly rows of men. "Right face!" "Forward... march!" The commands were repeated by a multitude of voices at various sites across town. In an instant, the formations shifted into columns of four, and each brigade began merging into its division. Pickett's division remained in the city, but the rest of General Longstreet's I Corps moved down the road towards the small town of Gettysburg.

The men were lean and tan. Their clothing was dirty and worn. No two seemed to be dressed alike. Many wore homemade shirts rather than uniform jackets. Patches adorned every garment. The only items not mended were the vast number of sky blue Federal trousers, obviously stripped from the Union dead in previous battles. The variety of hats and the assortment of colors were endless. Some soldiers were barefoot. The only semblance of a uniform was the inevitable toothbrush stuck in the second buttonhole of a jacket or in the breast pocket of a shirt. In stark contrast to their clothing, the Enfield or Springfield rifles on each man's shoulder were bright and clean. Northern civilians peered out doors and windows at these unkempt troops and marveled how they had defied the power of Federal arms for so long. The long line of marching rebels seemed endless to these mortified Northerners.

The tiresome march through the mountains was stop and go. Despite pleas from the ranks, the customary ten minutes' rest each hour was not granted. The view from the crest, however, erased every soldier's fixation on the heat and fatigue. As the column started to descend the high slope, the distant rumble of cannon fire echoed from the east. Their steps gained new purpose. Every eye strained to capture the scene before them. The gentle rolling hills were colored various shades of rich green. Other fields were gold with ripening oats and wheat. The blue sky above the distant town was inscribed with the distinctive gray puffs of smoke from shells bursting in the summer air.

Excitement electrified the ranks. The Army of Northern Virginia had never tasted defeat. Perhaps the end of the war was in sight. Father no longer cared about the outcome of the war. He only imagined that he was seeing the end of his distress. He fantasized that out there, in an unknown Yankee cartridge box, was the bullet that would end his pain. An unnatural peace invigorated his steps. He was eager to arrive at his encounter with that bullet.

Long shadows gave way to the darkness of night, but the column pushed on. Men stumbled and cursed. The only response from the officers was "Close up." The column kept its pace toward another rendezvous with the death angel.

Around midnight, Benning's Brigade stopped. Other Confederate units already were asleep on the ground. The tired veterans dropped to the damp clover without removing their equipment. Conscious that his death might come the next day, Father slept well. However, the night's bivouac was brief. At three o'clock in the morning, the march resumed. After covering only three miles, the column again halted. The weather was agreeable. At seven o'clock the temperature was 74 degrees. The sky was overcast, and a mild breeze blew from the south. The soldiers' mood grew more somber. The sights, sounds, and smells from earlier fighting vanquished any illusion of what the day would hold. At one o'clock in the afternoon, the division once more resumed its movement. The delightful morning had been replaced by a scorching daytime heat.

As the march moved closer to the enemy, decks of cards, dice, and other unnecessary items were tossed into the bushes along the route. Father thought about reaching down and picking up a pack of cards. Having them in his pocket might tip the balance of fate in favor of his death, but fear of stumbling assuaged the attraction. Then he saw something so tempting he could not resist picking it up.

On the ground was a small *carte de visite*, a photographic print glued to a cardboard back. This one had a woman's picture. She was not particularly attractive, but her pose was explicitly obscene. Her skirt was pulled above her waist, and she did not wear undergarments. Her legs were placed so that her genital area was clearly exposed. Father reached down and picked up the print without breaking stride. Partially unbuttoning his jacket, he inserted the lewd photograph in the pocket over his heart. The deed gave him a curious sense of satisfaction. Father imagined that possession of the pornographic picture would ensure that he would be killed in the looming battle. And his agility in grabbing an item off the ground while marching generated personal pride.

Colonel Harris's voice roared, "On the right! By files into line. March!" The front four men in the regiment's column turned sharply to their right. They carried out an intricate choreographed move and a line of battle began to form. Behind them the next four men peeled off and found their place in the battle line. In this manner, the regiment's line was extended to its full length.

As Hood's division approached its line of departure, Federal batteries opened fire. The Second Georgia advanced by the right flank to its position in Benning's line. The Seventeenth Georgia formed on the left of the Second. Directly in front of the regiment, an Alabama brigade already was in a line of battle. A small ridge in front of these Confederates prevented the Georgians from seeing the terrain they would cross. The men took off bedrolls and knapsacks but kept leather accouterments, canteens, and haversacks. They placed the discarded items in piles behind the formation and hoped they still would be there later.

By four o'clock that afternoon, the entire division was formed into a line of battle. Federal artillery intensified its fire. Most of the shells struck the left end of the line, where they created havoc in the Texas regiments. Confederate guns at each end of Hood's line answered their fire. At four thirty, the division was ready to attack. Scarlet banners snapped in the gusting wind common to the battlefield. The fourteen hundred men in Benning's Brigade were hot and thirsty. Few of them could see General Hood take his place in front of his old Texas brigade. None could hear his brief speech. Nonetheless, his command to fix bayonets was repeated by subordinates, and soon the clanking of metal against metal undulated across the fields. By now, smoke obscured the entire front. The Alabamians moved forward and vanished into the haze.

The voice of "Old Rock" roared, "Attention! Shoulder—arms! Right shoulder shift! Guide center. Forward!" Colonel Harris repeated the command, and the Second Georgia stepped off, ready to meet the enemy. Father was eager to find the bullet that would end his despair. The regiment maintained splendid alignment as it advanced. Harris rode twenty yards in front of his men.

Four hundred yards ahead of the brigade, the Confederate line was in trouble. The Georgians charged with a yell. Harris's horse was shot, and the colonel hurtled to the ground several feet in front of the fallen animal. Harris jumped up, drew his sword, and cried, "Forward men!" Now on foot, he continued to stay twenty yards ahead of his regiment. General Benning paced back and forth in front of the brigade shouting, "Give them hell, boys, give them hell." The Second Georgia crossed a small creek and moved into a deep gorge. The formation began to come apart in the grotesque landscape of large boulders and patchy underbrush.

Nonetheless, the Second pressed forward along the rock-choked banks and undergrowth, driving towards the enemy before them. Father heard a Confederate to his front cry above the din of battle, "There is Benning; we are all right now."

Quickly, Father and the rest of the Second passed through the ranks of an exhausted Alabama regiment. The formation completely disintegrated as individuals hid behind rocks and trees. The Federals on the cliffs above poured volley after volley into the regiment. Members of the Columbus Guards were among the dead. Harris ordered the regiment to attack a small hill called Little Round Top. He started forward one more time. However, few of his men followed him. Father was one of the few who did. Resolved to die on the battlefield, this seemed like the perfect opportunity.

Suddenly Harris fell, killed instantly when a bullet pierced his heart. Father saw him fall but kept going. However, a moment later, he slipped on a slick rock. He tumbled to the ground. Dazed, Father made no effort to get up. Exhaustion replaced depression. He lay there unable to move and awaited the outcome of the fighting. Even in the roar of battle, he could not remain conscious. Father drifted off amid the carnage that surrounded him.

By now, the Second and Seventeenth were separated from the brigade. Their advance stalled in the face of a Yankee counterattack. The two Georgia regiments fell back a short distance to a more defensible position. They bit cartridges, rammed them down hot muzzles, and fired. The Georgians found themselves in a murderous crossfire. Two cannons three hundred yards to their front also opened on them. Iron balls ricocheted off granite boulders and tore into human flesh. Still, the Georgians retained their position. A burial detail later named the spot the Slaughter Pen. Amid the bloodshed, the Second and Seventeenth Georgia repulsed seven attacks. Finally, they heard the unmistakable rebel yell from the crest of the ridge on their left. The rest of the division advanced as Union resistance crumbled. The Second and Seventeenth Georgia renewed their attack up the gorge. Outflanked, the remnants of shattered Union units withdrew to higher ground.

As the Confederate line passed by, Edwin Anderson heard a familiar voice. "Father, wake up. It's time to move on." Father looked up. It was John Lindsay. Lindsay extended his right hand. Father grasped it and pulled himself up. The two comrades quickly rejoined the rest of the Columbus Guards attacking the small knoll where the Federals were reforming. The brigade advanced into the valley beyond the rocks where they had fought most of the afternoon. They crossed a small stream but were unable to move up the hill in front of them.

"It's time to move on." Lindsay's statement seized Father's mind. Perhaps God was trying to tell him something. *'It's time to move on.' Lord, I guess it is time to move on. But where will I go?* Father reached back into his pocket and started to pull out Polly's letter. He lifted it a few inches, hesitated, and then pushed it back securely. Then he remembered the pornographic carte de visite he had picked up on the roadside. He discreetly pulled it out and tossed it among the rocks.

The Second Georgia had experienced bloody fighting during that second day at Gettysburg. That night, Benning adjusted his line and removed as many of the wounded from the battlefield as possible. Father and the other men in the ranks listened to the noise of the enemy throwing up breastworks. The sound of rock hitting rock signaled the construction of formidable defenses. The ensuing battle promised to be even more ghastly than what they had just survived, but fortunately Benning's Brigade did not renew their attack the next day. Instead, the brigade's pickets spent the day skirmishing with the enemy, but no general engagement erupted on their portion of the battlefield. Late that afternoon, the brigade withdrew back to the ridge from where they had launched their attack the previous day. Bedrolls and knapsacks were promptly retrieved from the piles where they had been dropped.

The next morning, the division formed a line of battle that straddled Emmitsburg Road. It was the Fourth of July, but no one celebrated the holiday. Instead, the men in the ranks hastily threw up breastworks. Around midnight, Hood's division commenced retreating back to Virginia. Benning's Brigade was its last to withdraw. Lightning illuminated their path. Father spent a miserable night, wet and fatigued. Torrential rain was falling. Grudgingly, his feet swung forward as he tried to keep up with the man in front of him. In the inclement weather, the pace was erratic. Men collided as the column came to an unforeseen halt when someone tumbled to the ground. During these unintended stops Father dozed off, standing erect in the ranks.

The invasion of Pennsylvania had been more disastrous than the previous year's invasion of Maryland. Sharpsburg had been a draw, but Gettysburg clearly was a defeat. For only the second time since General Lee had taken command, the Army of Northern Virginia had retreated. Heavy rain continued falling. When the army reached the Potomac River, it was impassable because of its swollen waters and swift current. The Union army caught up with them there on July 12.

Strangely, the Yankees did not attack. General Lee used the respite to build a makeshift pontoon bridge across the river. It was a rickety affair, but it sufficed. The next night, Lee's army crossed into Virginia and safety. By then, Yankee burial details already had placed over 2,592 Confederate soldiers in graves near Gettysburg. Edwin Anderson was not among them.

Back in the relative safety of Virginia, Father contemplated what had happened at Gettysburg. John Lindsay's words were still etched in his memory. "It's time to move on." Father no longer was quite so bitter at God, but he still was disillusioned. The staunch Christian conviction he had held before the war had vanished. His days as a Baptist preacher were over. He still believed

God existed, but God now seemed so distant. Religion no longer had any relevance.

One afternoon, Father read Polly's letter again. He wondered what mysterious force it held on him. Her letter reminded him of the one from Mr. Lewis. Although the fire had incinerated Lewis's letter, Father felt obligated to reply to it. He borrowed paper and pencil from John Lindsay and began to write:

South of the Potomac River
July 17, 1863

My Dear Father-in-law,

   By now you are well aware of events in Pennsylvania. It would be easy to blame my failure to acknowledge your letter upon my military obligations. However, in truth I must confess that I have been paralyzed by grief and self-pity. Ann meant more to me than anything else in life. Charlotte and James were the natural expansion of our love. There is a void in my heart that their absence has created. It will be there until the Lord reunites us on the other side of Jordan. I don't know how much longer this cruel war will last. It seems as if it will go on forever. However, you are now the only family I have in this world. If you have no objections, if I survive the war, I would like to come and visit you at Stillwater. Perhaps it is not too late for us to become ~~friends~~ family.

Your obedient ~~servant~~ son,
Edwin

P.S. Is Polly still living with you at Stillwater? I made a promise to Richard before he died that I would see after her needs if he were killed.

A few days later, at Culpeper Court House, Virginia, the brigade was issued replacement uniforms. The soldiers cheerfully discarded the rags they had worn into Pennsylvania. The new uniforms dramatically transformed the appearance of Longstreet's entire corps. For once, everyone was dressed virtually alike. Each man retained his previous headgear, predominately old battered slouch hats, but the coats and trousers were all the same, a cadet gray shell jacket and sky blue trousers. The jackets were typical Richmond Depot, with shoulder straps and two belt loops. They were waist length with nine brass buttons on the front, each one regulation with a block "I" for infantry stamped on the surface. What made these particular jackets distinctive was the color. The hue in the dye gave them a faded blue color, not unlike that of Federal sack coats. Combined with the sky blue trousers, the new uniforms differed from the Yankee uniform in appearance only in the length of the jacket.

The new uniforms inspired humorous banter among the soldiers. The serious-natured Fogle was not amused when John Lindsay asked, "Hey Sarge, where did you get that Yankee uniform?" Thomas Chaffin retorted, "Off of two dead Yanks!"

"*Two* Yankees?" a puzzled Lindsay asked.

"Yeah. One got shot in the behind and got blood all over the bottom of the jacket and the seat of his britches. So I tore his coat off at the waist. The other got shot in the back and messed up his coat. So I took his pants."

Lindsay laughed, shook his head, and said, "Good, Chaf, real good."

Father didn't share in the joking. His appetite had not returned. Even though he realized that he must move on, he didn't know how. The letter to James Lewis had only been a first step. The death of his family had ushered in anger towards God. At Gettysburg, when his effort to commit suicide failed, the anger gave way to apathy. Several times, he pulled his Bible from his coat pocket and tried to read, but the pages seemed filled with empty words. One day though, he inadvertently opened to the seventh chapter of Ecclesiastes. His eyes fell on verse 14—"In the day of prosperity be joyful, but in the day of adversity consider: God also hath set the one over against the other." Father did not finish reading. The bitterness returned with vengeance. *I have just read God's confession. God was responsible for Ann's death!* Father no longer was angry or apathetic. Now he was unequivocally hostile. God had become his enemy. At that moment, "Father" Edwin Anderson started another war, one between him and God.

CHAPTER SEVEN
"The most frightful consequences"

FATHER'S WAR WITH GOD DID NOT RELIEVE HIM FROM fighting that other war in which he and his comrades were engaged. Gettysburg had been a Union victory, but morale in the Army of Northern Virginia remained strong. The men in the ranks were confident of their ultimate victory. They were certain that "Marse Robert," as they affectionately referred to General Lee, would recapture their glory soon. By early September, all signs pointed to something big in the works. The soldiers had been issued forty rounds of .577 caliber ammunition for their Enfield rifles. They also were instructed to prepare three days' worth of rations.

The ammunition came packed in four small paper packages, each containing ten cartridges and ten brass percussion caps. Father placed one package into each of the lower compartments of the two tin containers inside his leather cartridge box. He opened the two other packages and removed the cartridges, which consisted of a paper tube containing a single lead Minie ball and black gunpowder. The empty end of the tube was flattened to form a tail that was folded down along the side of the cartridge. Father positioned these cartridges vertically in the tin containers' top compartments so that in the heat of battle, he could open the flap of the leather cartridge box, reach in with his right hand, and grasp a single round at the paper fold. He took the twenty percussion caps from the two packages and put them in the small leather pouch on his belt.

After Father was certain his ammunition was in order, he grabbed his haversack and ambled over to a small group of soldiers huddled around a blazing campfire. The smell of burning wood mixed with the sweet aroma of bacon filled the air. As Father knelt down at the only vacant spot around the fire, smoke engulfed him. His eyes burned, so he jerked his head away. The abruptness of this movement caused him to lose his balance and topple over. The rest of the men laughed, all except young David Moses. Father's tumble bumped Moses's right arm and caused him to drop an iron skillet filled with bacon. Some of the bacon spilled onto the ground, leading Moses to utter a loud expletive. His profanity only amplified the mirth of the others.

John Lindsay chuckled and quipped, "What's a matter, Father? You been drinking that red eye again? Ole sarge'll have you bucked and gagged."

Father, now squatting before the fire, ignored the jest. He reached into his haversack and pulled out a frying pan that he had fashioned by taking apart a Federal tin canteen. A slot had been cut in a stick so that a canteen shell half could be inserted into it. The stick served then as a handle and the canteen shell as the pan. Father took his bacon ration out of the haversack and began laying it out in the homemade skillet.

Moses's red face had diverted Lindsay's attention away from Father, and he said, "Look pards, the fresh fish is about to have a conniption fit. He's fit to be tied!"

Moses had joined the company after Gettysburg during the regiment's recruiting efforts near Richmond. He was only seventeen years of age. When the other men around the fire were fighting at Gettysburg, he had been a student at Washington College in Lexington, Virginia. He had joined the Columbus Guards because of an old newspaper article about their Zouave drill at Jefferson Davis's inauguration. He had not yet learned of the esteem the company held for their senior veteran, and he smarted off, "This old man…"

Before he could finish, Lindsay cut him off, "Old man? Maybe, but sonny boy, this old man is on his second war. If you don't wish to be sold to the Dutch, you best learn from him."

"Sold to the Dutch, huh?" inquired Moses.

"Killed by one of them German immigrants Lincoln hires to fight this war. Yankee recruiters stand at the foot of a gangplank whenever a ship arrives from Europe. Then they sign the Germans up for the army as they get off the boat. Most of them don't speak English. So they don't understand what they are doing," answered Father as he turned his bacon with a fork.

"Really?" asked the bewildered young recruit.

"I can't say for sure, but we've captured more than one prisoner who did not speak American," asserted Chaffin.

Father removed his frying pan from the fire, took out the bacon, and wrapped it in a piece of cloth. He placed the wrapped bacon in his haversack and poured the grease onto the fire, causing a momentary racket when it flamed up. He then withdrew a small cloth bag and a small square piece of oilcloth cut from a captured poncho. After scooting back from the fire, he spread the oilcloth on the ground and poured coarse cornmeal from the bag onto it. Mixing the cornmeal and some salt with water from his canteen, Father made a paste and shaped it into a thick disk. He dropped his hoecake onto the homemade skillet and set the pan on the coals of the fire to bake. Captain Ellis stopped by just as the group was finishing cooking.

"How are you boys doing?" Ellis asked. He smiled as they responded with a chorus of the usual jokes and grumbling. Turning to Father, the captain asked, "Ed, how are you holding out?"

Father hung his head and answered, "Making it, sir. I'll be all right."

"Old friend, don't feed me that balderdash. I know you too well. We'll talk soon. In the meantime, sew these on your sleeves."

Captain Ellis tossed Father a pair of sky blue corporal's chevrons. Father caught the chevrons but stretched out his hand to return them saying, "Roswell, I don't want any stripes…"

Ellis interrupted him declaring, "That's Captain Ellis, Corporal. I'm afraid this time, you don't have a choice. Seems General Benning saw your row at Gettysburg. I told him that promoting a parlor soldier like you was humbug, but the general told me to toe the mark. So stop bellyaching and sew them on your duds."

"Yes, sir," Father replied meekly.

Then Ellis pulled a pocket watch from his jacket, checked the time, and continued, "Gentlemen, you better get some rest tonight. We're moving out before dawn."

Only a tint of pink on the eastern horizon was showing when the brigade broke camp and headed toward Orange Court House, the town that served as General Lee's Virginia headquarters. The day was still young when the column came to a stop. Colonel William Shepherd had replaced the deceased Colonel Harris after Gettysburg. He gave the command, "Second Georgia! Front!" In an instant, the column of four men abreast transformed itself into a line of two ranks. They stacked arms and were given the command, "In place, rest!" The Seventeenth Georgia formed on their left. The Fifteenth and Twentieth Georgia Regiments fell in behind the Second and Seventeenth.

Directly in front of the brigade lay the worn tracks of the Orange and Alexandria Railroad. The men in the ranks watched with fascination as a locomotive backed a string of tobacco-colored boxcars onto the siding. All of the boxcars' doors were open, disclosing empty interiors. Amid the sounds of screeching wheels and banging metal, the train of battered cars quickly came to a rest. The crew stepped down from the locomotive cab. The engineer inspected and oiled the engine. His fireman poured water into a purple tender with gold-leaf trim while the brakeman walked down the string of cars checking wheels and couplers. The conductor walked over to General Benning. The commanders of the four regiments ran quickly to join their conversation. When their discussion ended, the regimental commanders rejoined their soldiers.

By this time, the troops had guessed they were the train's cargo. When Colonel Shepherd approached the Second Georgia, he yelled, "Officers' call!" The ten company commanders and their lieutenants quickly gathered around him. Occasionally, the huddled officers turned and looked at the boxcars. Shepherd pointed to one of the open ones. The commanding officers of Companies A and B saluted. Then they and their lieutenants returned to their troops. Shepherd pointed to another car, and the scenario was repeated with the next two companies. When the colonel spoke to Ellis, the men of the Columbus Guards watched intently so they could identify their car. As Captain Ellis and the company lieutenants walked back to their men, non-commissioned officers moved reflexively to receive their instructions.

Meanwhile, the enlisted men visually surveyed the car they assumed belonged to the company. It was a standard twenty-eight-foot long wooden car. Several boards of siding had recently been replaced and left unpainted. The car rode on a pair of wooden frame trucks, but only the one facing the locomotive had brakes.

Their scrutiny was interrupted by the brigade bugle. As the ranks snapped to attention, General Benning's voice bellowed, "Brigade! Attention!" Regiment commanders responded, "Battalion! Attention!" Along the line, company commanders echoed in unison, "Company! Attention!" A series of commands followed as the stacked rifles were taken and an impressive martial display of power stood at shoulder arms along the railroad tracks.

Gazing proudly at his brigade, Benning once more spoke in a loud, clear voice. "Gentlemen, take charge of your regiments and board the trains." The commanding officers of the four regiments saluted. Colonel Shepherd turned and faced the Second. He pointed at some boxcars and said, "Into the house cars. We're taking a train ride."

Ellis pointed to the car the men had spied earlier and said, "Columbus Guards, on the roof! Company H got the inside." He paused briefly and added, "Hold onto your muskets. You will need them."

Father climbed up the ladder on the end of the old car and stepped on the tin roof, but the leather sole of his brogans caused him to slip. As he started sliding off the car, he reached and grasped the wooden roof walk. Simultaneously, several hands grabbed his jacket and arms. Surprisingly, he still clutched his rifle in his left hand.

"It's not your day is it, Father?" snapped Lindsay.

"It's these brogans. Made me slip at Gettysburg. Knocked me right out then," replied Father.

About that time, a roar of laughter erupted on a car assigned to Company F. The men on Father's car twisted to check out the reason for their amusement. A less fortunate comrade was knocking dirt from his uniform after tumbling off the car.

"Watch your step boys," Sergeant Fogle hollered. "Army shoes ain't designed for walking on tin roofs. One of you might fall off these here cars and break your leg."

"Break a leg, nothing! Might break my neck," responded an unidentified voice on the other end of the car roof.

"The army says necks are okay. You can still shoot without a head," cracked Lindsay, "but you can't march without a leg." The habitual chuckles followed.

Once the men had settled in their assigned location, they started the usual speculation and gossip about the movement. Alongside the track, Robertson's Texas Brigade was moving into the spot the Georgians had just vacated. It looked like Hood's entire division was on the move.

Colonel Shepherd and Captain Ellis walked by with the conductor on his inspection of the loaded train. They ignored the queries from the regiment. A few moments later, amid the hissing and bellowing of its locomotive, the train lurched forward. The sudden movement joggled its human cargo, but no one fell off. As the rhythm of the engine's chugging increased, the train slowly gained speed. Captain Ellis came running alongside Father's car. Ellis reached up, seized a grab iron, and swung himself onto the car's stirrup step. Cheers went up from the men on the roof. Ellis stepped on the end sill of the car and scampered up the ladder.

"Captain, on behalf of the O and A railroad, I welcome you to our plush first-class passenger car," Lindsay smarted off. "As you can see, this car has the latest in travel accommodations. We've removed the walls so as not to obstruct your 360-degree view of the countryside. We've raised the seating so you can see over the other cars and not miss any of the local wonderments."

"Lindsay, are you working for the railroad now?" asked Ellis.

"Well sir, I figure it's a might better than fighting in the army," Lindsay replied.

"Now Mr. Lindsay, I want to register an official complaint," inserted Chaffin.

"Well sir, what do you find so unpleasant with our transportation?" Lindsay responded in a mocking business-like voice.

"Well, your locomotive is blowing smoke into my face. It is spitting hot cinders onto my new Sunday go-to-meeting suit. And these here seats need cushions," answered Chaffin.

"Well sir, our designers are working on these issues. In fact, they already have designed solutions for each and every one of them. Unfortunately, Mr. Lincoln's navy has blockaded all of the ports in the Confederacy, and we cannot get the raw materials we need to implement the designs. So sir, I suggest you discuss all these inconveniences with Mr. Lincoln," teased Lindsay.

"What about this here smoke?" sneered Chaffin.

"Why of course. We had eliminated all smoke on our locomotives just for you, sir. However, the army officers made us reinstall the smoke. They say army regulations mandate smoke burn all privates while in transit to new duty postings," retorted Lindsay.

"A smokeless locomotive," mused David Moses. "I suppose one day people will ride in passenger cars that fly through the air. What do you think, Father?"

"Oh, I don't know, David. When I was a kid, lots of people thought trains were impractical, but look at them now. I once saw a balloon break loose and fly twenty miles before it came down. People can do lots of things that other folks don't think can be done. I suppose one of these days, somebody will figure out a way to operate a steam engine without smoke, and somebody else may even find some way to make a passenger car fly," replied Father.

The futuristic jesting soon died away. Occasionally, the men speculated on their destination. The cars rocked back and forth as the train trekked along worn-out tracks. Forty minutes after leaving Orange Court House, the train reached Gordonsville, Virginia. There the train turned onto the Virginia Central track and headed east toward Richmond. Father looked longingly at the tracks going west. He imagined traveling them to Lynchburg, then Knoxville, then Chattanooga, then Atlanta, and finally to West Point, Opelika, Girard, and Columbus. Ellis recognized the homesick expression on Father's face. "Yanks took Knoxville a week ago. If we go back to Georgia, we'll have to go the long way."

"What's up, Roswell?" asked Father.

"I don't know, Ed. But something big is happening. Our whole corps is on the move now." Ellis paused for a moment and then added, "Except maybe the survivors of Pickett's division. They're played out and not fit for much after Gettysburg."

That evening, the train pulled into the depot near Broad and 17th Streets in Richmond. After unloading, the brigade formed up and marched through the city. When they reached the Richmond and Petersburg depot on the south side of town, rolling stock composed of every imaginable type of railway vehicle was standing on the main and sideline tracks. Coal cars were coupled to passenger cars. Platform cars were coupled to baggage cars. These in turn were coupled to boxcars.

The brigade stacked arms and fell out. Details collected canteens and went in search of a water pump to fill them. Father reached into his haversack and broke off a piece of cornbread. He unwrapped what was left of the bacon—he had eaten some at breakfast and some on the train—and began chewing the salty meat. The fare hardly compared to meals at Frederick Wilhelm's restaurant in Columbus, but his system had grown accustomed to these stark rations. While he was eating, Sergeant Fogle handed Father four hardtack crackers and a slab of raw salt pork. He stuffed them into the haversack with the cornbread. When the canteen detail returned, he gulped down water to wash down the rest of his evening meal.

The brigade did not tarry long in Richmond. Well before midnight, they boarded one of the parked trains and headed south. Father and his company were assigned a flat car. They wrapped up in their blankets and soon were fast asleep.

Father awoke shortly before dawn. Roswell Ellis already was awake. "Good morning, Ed," he said cheerfully.

"Good morning, Roswell. Where are we?"

"Somewhere in North Carolina. We passed through Gaston a few minutes ago," Ellis answered.

"Where do you suppose we're headed?" Father inquired.

"My guess is Tennessee. Remember back at Gordonsville when we were dreaming about Georgia and I said we would have to go the long way? Well, it appears to me that is exactly what we are doing."

Ellis's conclusion made sense. Several newspaper articles recently suggested reinforcing Braxton Bragg's Army of Tennessee with troops from Robert E. Lee's Army of Northern Virginia. Camp gossip also conjectured such a move was likely. Others on the car were waking up. John Lindsay spoke first. "What's going on?"

"The captain says we're going to Tennessee," answered Father.

Before the company had time to digest the idea, a small hamlet came into sight. The locomotive blew its whistle and maintained its speed as it rumbled past the station. The placard on the depot read, "Littleton." A few passengers were standing on the platform waiting for the southbound mail train. At first, the sight of the long freight train filled with soldiers from Lee's army startled them. However, before the last car cleared the turnout for the parallel sidings, they were cheering wildly for the famed veterans of so many legendary battles.

Through horseback and telegraph, word of the train's movement spread faster than it traveled. Crowds began to gather at each station. Engineers were forced to slow their engines for fear of killing large numbers of civilians. Men doffed their hats. Women waved white handkerchiefs. Some of the younger ones blew kisses. Children waved small Confederate flags. A few of the small boys stood frozen in awe of their heroes. As the train progressed south, the crowds grew in size.

At one station, a man of military age wearing an elegant civilian frock coat raised his derby hat. Before he could replace it on his head, Lindsay grabbed it. He replaced his tattered slouch hat with the new acquisition.

"Fellars, how does this highfalutin hat look?" he asked.

"Lindsay, that's stealing," replied Ellis.

"No sir, I just requisitioned it. That big bug peacocking about should be in uniform instead of those duds. Way I see it, giving me his hat was his way of paying me to be his substitute," asserted Lindsay with an insincere straight face.

Everyone burst into laughter. Some wealthy men who should have been in the army evaded the draft by paying substitutes to fight in their place. Veteran soldiers held such cowards in great contempt. Everyone on the car simply concluded that the man had received some small token of justice by the loss of his hat.

By dusk on September 9, Benning's Brigade reached Raleigh, North Carolina. Unknown to them, that same day Rosencrans's

Union Army of the Cumberland entered Chattanooga. Father and the men in Longsteet's corps were destined for north Georgia, not Tennessee. Upon reaching Raleigh, the brigade said goodbye to their flat car. Benning led his men through town to the North Carolina Railroad station.

While they waited to catch another train for the next leg of their journey, some of the members of the brigade staged a raid on a local newspaper, the Raleigh *Weekly Standard*. The paper's editor, William W. Holden, was of uncertain war opinion and was considered unpatriotic by most members of the brigade. His office was smashed. Type was poured out, and some equipment was damaged. The Raleigh *Progress* accused "Rock" Benning, an ardent secessionist, of leading the mob, but The Atlanta *Intelligencer* investigated the report and concluded it was baseless.

The day after the incident, a mob wrecked the *State Journal* office in retaliation, causing North Carolina Governor Zebulon Vance to write Jefferson Davis, "Please order immediately that troops passing through here shall not enter the city. If this is not done, the most frightful consequence may ensue." By then, the brigade that caused this uproar was moving through South Carolina.

Word of the brigade's approach continued to travel faster than the dilapidated trains on worn-out track. The crowds along the right of way increased with every passing mile. Father's train stopped in Chester, South Carolina, to refuel and fill the tender's water tank. The veterans of Sharpsburg and Gettysburg leaped down from their cars. They stretched cramped muscles and laughed about events at the previous stop. Civilians stormed their ranks. Old men patted Benning's soldiers on the back and praised their military prowess. Young boys sheepishly reached to touch the famed warriors. Father and the others politely acknowledged this attention but moved promptly to female members of the crowd.

The older women handed out homemade cakes and pies. One local farmer poured fresh milk into the soldiers' tin cups to wash down this epicurean feast. More than one soldier stole a kiss from the numerous teenage girls and young ladies who flocked to admire the men of Robert E. Lee's legendary Army of Northern Virginia.

The atmosphere was electric. Even Father was swept up in the moment. One young lady caught his attention immediately. She stood with her back to him. Most of the women wore bonnets or had their hair wrapped in snoods, but this woman wore no millinery, and a row of golden curls dangled down the back of her neck from shoulder to shoulder. She reminded Father of Ann who had worn her hair in the exact same fashion to several balls they had attended before the war. For a moment, the memory eclipsed his sadness. He started to call out Ann's name, but before it escaped his mouth, the woman turned. Her hooked nose and rough face destroyed the illusion. Ann's features were delicate, and her snowy white complexion was smooth. Even so, Father could not evade the gaiety along the railroad tracks.

He felt a soft feminine hand clasp his. He turned to find a mysterious woman staring up at him. She appeared older than the rest of the ladies dispensing affection. Father guessed she was in her late twenties or early thirties. Although stocky in build, her proportions were pleasing to his eyes. She wore a light blue calico day dress that accentuated her figure well. Her eyes were dark brown and invited a man to approach her. But it was her hair that caught Edwin's attention. It was fiery red and framed her face beneath a dark blue split bonnet. Father easily squeezed her up against him and thought how wonderful holding a woman was.

"Suh," she said softly, "I-ah hope your intentions are honorable."

"Well, even if they are not, I am sure the army will not allow me time to carry them out," Father joked.

The woman giggled and said coyly, "Too bad." She extended her arms around his neck and rested in his embrace.

"Madam, you are right about that," snapped Father.

"I-ah am Adeline, Adeline Knight," she said in an exaggerated southern drawl. "And to whom do I-ah have the pleasure of addressing today?"

"Father…I mean Edwin Anderson," answered Father.

"Father?" she asked sarcastically.

"Yes, Miss Knight. I presume it is Miss," replied Father. "It's a soldier's joke. I'm somewhat older than most of the boys."

"Yea-is, I-ah reckon I-ah can see that. It twas one reason I-ah picked you out. I-ah like maturity in my men," she stated.

"Men? So I am not the first?" teased Father.

"Nope. I-ah was engaged to Rufus McDonald."

"Rufus McDonald? What happened?"

"He went and got kilt at Pittsburg Landing," she answered. "I-ah wont y'all to kill as many of them murdering Yankees as y'all can."

"I'll do my best."

"Good," said Adeline. Then she reached up and kissed Father on the lips. He kissed her back. A sensation he had not felt in two years flooded over him. He instinctively squeezed Adeline more tightly against his body. As she did, he became very conscious of her feminine form. His kiss became more passionate.

The train's conductor interrupted their romance by yelling, "All aboard!" His call set off a chain reaction.

"Brigade!"

"Second Georgia!"

"Columbus Guards! Fall in!"

Father hesitated. He did not want to let Adeline go. Then he felt a man's hand on his shoulder. Sergeant Fogle barked, "Let's go, Father."

As Father released Adeline Knight, she asked, "Ca-an I-ah wri-ate to you, Edwin Anderson?"

Father climbed back onto the boxcar roof, turned, and yelled back, "Yes, address your letter to me at Company G, Second Georgia Infantry, Benning's Brigade, Hood's Division, Longstreet's Corps, Army of Northern Virginia."

"Company G, Second Georgia! I-ah right sure I-ah can fin' yo'!"

"Correct! Benning's Brigade, Hood's Division, Longstreet's Corps, Army of Northern Virginia," yelled Father.

"Benning, Hood, Longstreet. I-ah have yo'!"

Adeline's voice was drowned out by the crowd's cheers and dozens of other similar conversations. Father dared not hope she actually would write. More likely she would forget the address. Nevertheless, he kept his eyes focused on her as the train pulled away. She was still looking at him when the train rounded a bend in the track and left her sight. She opened her purse and pulled out a small lead pencil and a tiny scrap of treasured paper—the war had made even this common commodity rare—and wrote: *Edwin Anderson, Co. G, 2nd Geo Inf., Benings Bgd, Hoods Div, Longstreet Core, ANV.*

On the roof, John Lindsay inquired, "You engaged now, Father?"

"Yeap," Father asserted jovially. He thought of Adeline's red hair. It was not the same shade as Polly's, but it sure brought back memories of Polly standing in the hallway that day so long ago. He reached into his pocket. Her letter was still there. Teasing about matrimony and recollections of the hallway in the parsonage triggered reminiscences of Ann. Over the next few hours, Father's despondency returned. He stared out into space taking little note of the scenery around him.

Benning's Brigade was the vanguard of Longstreet's corps from the Army of Northern Virginia. The new uniforms gave the entire corps a standardized military appearance unknown in the Army of Tennessee. Father once again was perched on the roof of a boxcar on Saturday, September 12, as the train approached Atlanta on the Georgia Railroad. The church spires of the city were clearly visible on the horizon. Father watched as the train rolled past an unfinished brick plantation house adjacent to the tracks and through a railroad cut in the red Georgia clay. In less than a year, this tranquil site would be a battlefield. But today, the Federal army was nearly 150 miles away in the northwest corner of the state.

The train slowed as it entered the city. Father noted the residential community seemed oblivious to the war. He turned to take in the massive car shed that dominated this rail hub. A white clerestory ran the length of its curved roof, and tall lightning rods reached from the roof towards the sky. The train was heading to one of the three arched openings that penetrated the end of the building. The center opening was half the size of the other two. Both were wide enough to accommodate two tracks. Father's train entered the left portal on its left track. Looking across the adjacent track, Father observed a loading platform that ran the length of the building. Down the center of the platform was a small brick building that contained waiting rooms and railroad offices. The platform was crowded with soldiers and civilians.

Of special interest to many of Father's comrades was a bar erected by laying wood lumber across wooden barrels. This makeshift counter was adorned with red, white, and blue bunting. Above it, hanging from the superstructure, was a large off-white cloth banner. "SOLDIERS EXECUTIVE AID ASSOCIATION" was emblazoned on it in fancy maroon lettering. Beneath that title in slightly smaller letters of the same font was "FOR THE RELIEF OF THE ARMY OF TENNESSEE." Behind the bar, well-dressed society ladies in hoopskirts were serving soldiers milk, coffee, and lemonade from wooden buckets. Young girls in plain cotton dresses weaved among the throng of thirsty soldiers to dispense cakes and fruits from baskets.

Father looked around, absorbing as much of the picture as possible. Above him, massive curved trusses supported the roof. Locomotive smoke filled the space and burned his eyes. Turning his head to see behind him, he observed a brick colonnade of arched openings. Through these openings, he could see more of the city. His sightseeing ended abruptly as officers started issuing commands. Father stood up and moved across the canvas roof of the boxcar. In front of the colonnade was another loading platform. The provost guard was clearing waiting passengers off it. Some were obviously disgruntled by their inconvenient displacement. Most were in awe of the unannounced appearance of these troops.

The brigade formed up and marched to a large park next to the car shed. A whitewashed picket fence surrounded the park. Inside the park the brigade stacked arms. Thereafter, they were allowed to roam within the park boundaries. The civilian reception in Atlanta was less cordial than the ones in the Carolinas and the rural parts of Georgia. The city had grown accustomed to troop movements. Still, the fence was lined with numerous viewers curious to see these fabled fighters from the Eastern Theater. More than one of the onlookers wore the jean wool uniform so common in the Western Theater.

The whole scene reminded Father of the time he witnessed P. T. Barnum's Great Asiatic Caravan, Museum and Menagerie. Only now he was one of the animals on exhibit. Many of Lee's soldiers engaged in conversations with the visitors along the fence. Father, however, was content to absorb the sights around him. A four-story hotel stood across the street from the north side of the park. "Trout House" was painted in large block letters on the fourth floor, with a window between each letter. A three-story brick structure stood beside it. This building had a Masonic emblem in its gable. Various business signs indicated other occupants.

The western end of the park was opposite the brick side façade of the three-story Atlanta Hotel. Another street bordered the park's east side. The city east of the park was more open with lower buildings. Father and the Columbus Guards remained in the park until Thursday when they boarded the Western and Atlantic Railroad for the trip to north Georgia. Additional ammunition was issued to the brigade. Fresh rations also were disbursed. These were eaten or stuffed in haversacks. The interaction with the city's residents continued, but mostly the men in the ranks were aggravated by the delay. They watched as Gregg's and McNair's Brigades from Joseph Johnston's command in Alabama and Mississippi boarded slate-blue cars on the Western and Atlantic and vanished from sight going north.

Eventually, Longstreet's corps received orders to move north. Robertson's Texas Brigade loaded first. Benning's Brigade followed a few hours later, and the Columbus Guards took their assigned place on the train. On this trip, they rode inside a battered boxcar. Its slate-blue paint had faded to various lighter shades. "W.&A.R.R." was stenciled on the side wall to the left of the door, and "926" was painted on the wall to the right. Father was among the last members of the company to board. He tossed his musket to John Lindsay and reached up his right hand for help. Roswell Ellis grabbed it and pulled him up. The three sat on the floor in the doorway, their feet dangling outside the car. A few boards on the side walls were busted, leaving narrow vertical openings. Some soldiers quickly enlarged these openings with little consideration for the damage they were causing. The mood was far more somber now. No one had any illusions about their destination. Some men on this northbound train had an appointment with death somewhere in north Georgia. This time, Father hoped he was not one of them. His encounter with the mysterious Adeline Knight had provided a new incentive for living, but his war with God remained unresolved.

As the train rumbled through Marietta, Father observed a four-story brick hotel on the east side of the track. A woman with red hair was standing in front of it. Her petite figure attracted the attention of soldiers on the trains. So many voices were screaming simultaneously that it sounded like one continuous roar. The woman caught Father's attention as well, and for a moment he imagined she was Polly. But what would Polly be doing in Marietta?

The train stopped when it reached the tunnel through Chetoogeta Mountain, a rugged ridge that traversed the railroad's path. To avoid getting knocked off the train, the companies on the roofs unloaded and marched through the stone portal to the far side, over 1,447 feet in the distance. The usual banter was exchanged as those inside the cars watched their comrades pass by. One member of the Seventeenth Georgia looked up at Father and joked, "Have a nice ride, old man."

"Don't get lost in the dark or you'll miss your train," Father snapped back.

"Grab hold of the man in front of you when you get inside," Lindsay added.

After the column cleared the far side of the tunnel, the train eased its way through the passageway. Smoke filled the tunnel and made breathing arduous for the men inside the cars. Their eyes burned. They coughed and envied those already on the other side of the mountain. Once through the portal, the train came to a stop again. The troops who had marched through earlier climbed back up onto the roofs of the cars. While they scurried up the ladders, Father checked out the stone depot. It looked more like a warehouse than a proper depot. A sign on the end of the building identified the location as Tunnel Hill.

A voice from the other side of the car asked, "What are all those new wooden structures?"

"Looks like a hospital, but I don't see no yellar flag," someone answered.

Father turned and saw several recently constructed buildings. They appeared abandoned. However, before further investigation, his attention was diverted to a two-wheeled cart being pulled down the road by two spotted oxen. Behind it, a gaunt milk cow plodded along, connected to the cart by a thin rope. The cow's copper bell was dinging out the cadence of each step. The cart had lost all its paint long ago. It was stacked high with baskets, blankets, and crude handmade furniture. Five small children dressed in homespun were perched on top of the pile. Sad eyes gazed out from dirty faces. Another child, a boy of no more than ten, walked alongside the oxen. He used a cane pole to guide the massive beasts. Behind him was a woman. Her washed-out green dress was unadorned. An unpretentious wool cape draped her shoulders. Another of those ubiquitous split bonnets hid her face until she glanced over at the train. Her haggard face made her look much older than she was. She clenched a corncob pipe in the corner of her mouth. Her expression seemed to ask the troops, "Where have you been?"

Every man on the train recognized the woman and her children. They did not know them by name, but they had encountered the same sort of wretched souls in Virginia. The woman and her children were refugees, some of the hundreds of civilians fleeing before the Yankee invasion. The soldiers on the train suspected the woman's husband also was a Confederate soldier. The mood turned solemn as the locomotive sounded its whistle and crept north. In Virginia, these callous veterans might have overlooked refugees, but this was not Virginia. They were now home in Georgia. If they did not turn back the Union army, their families might soon become refugees, too.

The train chugged to a halt at Catoosa Station late Thursday evening. From here, the men from Robert E. Lee's Army of

Northern Virginia would march to join Braxton Bragg's Army of Tennessee, only a few miles distant. Together they hoped to find the Union Army of the Cumberland lurking somewhere in the dark woods of North Georgia. Fresh hope for the Confederacy now rested upon the outcome of their encounter. For once, the Confederate Army would enjoy numerical superiority.

CHAPTER EIGHT
"Dogged resolution"

DARKNESS OBSCURED THE AREA AS FATHER AND THE rest of the Columbus Guards climbed out of the slate-blue boxcar. Unloading in the dark caused more than one man to slip and fall. His inevitable yell provoked laughter among his comrades. Above the din, Father heard Benning shout "Brigade!" Others heard it, too. The chatter and laughter gave way to the sound of shuffling feet.

Colonel Shepherd's voice pierced the night air, "Second Georgia!"

The habitual echo of company commanders responded. "Columbus Guards!" Roswell Ellis shouted.

Father promptly rushed to find his spot in the formation as everyone anticipated Shepherd's next command. "Fall in!" The chaotic activity and loud noise of unloading quickly ceased and gave way to four regiments formed parallel to the track. Each regiment stood in a single line, two ranks deep. In the center of each line, a color sergeant held the unit's battle flag. Each banner was rolled around its flagpole and encased in a canvas sleeve.

Benning proudly surveyed his men. Even in the darkness the formation exuded power. The command "Fix bayonets!" was followed by the sound of metal clicking against metal. Instead of the presumed "Right face! Forward, march!" his command was "Stack arms." Father lifted his rifle and instantly placed his bayonet against John Lindsay's. Americus Ham positioned his between the two. Father took it and swung it forward, locking the three. He and Lindsay placed the butts of the three guns on the ground. A fourth gun was leaned on the stack, giving it the appearance of the poles in an Indian teepee.

Shepherd instructed the men to remain in the immediate vicinity and get some rest. The temperature plummeted during the night. By dawn it was near freezing.

Gathering wood and starting campfires was the first order of business. A provost guard kept a close eye on the railroad's firewood piles to ensure the locomotives maintained sufficient wood for fuel. The men were relegated to other sources. Fence rails, fallen limbs, and civilian firewood were burned for heat. Between the cold weather and anticipation of a coming fight, the men in the brigade didn't rest well. On September 18, Father was awake before reveille. He had just put another log on the fire when the bugle sounded.

Time passed leisurely that Friday. As the day wore on, the distinct sound of gunfire became audible in the distance. Father intuitively opened his cartridge box. Twenty rounds occupied the top compartments of its two tins. Lifting up the tins, he discovered the cartridges in the bottom compartments were still in their paper packages. Ripping each one open, he systematically placed the individual rounds in the lower section of each tin and moved the caps to his cap pouch. Then he pulled out of his pockets the two packs that he had been issued in Atlanta. He glanced at the label for the first time, "10 cartridges, Enfield-Springfield Minie, or Rifle Musket, Calibre 577 or 58, Conical Ball, Columbus Arsenal, 1863." He had seen hundreds of comparable labels during the last two years.

A gloomy mood descended on him as he read the word "Columbus." Memories of Ann flooded his mind. He could feel anger swelling as the reminiscences grew. His bitterness at God for taking Ann from him competed against a lifetime of believing that God was good. He recalled the numerous times he had counseled grieving church members. He had encouraged them to trust a loving God's providence. Now he wondered if he had been right about what he had said. Or had he done them a disservice by feeding them lies? This confusion over what he had once believed to be his divine calling only added to Edwin Anderson's pain.

Clutching the paper package, Father listened intently to the distant firing. He managed to shift the focus of his anger. Even in his spiritual wilderness, he realized the futility of challenging the deity. But the cursed Yankees were a different story. Father blamed them for this hated war that had separated him from his family. Why did they refuse to leave the South alone? Father had opposed secession, but Georgia had chosen to leave the Union. The people had voted for independence in a free election. Now states distant from Georgia were attempting to overturn that election with bayonets and bullets. Father systematically counted the rounds in the top compartments of his cartridge box. As his index finger touched each round, he thought, *Here's your ticket to Dixie, Yank. I'll personally deliver it to you for all the grief you have caused me.*

Benning's Brigade remained near the railroad until sunset. Against the backdrop of a red western horizon, bugles sounded. Drums began beating the long roll. Adrenaline surged as troops fell into formation. Commands were shouted, and the formation expeditiously became a marching column, snaking its way along the primitive road in the darkness. Leather soles stirred up clouds of dust, choking the men in the ranks. The column plunged into the north Georgia forest and was swallowed up in the woodland's deep blackness. The men were guided almost entirely by the sound of the soldier directly in front of them. Repeatedly, they reached out to touch him. Occasionally the noise of someone tumbling, followed by a chorus of profanity punctuated the rhythm of shuffling shoes. Laughter erupted until officers and sergeants, in muffled voices, commanded, "Quiet in the ranks." The pace was steady.

The brigade reached Chickamauga Creek in the vicinity of Reed's Bridge around midnight and went into bivouac. At night, the men were unable to discern their surroundings. Weary soldiers jockeyed to find an available spot to lie down. They removed backpacks or bedrolls and spread their blankets on the ground. Canteens and haversacks were taken off and placed where they could be retrieved quickly. Leather cartridge and cap boxes stayed on the soldiers. Rifles were not stacked. Instead, each man slept with his weapon. The proximity to the enemy dictated the need for an instant response to every contingency. The night was again extremely cold, but no fires were permitted until dawn. Father rolled up in his blanket and ground cloth and slept well. The next morning, frost covered the sleeping soldiers, as well as the ground.

Father was up early, as usual. He looked around at his surroundings. The brigade was in old growth hardwood with little undergrowth. A wooden bridge crossed a steep ravine. Sluggish yellow-green water flowed down a creek about ten or fifteen feet below the bridge.

Father built a small fire in order to prepare breakfast. He poured water from his canteen into a tin cup and set it at the edge of the fire. To the west he heard sporadic gunfire. *Nervous pickets*, he imagined. He pulled a small cloth bag filled with a few precious coffee beans from his haversack. He also took out his homemade frying pan. Father left the stick in his haversack and put the canteen half on the ground. Then he poured half the beans into it. John Lindsay sat up and looked blurry-eyed at the fire.

"John, want some coffee?" asked Father.

"You got coffee?" replied Lindsay.

"Yes, and I'll share it with you," replied Father.

"Dang, Father. Beats me where you get this stuff. I've been drinking roasted peanuts and you come up with real Yankee coffee beans."

"I'll never tell," teased Father.

A civilian had given the beans to him in the Carolinas. He imagined a blockade runner had slipped it in past the Federal fleet off Charleston. Father grabbed his bayonet and, using the socket end, pounded the beans into coffee grounds. When the water started to boil, Father dumped the grounds into a stained piece of cloth, tied its corners together, and placed the makeshift bag in the cup of steaming water.

Father took Lindsay's tin cup and emptied half of the brown liquid into it. Then he took a hardtack cracker from his haversack and dipped it into his coffee.

"That won't help," smirked Lindsay.

Father smiled and bit into the biscuit. Lindsay opened his haversack and took out a broken fragment of hardtack. When he finished eating, Lindsay picked up his canteen and said, "Give me your canteens boys. I'm going to make a water run down to that creek."

Lindsay was climbing up the bank of Chickamauga Creek when the long roll sounded. Father had already tied up Lindsay's bedroll. He took his canteen and handed Lindsay his accouterments. As soon as the brigade was formed, it crossed Reed's Bridge. The sound of gunfire to the west had grown into a loud roar when the brigade moved off the road into the tangled woods. The men expected to be thrown into the fray, but General Hood held the brigade in reserve most of the day.

With little to do, the role was torture for the men. Most had discarded their decks of cards and dice, but a few souls were brash enough to risk having vice paraphernalia sent home with their personal effects if they were killed. These few plucky individuals initiated poker games or shot craps. Many men took out pocket New Testaments and read holy writ for solace. Most engaged in the empty banter that masked their worst fears. All the while the distant rumble of gunfire beckoned them to leave their haven of safety and share in death's grim harvest.

Late that afternoon, the brigade was ordered forward. Bugles blew the call to assemble. Drums beat out the steady cadence of the long roll. The commands were so familiar that each man responded automatically. The four regiments of the brigade formed into a single line of two ranks facing General Benning. He ordered the colors uncased. Four red battle flags, each approximately forty-eight inches square and made of bunting, marked the location of the individual regiments in the line. All four flags had a dark blue St. Andrew's cross on a red field. The cross was trimmed in a half-inch-wide white edging and bore thirteen five-point stars. The leading edge of each flag was bound with a two-inch wide canvas. Three whipped eyelets provided a place for tying the flags to their staffs.

The Second's flag was bound on its three other sides with an inch and a half of orange bunting. At the center of the lower edge, a white cotton strip was sewn. It was about three by eighteen inches with "2ND. GA." painted in black. Over eighty bullet holes in the banner testified to the ghastly fighting in the Slaughter Pen at Gettysburg. In battle, these flags served a pragmatic function. They enabled commanders to locate specific units and identify the placement and movement of individual soldiers. No less practical was the emotional bond they generated. Each regiment's colors embodied the spirit and pride of the unit. Carrying the colors was a great honor. Soldiers willingly sacrificed their own lives to preserve the flags.

As Father watched the Second Georgia's flag flapping in the wind, extreme pride swelled up inside. At that moment, no greater honor could be found than standing beneath the folds of that flag.

As usual, the Second was on the extreme right. Commanders took their positions directly in front of their respective companies. Soldiers focused their eyes and ears upon the commanding officer of their regiment. Lieutenants and sergeants formed behind the line. The brigade was like a tightly coiled spring ready to explode. Benning's voice bellowed, "Brigade! Attention!" Down the chain of command his orders echoed. Father responded as Captain Ellis shouted, "Company! Attention!" The butt of Father's Enfield rested on the ground, his right hand firmly gripping the piece below the middle band. "Shoulder…arms!" Father's right hand lifted the rifle vertically. His left hand moved across his body, gripped the weapon, and continued lifting it. Simultaneously, his right hand released the rifle and dropped to his side, grasping the swell of the stock with his thumb and forefinger firmly embracing the trigger guard. The barrel rested against the hollow of his shoulder.

The command, "Right…face!" caused every man in the formation to move. John Lindsay on Father's right shoulder pivoted on his left heel and sharply faced to his right. Behind him, J. H. Hicks performed the same movement and then shifted one step to his right. Father likewise pivoted and stepped between Lindsay and Hicks. William Moses, who was behind Father, stepped up to the right shoulder of Hicks. Instantly, the two lines had changed into a column of four ranks.

Benning lifted himself erect in his saddle. He slowly surveyed the length of the column and then in a clear, audible voice commanded, "Brigade, forward…march!" Every left foot stepped out. Benning wheeled his horse to his left and galloped to the head of the column. The column changed to route step as it marched down the dirt road. The tread of so many feet kicked up swirls of dust, making breathing difficult. The monotonous sounds of clanging canteen cups and shuffling feet marked the column's progress. The forest canopy covered the road for most of the march, shielding the men from the afternoon sun but blocking any cooling breezes. Sweat rolled down Father's forehead and stung his eyes. He tried to gauge the severity of the fight from the sound of the gunfire. Its volume and the rapidity of the brigade's advance were ominous signs. The column passed increasing numbers of wounded moving in the opposite direction. Bloody work lay ahead.

Two miles down the road the pace slowed. Benning called his brigade to attention. It soon burst out of the dark woods into an open field. The noise prevented Father from hearing the commands of Colonel Shepherd or General Benning. He strained to hear Captain Ellis. On a slight rise to his left, he could see Robertson's Texas Brigade. The familiar battle flags of the Army of Northern Virginia snapped in the wind. Ellis's voice interrupted any further observation. "By company into line! March!"

Father's left hand seized his Enfield's barrel and stock, lifting it against his right shoulder. His right hand grasped the butt plate, and he raised it until its hammer was even with his neck. At the same time, he sprinted to his left to find his place in line. The company transformed back into a line of battle. Father was in the front rank between Eugene Steward and John Lindsay. When they reached the ridge where the Texans stood, Benning halted and dressed his troops so that his battle line was perfectly straight.

The pause provided Father an opportunity to survey what lay ahead. About 350 yards in front of him, a dirt road ran parallel to the brigade line. Across this road was another field. Both fields were bordered by split-rail worm fences, but these mostly had been knocked down. Bodies of dead and wounded in both blue and gray uniforms littered the two fields. Across the road the ground descended into a small ditch and then gradually rose to a higher ridgeline. This hill was covered in dense woods. On the left side of the field, just across the road, stood a small log cabin. Behind it was another small wooden structure. Blue-coated infantry held both buildings. An artillery battery at the wood line supported them. Its guns could sweep the entire field. *Not good*, Father thought.

Again Ellis's voice interrupted his thoughts. "Company... load." Father placed his Enfield's butt plate on the ground directly in front of his body. With his left hand, he held the rifle vertical at a slight angle, barrel facing the enemy. With his right hand, he pulled down on the leather strap that secured the flap of his cartridge box. Once the flap was free, he reached inside and pulled a single .577 caliber cartridge out of the tin. His thumb flipped out the tail of the paper cartridge as he raised it to his mouth. Biting down on it, he ripped off the back portion of the paper. Black powder inevitably spilled against his tongue and lips, staining them and leaving a nasty sulfur taste in his mouth. He quickly poured the rest of the powder down the gun's barrel. Next he pushed the lead Minie ball into the barrel, pulled out his musket's ramrod, and shoved the bullet down the tube. After returning the ramrod to its slot in the stock, Father held the musket in his left hand and pulled its hammer to half cock. Reaching into the leather pouch on his belt, he took out a small brass cap and seated it on the nipple of the musket. The whole process took him less than fifteen seconds. When he finished, he returned to shoulder arms.

Father glanced at Lindsay. The redhead winked back at him. Both men were scared stiff. They were keenly aware of the high odds that they could become casualties in this fight. The urge to run away tugged at each man, but neither would let down his friend. It was this sense of obligation to his fellow warriors that enabled the soldier to overcome his natural instinct for self-preservation and stand and fight.

With the command, "Charge...bayonets!" the front rank of the entire brigade line snapped their rifles to their right side at a forty-five-degree angle toward the enemy. Each man emitted a low guttural growl. "Forward...march!" and the brigade stepped off. About one hundred yards from the house, bugles passed the command to halt. Over two years of military service had taught these veterans to understand the brass instrument's notes as well as verbal orders. In combat, its sounds could be distinguished when human voices were lost in the noise. Today Sergeant Fogle was standing behind Lindsay and Hicks, so Father had no trouble hearing him parrot commands. "Ready!" Father's thumb pulled the hammer on his rifle to full cock. His right foot shifted. The inside of his right shoe touched the heel of his left foot so that his feet formed a "T." Fogle shouted, "Aim!" Father brought the Enfield up into the firing position. He aligned his sights on a dark blue figure directly in front of him. He felt Moses's left hand rest against his right shoulder. He glanced and observed Moses's Enfield pointing toward the enemy. Father's ear was aligned between the second and third bands of his comrade's rifle. "Fire by files! Commence firing!" The two rifles on the right end of the line discharged. Then the next two fired. An instant after Lindsay's and Hicks's rifles discharged, Father heard Moses say "Fire." Father squeezed his trigger. Their weapons fired simultaneously. A white cloud of smoke obscured Father's vision, so he could not see if he had hit his target. He reached into his cartridge box and pulled out another round.

As Father reloaded, he heard Fogle yell, "Fire at will boys. Pour it into them." Each man was firing as fast as he could reload. The soldiers in this line of battle had honed their skills for almost three years. They fired an average of three aimed shots per minute. The Federal troops defending the small farm were returning fire at a similar rate. The sound grew deafening as individual shots faded into one loud roar. Rifle barrels heated until they burned human flesh. For the moment, Benning's Brigade had the superior force and gradually gained dominance, but neither side could maintain this intense fire indefinitely. Sooner or later one side had to give.

When the Federal fire began to weaken, Benning's bugles sounded cease fire. Then they called the brigade to attention. Father clasped his Enfield in the shoulder arms position. His right shoulder touched Lindsay's left. His left shoulder pressed against Steward's right. "Forward at the double quick! March!" Once again the line moved forward. Its pace was faster. With the command "Charge!" it broke into a run. As they raced toward the houses, their voices let loose the distinctive high-pitched rebel yell. Hundreds of voices screaming "Wah-whoo-ey, wah-whoo-ey!" created crescendos that raised the hair on the back of every Yankee who heard it.

The Federals around the house fired round after round into Benning's charging brigade, but the Georgians were too strong and determined. The Federal defense of the log cabin and its outbuilding ended as the Confederate tidal wave swept over the small farmstead. Its blue-coated defenders raced across the field behind the house towards the wood line on the other side. Having taken his objective, Benning dressed his line and waited for reinforcements so that he could continue his advance. Standing exposed in the field, Father could see log breastworks at the edge of the woods. A Federal force nearly five times stronger than the greatly depleted ranks of Benning's Brigade was behind those fortifications. They were supported by two more artillery batteries. The Confederate line poured musket fire into the foe briefly. Maintaining the formation was suicide. Father and his comrades did not break and run, but they did seek cover. Some hid in the farmhouse and its outbuilding. Others found shelter behind trees or stumps. Most ended up in a dry stream bed. Father, Lindsay, Steward, Moses, and Hicks huddled against the far bank of this ditch.

Lead bullets made a loud crack as they ripped into log walls and tree trunks. They kicked up small puffs of dust as they ricocheted off dirt fields. Occasional expletives punctuated near misses. A dull thud or a painful shriek disclosed a more tragic result. The pitiful moans of the wounded competed with the noise of battle. Father held his rifle above his head, pointed it in the general direction of the enemy and pulled the trigger. He struggled to reload in his cramped quarters. Mostly he tried to make himself as small as possible. The first Federal battery was wreaking havoc, pouring canister into the ditch.

When the devastating fire slackened, Fogle yelled, "Here they come. On your feet, boys." Father peeked over the lip of the ditch. Down the slope of the field came a Federal brigade in a line of battle. No orders were needed. Every man knew what to do. They loaded and fired as rapidly as possible. The Federal attack stalled and then fell back to the safety of their breastworks.

As the sun slid behind the western hills, the carnage ended temporarily. Benning withdrew most of the brigade to the east side of the dirt road. They reformed in the dark woods behind a one-room log schoolhouse. The Second Georgia remained on the brigade's right flank but did not re-cross the road. Father was exhausted, but he was alive. He didn't remove his accouterments that night. He still fell asleep easily. He didn't sleep long, though. Sporadic gunfire constantly alerted one that danger lurked in these woods. The temperature again plummeted. Frost formed on the ground, and a cold north wind whistled through the trees. Men shivered in wool uniforms soaked in human sweat. Tonight there could be no fires to bring temporary relief. The night was pitch black and their flames would only draw enemy gunfire. Most disturbing was the terrible sound of the wounded. Moans of pain and cries for help were inescapable torment for the men still in the ranks. They heard more than one dying voice crying for his mother. Tomorrow their own voices might be added to this morbid symphony.

On the second day at Chickamauga, Father awoke in the early morning hours with parched lips and a swollen tongue. He sat up and pulled the cork stopper from his canteen. He drained the last of its contents and wondered how he would do without water. He reached into his haversack and pulled out a hardtack cracker. As he chewed on the tasteless cracker, Fogle tapped him on the shoulder and said, "Father, is that you?"

"Yes, Theodore, it's me."

"Give me your canteen. I'm taking a detail down to the creek for water."

"Here, thanks."

Father dozed off once more. It was still dark when Fogle shook his feet. The sergeant returned his canteen and softly said, "Wake up, Father. We're pulling back again. Be as quite as possible. We don't want to alert the Yanks."

Shortly thereafter, Captain Ellis came up and said, "Okay, boys, let's go. Move quietly through these woods until you get to the road. We'll form up there." A second later, Ellis spoke directly to Father, "Colonel Shepherd was hit yesterday. I don't think it's too serious, but Major Charlton has assumed command of the regiment."

The moon cast a pale blue light on the road and the field beyond. The brigade had no trouble reforming in the moonlight. Smoke still hovered low over the area. The cries of the wounded were clearly audible. Somewhere behind them a quivering voice was calling softly, "Momma, Momma, where are you, Momma?"

"Damn, I hate that sound," muttered Lindsay.

"John, watch your language," chided Father.

"I forget that you're a preacher sometimes," Lindsay responded. "I hate hearing those poor boys suffer."

"Well I am, and I should be in the pulpit today instead of wandering aimlessly in these woods. But me being a preacher has nothing to do with your cursing. I told you to watch your language because you are a better man than that."

"I just imagine all of them that you can hear are Yanks," said Moses.

"Wouldn't help," replied Lindsay. "I can't even stand thinking about Yankees suffering out there alone in the cold and dark."

Their conversation was interrupted when Ellis whispered, "Quiet in the ranks."

By dawn the brigade was on the road again. It retraced the previous day's route for a short distance. When Benning came to an intersection deep in the woods, the column turned left onto a road that seemed to go north, veering slightly to the east. The road was more like a farm lane, barely wide enough for a column four-men abreast to pass through the heavy forest. Less than a mile away, this road intersected another east-west road. On the southeast corner of the intersection was a small farm with one of those omnipresent log cabins. Just before reaching the intersection, the column halted.

When the command "Front!" was given, Father made a left face and stepped up between Steward and Lindsay. The brigade now stood in a line of battle facing due west. General Benning moved them forward into the woods, an area of more old growth with little underbrush. Moving only a few yards into the trees, Father was still able to see the road behind him. In front of Benning were the other two brigades of their division – General Jerome Robertson's Texas Brigade and Colonel James Sheffield's Alabama Brigade.

Benning barked a command and his subordinates repeated it. "Fix bayonets!" Father's left hand mechanically fell to his side and grasped his bayonet. He withdrew it from its scabbard and again affixed it to the barrel of his rifle. The clicking of metal against metal as hundreds of men carried out the same drill echoed through the trees. A chill ran up Father's spine. He never could get used to that sound. The brigade stacked arms and was allowed to break ranks.

A short time later, Father heard the shuffle of marching feet. Dust filled the air again as another brigade trudged up the road. The newcomers continued up to the intersection and turned left. Father joined others standing along the side of the road to observe these westerners up close. They carried strange blue battle flags that were smaller than the square red battle flags of the Army of Northern Virginia. Instead of the familiar blue St. Andrew's cross, they had a large white disc. A three-inch-wide white border framed the banner. Father took a closer look as the second of these flags passed him. On the top border, painted in black, was the word "PERRYVILLE." On the bottom was "MURFREESBORO." In the center of the disc, two crossed cannons were also painted in black. Father heard someone say the cannons indicated the regiment had captured an enemy artillery battery. Above the cannons was "17TH TENN"; below was "REG'T."

The men in the column didn't seem to have a standard uniform. No two soldiers were dressed the same. Some had homespun jackets. Others had on homespun sack coats. One man even had a ticking-striped frockcoat. Many wore government-issued shell jackets. However, even these varied. Some had dark blue standup collars; others had collars of the same fabric as the coat. Some had visible pockets; others did not. Some had brass buttons; others had wood buttons. Some had dark blue cuffs on the sleeve; others did not. Some were wool; some were course jean wool. Some were gray; some were butternut. Others had a salt-and-pepper appearance that resembled burlap. Their pants were even more diverse. Several, such as a green plaid pair, obviously were civilian trousers. Even their equipment varied. However, their muskets were well-cared-for Enfield rifles, same as those carried by the Second Georgia.

As the westerners moved by Benning's Brigade, the two units exchanged the usual banter of two friendly competitors, but it was subdued today. The carnage on Saturday had created new respect for each other. The knowledge of what lay ahead forged a strong bond between them. Soon the curiosity of the men from Virginia was satisfied, and the crowds of soldiers lining the road began to disperse.

Thirty minutes or less after the column vanished into the forest, drums pounded out the long roll. Father and the rest of Benning's Brigade formed up in their line of battle. They removed their rifles from the stacks and came to attention. General Benning rose up in the saddle of his horse and bellowed, "Brigade!" His voice was followed by the customary chorus parroting the command. Charlton's "Second Georgia!" didn't sound right. Father was sure it only was his unfamiliarity with the new commander's voice, but still it gave Father an ominous premonition. He turned to Lindsay and serenely said, "John, if something happens to me, write Mr. Lewis."

Lindsay, for once, was speechless. His expression turned gloomy and he simply nodded. More often than not, these premonitions turned out to be right.

Around eleven o'clock, heavy skirmish fire could be heard from the direction of the Tennesseans. Cannon fire added its big bass voice to the deadly concert. About ten minutes passed. Then the volume of gunfire increased significantly. Benning gave the command, and his brigade again stepped off. Coming out of the woods, they glimpsed a spectacular panorama. Across the road was another log cabin. A rough picket fence marked its dirt yard. A split rail fence extended the fence line around a large cornfield. Most of it had been dismantled in the previous day's battle. Survivors of the Federal skirmish line stood disarmed, looking in shock at the advancing blue-gray line. Behind these Federal prisoners, the Texans and Alabamians of the division pushed up the hill behind the cabin. In front of them, the troops from the Army of Tennessee with their strange blue banners were running into the woods. Thousands of voices raised the rebel yell. The Federal line in front of them was evaporating before this onslaught. However, north of the road, a strong blue line was pouring lead into the flank of Sheffield's Alabama Brigade.

As Benning's Brigade crossed the road, the general shouted, "Brigade, right wheel! March!" The line of battle wheeled and faced north. It pushed across another dirt road and into woods with heavy underbrush. Vines caught accouterments. Briars scratched hands and faces. Keeping the formation became impossible. Still the brigade advanced. Bullets whistled by, removing foliage from tree limbs. The woods filled with white smoke as the two sides clashed. Father caught a glimpse of the stars and stripes. It was the last thing he remembered. He dropped to the ground unconscious. Blood oozed out of his forehead onto the dead leaves on the forest floor. For "Father" Edwin Anderson, the Battle of Chickamauga was over.

When Father regained consciousness, he tore open his clothing and inspected his abdomen for wounds. Then he discovered the blood from his forehead. He attempted to get up but collapsed from exhaustion. Lying amid the trampled underbrush, he noticed a dead Yankee gazing back at him. Father feared being captured by Federals, but unable to move, his mind drifted to memories of his dead family and earlier war battles.

When Father opened his eyes once more, the dead Yankee had not been moved. Father did not know how long he had been unconscious. The pain in his head had eased some but his eyes burned. They always did in battle. The sweat combined with the black powder smoke to form a caustic rinse. Now blood had been added to the formula. His throat was dry. He could taste the residue of sulfur that gunpowder had left on his parched lips. *Water, I need water*, he thought. He could feel the oval shape of his canteen lodged beneath him, and he realized how uncomfortable his body was. It reminded him of the numerous rocks and roots his bedroll always seemed to end up on at night. He struggled and eventually worked his weakened body off the canteen.

When he attempted to lift it to his lips, it refused to budge. His weight held its strap in place. After additional efforts, he managed to slide the canteen into a position where he could pull out its cork stopper. He lifted the canteen's tin mouth to his lips. The water was lukewarm but refreshing. He reinserted the cork stopper, rolled over flat on his back, and laid the canteen on his belly. He felt moisture and realized the stopper was not seated well. He pushed it once more and the canteen stopped leaking.

The water had helped. He could now hear the sound of battle. It came from the west and north. *West…that was the direction my regiment was moving when I was hit*, Father thought. *No, the Texans were going west. My brigade had turned north. If the battle is to the west and north, then I am behind Confederate lines*. For the first time the fear of capture subsided. Refreshed by the water and relieved by the knowledge he was safe behind his own lines, Father realized he must get to a hospital. He spotted his Enfield lying in the underbrush. The hammer rested on the nipple. The distorted brass cap indicated that the rifle had been fired. It was not loaded.

He crawled over to where it lay. Slowly, he twisted the bayonet lug, turned, and pulled. The bayonet came off, and he instinctively attempted to put it back into the scabbard on his left hip. He missed its mouth and the bayonet tumbled to the ground. Edwin hated the bayonet. Most soldiers did. They rarely used it for its intended purposes. Both sides abided by an unofficial understanding: I won't stick you if you won't stick me. So he just left it where it fell. Using the Enfield as a crutch, he pulled himself up.

The struggle to stand drained Father of all his strength. He stood dazed and bewildered, examining his surroundings. He thought that the rays of sunlight peeking through the trees would direct him to the open field where Benning's Brigade had entered the woods. Looking down at the dead Federal soldier, Edwin spoke, "Good bye, friend. I hope you are in a better place. I may join you soon." Using his Enfield as a walking stick, he started toward the light.

Father struggled through the woods until he reached a road. This was no farm trail. It was a wide and well-traveled main thoroughfare. The only roads like it were the one the brigade fought over on Saturday and the one they crossed at the commencement of the attack earlier that day. Father did not realize it, but they were the same road, the Lafayette Road. The two armies had fought for two days to control this north-south highway. Father looked around in an effort to find another landmark in order to gain a bearing on his location, but he was only aware of the forest surrounding him. Which direction should he go? His head was spinning, and he was uncharacteristically disoriented.

Father could hear gunfire across the road. He looked in the direction of the sound. There was an open field with a small farm on one side of the road, but he was disappointed to realize it was not on the same side as the farm they had passed earlier. A pale smoke hung in the field and forest. It obscured his vision, but the striped banner that he saw was unmistakable. The Federals were on both sides of the road! Edwin didn't know what to make of this development. Like most soldiers, he could only follow the battle where he stood. He had gotten lost in the woods and had wandered too far north. He was looking at the intact left wing of the Union army under the command of General George Henry Thomas. They had occupied this area for most of the battle, but Edwin Anderson had no way of knowing that. The last time he could remember Federals east of a major road was sometime the previous day.

Panic overwhelmed him. Instinctively he turned south, away from the enemy line. After following the road a short distance, he turned east and started to plunge back into the woods. Just as he did, he heard a dull thud and felt his legs buckle beneath him as he tumbled into a shallow ditch beside the road.

Oh God, my head hurts, thought Father. He attempted to lift his head, but it seemed too heavy. Questions and recollections merged in his mind. Reality and imagination mocked a vague memory of the day's happenings. Opening his eyes, he could not see anything. Darkness had swallowed his world. Had he lost his sight? Or had night come to the deep woods along Chickamauga

Creek? Lying still, he listened for clues to his situation. A strange symphony resonated in the blackness. He heard the usual insects and woodland creatures, but their chorus was overshadowed by the painful moaning of human suffering. In the distance, a deep bass voiced cried out pitifully, "Mother, oh Mother. They've killed your boy."

As Father listened to the sounds in the darkness, he slowly realized what he did not hear, the sporadic exchange of musket fire that always divulged the close proximity of the enemy. Except for cries of the wounded, the army was unexpectedly silent. That only could mean one thing. The battle was over and one side had won a decisive victory.

After Father had been hit, Benning's Brigade had pushed its Union foe back. In the process, they had overrun a Union artillery battery. With the capture of these guns, the brigade's active role in the battle had come to an end. In his official report a few days later, General Benning wrote that his "command fought with a dogged resolution." Ironically, when Father had turned back after seeing the two Federal flags, the brigade had been less than fifty yards away. But the dense undergrowth concealed its position and Father unconsciously walked away from the companions who had become his surrogate family. He needed rest to regain his strength. Tomorrow he must find a hospital. Otherwise he most likely would die. So he lay in the shallow ditch and slept.

CHAPTER NINE
"It was thought more prudent"

THE JULY 1 ALARM ALLEGING THAT YANKEES WERE across the river at Chattanooga had been premature. Their eventual arrival seemed certain however. The Army of Tennessee started marching into the city not long after the July 1 excitement had passed. Bragg had been outmaneuvered and had retreated from Tullahoma, Tennessee. Endless columns of filthy, ragged troops moved through the streets for days.

Around noon on Friday, July 17, a single officer rode down the street from army headquarters. He caught Polly's attention as she gazed out the hospital window. He was riding on a sorrel thoroughbred. The horse and rider were the epitome of graceful movement. The man wore a fine tailored gray uniform. Its left sleeve was folded up and attached to the shoulder. He guided his horse with his one surviving limb. Despite being an amputee, he sat erect and proud in the saddle. His neat military dress seemed out of place among the soldiers of the Army of Tennessee.

As he trotted past her window, the officer turned and looked at Polly. They made eye contact briefly. His white shirt collar accentuated his olive complexion. Two black eyes peered out from under the brim of a regulation sky blue kepi that was trimmed with gold braid and pulled down low over his forehead. The officer's face was framed with shiny black curls that hung down to his shoulders. A thin mustache and the popular Beauregard-style goatee completed the portrait of this mysterious cavalier. Polly was smitten.

She stuck her head out the window and followed the handsome knight-errant down the street. In her imagination, she visualized him coming into the hospital to find her. When he turned the corner and rode in the direction of the hospital's entrance, he only enhanced her illusion. Her daydream quickly evaporated as one of her patients called out for her assistance. This was real life, not a magazine serial novel.

A short time elapsed, perhaps fifteen minutes, and quite unexpectedly Dr. Dudley Dunn Saunders walked into the room with the mysterious stranger. Dr. Saunders had replaced Dr. Stout as the director of Chattanooga's numerous hospitals when Stout had been promoted. As the two officers walked down the aisle of the ward toward her, Polly noticed that the stranger's sky blue kepi was now tucked under the his right arm, which was folded across his abdomen. His pants were tucked in a polished pair of black riding boots. A crimson officer's sash was wrapped around his waist, and a foot officer's sword was suspended from his belt. His sword and spurs clattered as he walked. A faint smile appeared when he again made eye contact with Polly. Polly blushed.

Dr. Saunders, spoke first, "Mrs. Brenton."

"Sir?" Polly answered.

"This is Major Benjamin Larimer."

Larimer bowed his head politely and said, "Mrs. Brenton." The aroma of perfume drifted from the major's curls. Polly found herself strangely excited and simultaneously embarrassed, suspecting her own fixation was apparent to both the doctor and his visitor.

Dr. Saunders continued, "Major Larimer has just arrived here from Jackson, Mississippi. He is looking for a Captain Robert Bancroft of the Twenty-fourth Mississippi. Our records show him in your ward."

"Yes, sir," Polly replied. "He is in the corner next to the window. Sir, if you will follow me, I will gladly take you to him."

"Very well, Mrs. Brenton," said Saunders. "I will leave the major in your care. Major, if you require anything else, I'm sure Mrs. Brenton can assist you."

The striking Major Larimer saluted and said, "Thank you, sir."

Saunders returned the major's salute. He then turned and walked towards the hospital's front door. Polly thought to herself, *This handsome major must be important for the hospital director to escort him here personally. I best be on my toes.* Then she spoke aloud, "Come with me, please."

"Yes, ma'am. How is Bob…I mean Captain Bancroft doing?"

"He is doing very well. I am not a surgeon, so this is mere speculation, but I suspect he will be returned to his regiment soon." Polly felt confident of her diagnosis. She already had acquired a good sense of when a patient was showing signs of recovering or of dying. Bancroft already was healthier than many soldiers who had been sent back to the front. Polly escorted Major Larimer to Bancroft's bed. "Captain Bancroft, I have a visitor for you."

Bancroft looked up and recognized Larimer. The wounded captain grinned and said, "Ben, what are you doing here?"

"Checking on an old friend," Larimer answered. Larimer turned and said, "Thank you, Mrs. Brenton. Captain Bancroft and I were neighbors in Mississippi."

Polly excused herself and went to another patient on the opposite side of the room. Larimer pulled up a stool, and the two soldiers became absorbed in their conversation.

Polly's patient was a private from Tennessee named Ezekiel McDonough. His home was currently behind enemy lines outside of Nashville. His wound was mortal, and he had asked Polly to write his wife. It was a chore she forced herself to complete. Writing such letters brought painful memories of reading Edwin's letter that first time. Ironically, that same letter now had become an object of solace, her personal talisman to ward off depression. Perhaps in time, her letters would bring similar consolation to the relatives of those men who died in her care. But writing such words also spawned even more painful intuition about Richard's last moments. She knew that the words on the paper did not always match the reality of the death. Dying soldiers always seemed to portray their demise encouragingly.

Polly pulled up a cane-back chair and sat facing McDonough. She took a sheet of writing paper and placed it on a book in her lap. Using a lead pencil, she recorded his words verbatim. He was barely conscious and his breathing was labored, so the dictation was an agonizing process.

July 17, 1863
Chattanooga, Tennessee

My Dear Darling Millie,

I am dying. By the time you read this letter I will have gone to my eternal reward. I did not suffer too bad. I have asked Mrs. Brenton to write this letter since I am too weak to do it myself. She has been my nurse since coming to this here hospital. She is a fine Christian lady. Please tell Mother that I am ready to meet the Lord Jesus. My only regret is that I cannot see you and our children one last time before going. I love you. Please kiss the children for me. Good bye. I love you.

Your loving husband,
Zeke

Polly knew McDonough's statement that he did not suffer was for Millie's comfort. He had been shot while on picket duty. The bullet had entered near his navel and ripped through his intestines. He had been delirious much of the time since coming into the hospital. He frequently screamed in intense agony. Polly was amazed that he remained coherent long enough to dictate this letter. He passed out almost immediately after he finished speaking. She conjectured that he would not last the night. Instead of posting the letter immediately, she remained seated and gently wiped his forehead with a damp cloth. He was sweating profusely from a high fever.

She occasionally would glance up and look at Major Larimer. A couple of times she caught him looking at her. Larimer's smile was infectious. "Mr. Major, sir, I sure would like to get to know you better," she said to herself. The major stayed about twenty minutes. Polly did not get up until Larimer started to leave.

On his way out, Larimer stopped to thank her for her assistance. "Mrs. Brenton, I am grateful for everything."

"I was glad to be of service."

"Mrs. Brenton, if I am not being too forward, I understand that you are a widow."

"Yes, my husband, Richard, was killed at Sharpsburg."

"You have my sympathy."

"Thank you, Major. This dreadful war is taking too many husbands." Polly glanced at McDonough. Tears started rolling down her face. She tried to stop, but could not. Her own grief coupled with the task she had just completed was too much for Polly.

Larimer tried in vain to comfort her. "I am sorry. I did not mean to upset you," he said sheepishly.

"It was not you, sir. I cannot control myself after I write one of these letters," she replied. She reached into a pocket in the skirt of her dress. Since arriving at Newsom Hospital, she had started carrying Edwin's letter with her every day. She pulled it out and gestured with it as she spoke.

"From your husband?" he asked, stressing the 'your.'

"No, this was from his best friend. Richard died instantly." Suddenly a terrifying thought invaded her mind. It produced such horror that she turned pale and could not speak. *What if Edwin lied for my benefit? Was he trying to shield me from Richard's suffering?* Slowly, she became conscious of Larimer's voice.

"Mrs. Brenton. Mrs. Brenton. Are you all right?"

"Yes, I just felt a little faint momentarily. I am fine now." Polly looked at the empty sleeve of Larimer's coat. She wanted to ask him about it but was too embarrassed to do so.

However, Larimer sensed her curiosity and explained. "Yes ma'am. I lost my arm at Fort Donelson last year. I spent some time in a Yankee hospital. I guess that Federal doctor saved my life."

The idea that a Yankee doctor saved a Confederate officer struck Polly as inconceivable even though she had witnessed Confederate surgeons save the lives of numerous Union prisoners. Her own sanctimonious belief in Confederate moral superiority never allowed her to entertain the possibility that Union doctors might be equally human in their efforts. In her limited world view, Yankees were the malicious predators who killed Richard, not compassionate human beings. "Major, I had not thought previously that Yankees were capable of such humanity. You, sir, have given me something to think about."

"Mrs. Brenton, would you walk me to the door?"

Polly looked around. Everything in her charge was in order. "Yes, sir, I would consider it an honor."

The two walked slowly to the hospital entrance. Polly impulsively followed Larimer outside. He reached up to mount his horse and then stopped. He turned and said, "Well, if I am not being too presumptuous, I would like to ask you to dine with me this evening."

"Sir, I don't know you. It would not be proper," she responded. Inside she was thinking, *Oh yes, I want to. But I might get in trouble with Dr. Saunders if I do. Besides I don't know anything about you. You might even be a married man.*

"I assure you, Mrs. Brenton, that everything will be respectable. Let me introduce myself properly. My name is Major Benjamin Gustave Larimer from Shubuta, Mississippi. I am a widower. My wife died from small pox in 1861. I was a member of the Shubuta Rifles, now designated as Company A of the Fourteenth Mississippi Volunteer Infantry Regiment, Adam's Brigade, Walker's Division, Department of the West. Currently I am attached to the staff of General Joseph E. Johnston. I have been sent here by General Johnston to confer with General Bragg. I am to dine with General and Mrs. Bragg tonight and having feminine company…" Larimer paused for what seemed an eternity to him before continuing. "Well Mrs. Brenton, to be honest, your company would make it a lot less awkward for me. I am not sure what I will say to Mrs. Bragg. I have not been around ladies in nearly two years."

Larimer had stared nervously at the ground as he spoke. When he looked up, he saw Dr. Saunders returning to the hospital. "If it will help, I will ask Dr. Saunders for permission prior to picking you up. If I do not arrive by six o'clock, you will know that he did not give his blessing."

"Very well, Major. If Dr. Saunders grants us permission, I will dine with you and the Braggs tonight."

Polly had not seen Dr. Saunders walking up behind her. His sudden appearance startled her. She was even more startled when he embraced the idea of her dining with the handsome stranger from Mississippi.

Polly enjoyed the dinner. It was the first real entertainment she had allowed herself since Ann's death. The major picked her up outside her quarters. They rode to General Bragg's quarters in a polished vermillion carriage pulled by two less than admirable horses. The animals seemed more suited for a plow than an elegant carriage. Polly found Mrs. Bragg a wonderful hostess, totally different from her sour husband. His failing health was obvious and did not improve his disposition. Two other officers were present with their wives. When the men stepped into another room, the ladies gathered around an old piano and sang hymns and patriotic songs for an hour. As Polly and Major Larimer rode back to her quarters, she contemplated the evening. She smiled thinking, *What would Deacon Archibald think if he could see me now?* Archibald loved the Confederate States of America and hated her with equal passion. And tonight, his despised antagonist had dined in one of the highest circles of his beloved Confederacy. She could not hold back a slight chuckle.

When Larimer asked what was so humorous, Polly said, "Nothing important. I was merely musing about an old acquaintance."

Larimer did not press the matter further. He remained the perfect southern gentleman throughout the evening. Even though the dinner had cut into the time she had for sleep, Polly oddly was rejuvenated by the episode. She slept well and was eager to get to work the next morning.

Even the puritanical Kate encouraged Polly to pursue a relationship with Larimer. However, the two had little opportunity to discuss the matter in depth. The day after Polly dined with the Braggs, Dr. Saunders began serious evacuation of the hospitals from Chattanooga. He announced that the Newsom Hospital would move to Cleveland, Tennessee. Kate decided to transfer to the hospital at Kingston, Georgia. She departed Chattanooga on July 22. Polly planned to go with her, but Dr. Saunders personally asked her to remain in Chattanooga temporarily. He needed someone to supervise the convalescents that were helping with the move. She agreed, primarily because Major Benjamin Larimer was still in the city.

Over the next five weeks, Polly and Benjamin spent many hours together. In early August, they took a day long sightseeing trip to Rock City on Lookout Mountain. The couple carried a picnic lunch and ate it on a rocky overlook. For the first time since Richard had left to go to war, Polly began to laugh and find fulfillment in the company of a man. Nevertheless, a dark shadow hung over her thoughts. Watching young men die in the hospital only deepened her anguish over Richard's death. She feared the war would last until every man was dead. Her cynicism threatened to take away whatever happiness she might find, so Polly struggled to erect a wall of protection against her suitor and prevent developing too intimate of a relationship with Larimer. Still, she could not deny her attraction to him, and their romance began to blossom.

Polly's opinion about organized religion had altered little since arriving in Chattanooga. Polly realized that any disclosure of her own misgivings about formal religion might jeopardize her position within the Confederate medical service. Significant prejudice against women nurses still permeated southern society. Therefore, moral stipulations for female nurses were extremely stringent. A traditional Judeo-Christian religious affiliation was essential, so Polly dared not discuss her skepticism with anyone, not even Kate. Their friendship had picked up as if it never had been interrupted. It grew even stronger and more intimate as the two spent more time together in Chattanooga. Although she was Episcopalian, denominational identification was secondary in Kate's faith. Kate indisputably was a devout Christian and like Ann, the organized church was very important to her. She frequently attended worship in Baptist, Methodist, and Presbyterian churches. Polly had normally accompanied her until Kate had left Chattanooga.

President Davis proclaimed Friday, August 21, 1863, to be a day of prayer and fasting throughout the Confederacy. The Reverend Doctor Benjamin M. Palmer was speaking at Chattanooga's Presbyterian Church as part of the city's compliance with the president's proclamation. Reverend Palmer was an eminent pastor from New Orleans. His eloquent and compelling preaching was well known everywhere in the South, so the entire town was abuzz about hearing him preach.

Major Larimer asked Polly to attend the service with him. However, he was unexpectedly detailed for some special duty in Atlanta. His orders called for him to leave Chattanooga before daylight. Without him to escort her, Polly considered skipping the prayer service. She was not caught up in the euphoria over hearing Palmer. In her eyes, no one else's sermons seemed to measure up to Edwin's. But her absence at an event where this popular preacher was in the pulpit might attract unwanted queries, so Polly decided to attend this service despite Larimer's absence.

When she arrived, the sanctuary was nearly full. Polly looked around, searching for an empty space on a pew. She noted that even General Cheatham was in attendance. The general was better known for his hard drinking and profanity than for his religious scruples. Then she spotted Major Larimer…and the vacant seat beside him. Polly's heart raced as she discreetly strolled to his pew. She excused herself as she stepped over an elderly couple sitting on the end of the pew. She could see a sly grin on Larimer's face. Polly sat down and said, "Major."

"Polly."

"Major, I thought you left the city this morning."

"I was supposed to catch the morning passenger train to Atlanta at 2:38. But General Bragg has delayed my departure temporarily. I thought you had hospital duties today."

"Most of our patients have been sent south. So I was able to be here after all."

"It's good to see you here. Your presence makes my day so much brighter."

"I am glad to see you, too."

The service was beginning, so no further conversation was practical. Polly had trouble keeping her mind on the service however. It was too occupied contemplating the attractive Major Larimer. His companionship made her feel alive. Her romantic musings were interrupted by commotion in the street outside the church. Polly could not determine what was transpiring, but she realized she was not the only one distracted by it. Throughout the congregation, people strained to comprehend what was happening outside. Suddenly everyone heard what sounded like the peal of thunder. Then came a soft whistle and a loud explosion. The windows rattled. Panic seized the congregation. People jumped up to leave, but General Cheatham stood up and called to them. His voice had a tone and volume that delivered orders above the din of battle. He spoke with authority. Everyone stopped and turned to hear what he said.

"There's not a Yankee within fifty miles of here," he asserted.

Another peal of thunder punctuated Cheatham's claim. But this time, instead of a soft whistle, a loud shriek prefaced the explosion. The entire building shook violently. A few intrepid souls remained, but most people stampeded out of the building. Reverend Palmer continued praying as if nothing had happened.

Major Larimer bent over and whispered in Polly's ear, "I think we need to evacuate this place." She nodded an affirmative as he took her hand. Together they quietly walked to the rear of the sanctuary and out to the city street.

Chaos greeted them outside. People were screaming and racing aimlessly through the streets. The explosions were increasing in number and volume. Larimer and Polly glanced down the street toward the Tennessee River. On top of a ridge across the river, six artillery pieces were blasting away at Chattanooga. Each time they fired, a puff of white smoke engulfed the cannon and its crew. A breeze over the water quickly swept the smoke away. By the time Polly grasped what was happening, the Confederate defenders of Chattanooga were returning fire. The Yankee guns shifted targets to engage them. On either side of the Yankee battery, mounted troops in blue jackets trimmed in yellow waited patiently for an opportunity to advance. However, no movement was made over the next few days. The reason for this delay was not apparent to those still in the city. It was not due to the city's defenders. Most of them had abandoned the city.

Benjamin Larimer left Chattanooga the next day. His orders were again modified so he returned to Mississippi. His departure at the train depot was extremely difficult for Polly. It reminded her too much of the day Richard had left Columbus. Benjamin embraced and kissed her. They had kissed previously, but this was the first time in public. Polly tingled with each kiss. She wondered if she was falling in love. Or was it a biological reaction to male stimulation? Or was Ben an available substitute for Richard?

The Yankees continued to demonstrate across the river but made no effort to occupy the city. On August 23, 1863, Dr. Saunders wrote Dr. Stout, now the medical director for hospitals for the Army of Tennessee, "It was thought more prudent to abandon the Academy, Gilmer & Foard Hospitals as they were in range of the enemy's guns and got all their water from the river." By then the city was virtually empty of medical facilities.

By Thursday, September 3, 1863, Dr. Saunders had relocated the Academy, Foard, and Gilmer Hospitals to Marietta, Georgia, so Polly's services were no longer needed in Chattanooga. She stuffed her few personal items into a worn carpet bag. Since the hospital's wagons and ambulances had previously left Chattanooga, she walked down to the depot. She intended to purchase a ticket for Atlanta. From there she would decide where to go next. She considered a number of options. She might rejoin Kate, but she did not know where Kate was. The entire medical corps was on the move, and the location of hospitals was changing every day. She seriously thought about trying to go to Jackson, Mississippi, in order to be near Benjamin. However, the shifting military situation in Tennessee and Mississippi made such a trip dubious. As she entered the car shed, Polly heard someone calling her name. It was the telegrapher. He handed her a telegram from Dr. Saunders. He requested she come immediately to Marietta. Polly walked over to the Western and Atlantic ticket window and purchased the needed ticket.

"How long before the train leaves?" she asked the ticket agent.

"Can't say," he answered. "Schedule has gone up the spout. Everybody is skedaddling fo' ole Rosy gets here. It will be an hour or more before any passenger trains go south."

"I'm going to step outside and get some fresh air. The smoke in here is burning my eyes."

"Yes, ma'am, but don't go too far or you might miss your car, and I don't know when we'll have another one. The army has taken control of our trains."

"I'm just going to step over there," she said, pointing to one of the arched openings. "The army is not a problem. I'm part of the army."

The ticket agent looked at Polly with a puzzled expression. Polly reached into her pocket. Her fingers caressed Edwin's letter. Then she felt another folded paper. She pulled it out and showed it to the agent. It was her army pass identifying Polly Brenton as a hospital nurse.

"Ma'am, I'll keep an eye out fo' you. If you miss the conductor's call, I'll come get you personally."

"Thank you. You are so kind."

The tracks around the car shed were a beehive of activity with an unusual number of locomotives around the yard. Almost all were headed south. White vapor clouds towered above their large Radley-Hunter smokestacks. Steam billowed out from beneath their cylinders. The peculiar sounds of these mechanical monsters filled the air. The locomotive nearest to Polly backed into a string of freight cars. The couplers banged hard against each other. The brakeman dropped an iron pin into the empty hole of one coupler while the conductor affixed a red flag to the engine and climbed up into the last car. He waved his hand. The engine's whistle emitted three short blasts as the train lurched forward, its bell clanging a steady rhythm.

Polly watched the bustle of the railroad with fascination. These locomotives represented the pinnacle of modern technology, but they also were starting to reveal a serious weakness of the Confederacy. Despite shiny Russian iron boilers, polished brass, and bright colors, they were showing the wear and tear of over two years of war. They had been built in the North, and replacement parts for repairs were now difficult to acquire. Despite the obstacles, the loyal crews and workers of the railroad kept many locomotives running, even if they operated at a much slower speed.

As she surveyed the panorama, Polly's attention was drawn to the bold slopes of Lookout Mountain. Happy memories of her day at Rock City with Major Larimer inundated her mind, but also reminded her that the handsome Mississippian was hundreds of miles away. A sad dejection swamped her elation when she remembered Richard's separation and death. The war was disturbing what little joy Polly was beginning to find in life.

Only about ten minutes had passed when Polly heard the ticket agent speaking to her, "Ma'am, there's a problem with one of the trucks on the passenger car. We can't repair it before sometime tomorrow, if…"

"If ever," interrupted Polly.

"Yes, ma'am. I can put you in a boxcar if you don't mind. Otherwise, to be honest, I can't promise I can get you out of Chattanooga before the Yankees get in here."

"Oh well, a boxcar is better than living with the Yankees," retorted Polly. "Just point me to the right one."

The boxcar was in bad need of paint, and several boards were missing. Inside, the floor was covered with a layer of hay. A ladder was propped against the open door. Polly tossed her bag inside and climbed up the ladder. At the top, a hand reached out to assist her. Polly looked up with relief. The smiling face of Dr. Rhea, an assistant surgeon from the Newsom Hospital, was looking back at her.

"Welcome aboard, Mrs. Brenton."

The sarcasm in his voice was obvious. Polly looked around. About twenty passengers sat on the floor. A number of crates, trunks, and barrels were stacked in one corner. Numerous blankets were scattered around on top of the hay for the passengers to sit on. Everyone introduced themselves. Over the next few hours they developed a close camaraderie, one of those relationships formed out of shared adversity.

Despite the urgency of the situation, Polly's train only traveled at a maximum speed of fifteen miles per hour. It was almost midnight when it pulled into a siding at Dalton. The conductor jumped out of the car before it stopped. A few minutes later he stuck his head back in the door and said, "We're going to be here until daylight. The line is in too bad shape to risk running at night. There's no hotel available now, so I suggest you do the best you can and get some sleep."

How bizarre, thought Polly. *Not long ago I was dining with General Bragg. Now I am sleeping in a boxcar with total strangers.* She curled up in an army blanket and soon was sound asleep. The next morning, she sent Dr. Saunders a telegram informing him of her expected time of arrival in Marietta. Later that evening, Polly's train reached the city's depot. Saunders had arranged for a steward to meet the train and escort Polly to the new hospital, a four-story hotel adjacent to the railroad track.

Two weeks after Polly had arrived in Marietta, she stood outside her new hospital and watched a train rumble past, the third one she had seen that day. All three were filled with soldiers. They were packed inside cars and covered the roofs. The troops on the last two trains looked strange. Their military uniforms were so alien compared with those of the troops she had watched marching into Chattanooga a few weeks earlier. They also displayed a brash demeanor acquired through numerous victories. The men hooted at her like school boys when the bell dismissed class. More than one, in jest, proposed marriage. She had heard that these troops were from Lee's famed Army of Northern Virginia. She wondered if Edwin might be among them, so she strained to catch a glimpse of him but had no success.

Patients had been trickling in for days. On Friday morning, Dr. Daniel, the physician in charge of the hospital, came into the ward and told Polly to expect much larger numbers of wounded. He just had been informed that a major battle was being fought in northwest Georgia. Images of the soldiers she had watched the day before flashed before her. She wondered how many of those cocky boys would pass through her ward. She reached in her pocket and pulled out Edwin's letter. It had become ratty and stained in her skirt. Nevertheless, most of Edwin's handwriting was still legible on the envelope. She looked at it and prayed, "Lord, if Ed is in this battle, please take care of him."

CHAPTER TEN
"Able to bear transportation"

FATHER OPENED HIS EYES. HE COULD SEE. SO HE WAS not blind. The morning sun illuminated the soft features of a young girl beneath a faded pink bonnet. She was bent over, staring into his face.

"Charlotte?" Father asked softly.

"Mister, are you okay?" she inquired, oblivious to his question.

"Charlotte, is that you?"

"No sir. I-ah is Adaline, Adaline Brotherton. Didje you want a drank of milk? I-ah jest milked our cows. They didn't git kilt in the battle. So I-ah milked them. I-ah was totin' the milk back to Ma and Pa. They aim to share it with the Kellys. Do you know the Kellys? They live up the road from ourn cabin. We'uns, the Kellys, and other folks from around here hid in a gully nigh near a mile from here when the shootin' started. Anyway, milkin' the cows is my chore and just cause there's sojurs don't mean cows don't need milkin'. Anyway, I wuz totin' this milk back to the folks, but I sees all you sojurs hurt so bad, I says to myself, 'Adaline Brotherton, it ain't fittin' not to keer fo these po puny souls richeer.' So I jest brung a drank of this milk to yourn fellars."

Father chuckled silently as he listened to the young girl. She reminded him so much of Charlotte. For a moment, he indulged himself in memories of his deceased daughter.

"Mister, are you dyin'? Yourn face sure is covered in blood."

Adaline's voice recaptured Father's attention and his reminiscences faded. "Did you say your name is Adeline?" he asked.

"Yea-is sir. I'm Adaline, Adaline Brotherton."

The girl's name is the same as the woman in South Carolina, thought Father. She even spoke with a similar accent. The recollection of Adeline Knight unexpectedly motivated Father. Her name aroused memories of their embrace, and despite his injuries, he intensely wanted to kiss her again.

Adaline turned. An army ambulance slowly moved down the road toward them. Instantly, she jumped in its path and frantically waved her arms. "Stop, I've got a sojur that's hurt exter bad."

The driver pulled back sharply on the reins with one hand. With the other, he pushed hard on the brake handle. The horse stopped, but the momentum of the wagon propelled it into a hard bounce before it came to rest on the dusty road.

"Girl!" screamed the pudgy driver.

"I got a hurt sojur over in dat ditch," she calmly replied.

Father could feel someone poking at his thigh. He opened his eyes. The small girl was still there, but she was looking down at his leg. Behind her was a man. His hair was long and turning gray. He wore a brown kepi. Father concluded he must be in the army. The collar of his soiled jean wool jacket was dark blue. The jacket itself was gray with a brown tint. Tarnished brass buttons confirmed the stranger was a soldier. He quickly surmised that the man in the grimy uniform was from the Army of Tennessee. "Hey, leave my leg alone," Father snapped at the driver. "I got hit in the head."

"Easy, sonny boy, you have a fresher hole down here, too. God must have been watching over you. A fraction of inch over and it would have cut the artery in your leg. Still is a wonder you didn't bleed to death. I have put a bandage on it. Walter, let's get him on the stretcher."

Another man in another ragged uniform stepped into the ditch beside Edwin Anderson. He grabbed the wounded soldier under each armpit. The other man wrapped his arms around Anderson's ankles. Together the men lifted him out of the ditch and placed him on a canvas stretcher. They then grasped the wooden poles and picked up their charge.

"Oh! Oh! Let me tell my sojur bye afore you tote him away and I nary see him agin."

Edwin recognized the voice of his mysterious young benefactor. If she had not discovered him lying in that ditch, he may have laid there for days…likely he might have died there. He felt the stretcher lower slightly. Then Adaline peered over its side. Standing on her toes, she reached over and kissed his cheek. "Good bye, mister sojur," she said.

"What did you say your name was?"

"I'm Adaline, Adaline Brotherton, Mr. Sojur. What's yourn name?"

"Ed, Edwin Anderson."

"You git well now, Mr. Anderson. Y'all take good keer of him, y'all hear?"

"Yes, ma'am," the gray-headed soldier replied with an unmistakable grin.

Quickly, the two men carried Edwin to the rear of the army ambulance and pushed the stretcher into place. One of them—Anderson could not tell which—closed the canvas flap. A few moments later, the wagon moved briskly down the road. The vehicle's pace jolted its human cargo. Father heard a scream. For the first time he became aware of another man lying beside him on the floor.

The ambulance rumbled along the rough road, each bump causing Father's injured companion to writhe in agonizing pain. Blood-curdling screams accompanied every jolt. Lying flat on his back, Father observed the bright sun briefly illuminating the canvas roof of the vehicle before trees on either side of the road formed a leafy roof that blocked the rays.

When the light returned, the interior of the ambulance grew warmer. After a frosty night, the heat felt good, but everything else in the wagon precluded any enjoyment of the warmer temperature. The air reeked of human sweat and blood. The screams increased as the vehicle bobbed along. Father now felt severe pain himself. When the shaking of the ambulance intensified appreciably, Father guessed that they had turned off the road into a field. If so, his ambulance ride almost certainly was over. He would be at a field dressing station or at a field hospital, Father did not know which. In either case, he knew that his odds of surviving the two wounds were now greatly improved.

The flap on the ambulance opened, and the grungy gray-haired soldier quickly grabbed the stretcher. As he pulled it out of the vehicle, the other soldier stepped up to take hold of the opposite end. In the daylight, Father could see both men more clearly. The gray-haired man likely was too old for active combat service. Black corporal's stripes were crudely sewn on each sleeve. Father only glimpsed the man's partner as the stretcher slid by him. He was much younger. A large slouch hat was pulled down low on his forehead. Nevertheless, Father noticed a crude leather patch covered his left eye. He, too, was unfit for combat duty.

The two men carried "Father" Edwin Anderson's litter a few steps and halted. A third man approached the side of the stretcher and looked down at Father. He appeared to be in his early thirties. His blond hair hung in ringlets down to his shoulders. A trimmed beard and heavy mustache added to his knightly appearance. His dress, however, was anything but dandified. He wore an off-white linen shirt. His sleeves were rolled up, and his collar was unbuttoned. A blood-splattered apron covered the front of his shirt.

Seeing the blood on Father's face, he said in a matter-of-fact tone, "Head wound, corporal. Let's see if it's mortal."

"Sir, it's not. I checked. His head injury is only a flesh wound," the corporal argued. "The bullet just glanced off the skull. Look at his leg."

Glancing at Edwin's blood-soaked pants, the assistant surgeon responded, "Okay, it may need amputating. Set him over there, corporal."

"Yes, sir!"

"Sawbones?" yelled Father. "You ain't cuttin' my leg off. It doesn't need it!"

"Calm down, soldier. I'm the doctor, and I'll tell you what it needs. But no decision will be made until after I make an accurate examination of the wound. Let me check to see if it's still bleeding." The assistant surgeon untied the temporary bandage, pulled a pocket knife out of his trousers, and cut a slit in Father's pants. He ripped the cloth apart and in doing so, reopened the wound, which began bleeding again. He reached into a knapsack on the ground, took out a tourniquet, and applied it to Father's leg. "I don't want you bleeding to death. I guess the Almighty was watching over you. Corporal, put him down."

The two soldiers placed the stretcher down onto the ground. They carefully lifted Father off it and laid him on the grass.

The gray-headed corporal twisted his head back and said reassuringly to Father, "Now don't think too hard of Doc. He's been up for two whole days. I guess you are about the five hundredth bullet hole he has looked at. Then he goes over yonder and helps the other sawbones cut off arms and legs. It's a bloody mess, but it's the only hope y'all wounded soldiers have."

Without saying anything else, the two stretcher-bearers returned to their vehicle. It quickly disappeared, kicking up dust as it sped back to shuttling wounded from the battlefield to this field hospital.

Father lay amid dozens of other injured soldiers. Most wore the grimy jean wool so common in the Army of Tennessee. A few had faded blue sack coats. A Federal soldier lay beside and facing Father. His terrified eyes were fixed upon something behind Father. Father turned his head and glanced at a horrifying scene. Several men were holding down a wounded soldier on a table outside a log farm house. The curly-headed assistant surgeon was also there, standing at the man's head doing something. His victim sounded as if he were being tortured. Father tried to turn away, but some morbid attraction held his attention.

Pain, though, was not the cause of the man's distress. The small dose of chloroform used during surgery was a good anesthetic and prevented the patient from feeling any physical discomfort, but a side effect was a hallucination-filled delirium that caused screams of agony and involuntary writhing. Physically holding the patient down was necessary to keep him still during surgery.

The assistant surgeon moved in between Father and the table. A few minutes later, Father noticed the rhythmic back-and-forth movement of the physician's right elbow. It reminded Father of a carpenter sawing lumber. Soon thereafter, one of the men holding down the patient turned and flung the soldier's leg aside. It landed in a pile of amputated limbs with a muted thud. The sight sickened Father. He turned away. It did not help. Images of his own leg being tossed into the pile tormented his mind. He could see that the same thoughts plagued the Yank lying next to him. He tried to speak to the Federal. *Odd how circumstances changed one's perception*, he thought. Yesterday the two men were trying to kill each other. Today Father saw only a frightened human being and wanted to comfort him. However, he was too weak. No words came out, but he did recall Christ's words in Matthew 5:44, "But I say unto you, Love your enemies." He wondered how he would ever erase his religious past from his memory.

The assistant surgeon's voice maintained its monotone volume as he commanded, "Next." Two of the men assisting him approached Father, placed him on a litter, and carried him to the table. Father summoned every ounce of strength within him to get away, but to no avail. He was placed on the table. At one end, a man grasped both ankles tightly against the tabletop. Other men on each side held Father's wrists and pinned down his shoulders.

A man in a plaid brown and burgundy shirt stood at Father's head. In one hand, he gripped a cloth folded into a triangular pyramid shape. In the other hand was an open brown glass bottle. He reached to place the cloth over Father's mouth and nose, but Father jerked his head to one side. The man snatched up the cloth before it tumbled onto the table.

"Hold him still!" demanded the man in the plaid shirt.

The man on Father's left, a sergeant, released his shoulder and grasped his jaw. The man in the plaid shirt set the cloth over Father's mouth and nose. He turned the bottle and poured several drops onto the cloth. Soon the chloroform performed its work.

The men continued to hold Father against the table. The assistant surgeon stuck his finger into the wound on Father's thigh. He felt around and pulled out a blood-soaked patch of fabric. Then he took a small instrument from his pants pocket. It was a tapered steel rod with a dark wooden handle, very similar in appearance to an ice pick. He bent over and probed the hole in Father's leg.

"The bullet didn't hit the bone," he whispered. It had passed clean through the muscle. Using boiled horsehair, the assistant surgeon sutured the entrance and exit wounds. As he finished sewing, he again spoke in a strong authoritative tone, "Sergeant, have a nurse bandage the wound and set this patient over there by the smokehouse." The surgeon pulled a wine-red silk handkerchief from the other side pocket and wiped Edwin's blood from the instrument. He then returned it to his pocket. Walking away, he growled, "Too much time here. Sergeant, tell the nurse I said to put morphine on the wound and bandage it tightly."

The anesthesia already was wearing off. Father was becoming conscious of the pain in both his head and leg. Two men reached down and picked up Edwin Anderson. They did not bother putting him on a litter. Instead, they quickly lifted him by his legs and shoulders and laid him on the ground beside the entrance to the log smokehouse. The scent of ham still lingered in the air. It made Father hungry. He reached into his haversack and found a hardtack cracker. He broke it in half. Lying beside him was the man whose leg the assistant surgeon had amputated earlier. Father offered him half of the cracker. When the man nodded his head no, Father put the piece back into his haversack and began munching on the other half.

The warm afternoon sun felt good to Father. He lay quietly on the ground wondering what had happened. He raised his head enough to see both of his brogans. Relieved that the surgeon had not amputated his leg, Father relaxed. He felt light-headed and longed for sleep. He had just dozed off when he felt someone shaking his leg and heard a voice telling him to wake up. Instead of the now familiar corporal's face, a woman was looking back at him. An old faded split bonnet framed her face. Her skin was dry and wrinkled. She held a wad of snuff in the corner of her mouth. She was stroking Father's forehead. Unsure of what her presence meant, Father instinctively turned his head away.

"Easy there, sonny. I'm fixen to fix you up," she scolded.

"The only nurse I could find was this old woman," said a man standing next to Father. "She's one of the local refugees. She says she can help you." Father remembered the man from the table. He had held Edwin's head like a vise while the chloroform was administered. The man wore a battered butternut kepi. His pockmarked face was accented by a jet black full beard. His deep-set brown eyes revealed a tender compassion that contradicted his actions at the table. He was wearing a brown tinted jean wool shell jacket. White sergeant chevrons were sewn on each sleeve. His reassurance worked. Father relaxed.

"Sure kin, sonny boy," said the old woman. She didn't say another word but immediately tore several strips from a green checkered tablecloth she held in her hands. She flipped the strips across her shoulder and poured powdered morphine directly onto Father's wounds. As she worked, the sergeant became very talkative.

"The old woman didn't want to help you at first. She took one look at that uniform you are wearing and thought you were a Yankee. You know that jacket is almost as blue as an old Federal jacket. I had the darnest time convincing her that you is one of us. You are one of Longstreet's men, ain't ye? Those Confederate-issue "I" buttons were the proof in the puddin'. Never seen so many Confederates dressed just alike as you boys. What's your name?"

"Most of the boys call me Father. It's a private joke. My real name is Edwin Anderson, from Columbus, Georgia. I'm in Company G, Second Georgia Infantry...of Benning's Brigade."

"I knew you was one of those Army of Northern Virginie fellars. Those buttons gave you away. I'm Caleb Jensen from Mobile, Alabama. This here is General William Preston's field hospital. This here farm belongs to a man named Robert Dyer."

Edwin looked around. He started to speak but once again slipped away into slumber.

The next day, Father was jolted awake. He found himself on the floor bed of a wagon with three other wounded men lying beside him. The floor was covered in pine straw. Four other wounded soldiers sat at the front of the old farm wagon. One of them soon divulged that Edward Flewellen, medical director of the Army of Tennessee, had ordered all patients in field hospitals to be evacuated to the general hospitals, so all patients who were "able to bear transportation," the stock phrase for those well enough to travel, were loaded into whatever vehicle was available and moved to Catoosa Station or Ringgold for transportation to various hospitals operated by the Army of Tennessee.

The distinctive cadence of the horses' hoofs on the bridge planking confirmed to Father that the ambulance was crossing the creek that was to give its name to the bloody fighting of recent days. Chickamauga was a Cherokee word that more or less meant "river of death." After an agonizing ride, the rickety old wagon and its human cargo arrived at Catoosa Station on the Western and Atlantic Railroad. Four days earlier, Edwin had gotten off a train at this same station.

Today, no locomotive stood waiting to take Father away. A large field near the woodshed was covered with row after row of wounded soldiers. Two officers watched as Father's wagon was unloaded. He was the last man out. As he waited, he overheard them arguing.

"Sir, I need trains to move these men south," said one.

"Sir, I know, but..."

Before he could finish, the first officer interrupted, "No buts. These men need immediate transportation. Most of them spent last night in the open without blankets."

"Yes, sir. Most of the army did, too."

"Sir, do you realize it was below freezing last night? This morning these men were covered in frost. We had two die last night from the cold. Another night like that and we'll lose a lot more. Now get me some trains."

"Sir, there should be two coming in from Ringgold in the next hour. They're bringing ammunition to replace what the army expended Saturday and Sunday."

"How many cars?" asked the first officer. Father decided he must be a surgeon.

"Sir?" the other officer replied, obviously bewildered by the surgeons inquiry concerning the makeup of the two expected arrivals.

"How many cars, Captain?" repeated the surgeon. "Doesn't the Quartermaster Corps understand plain English?"

"Yes, sir," replied the second officer, obviously riled by the doctor's insult. "Twenty cars, I believe. Possibly as many as twenty-five."

"Sir, that will not do! No sir! It will not do. It will take forty house cars just to remove the men lying here now. Look at that road, sir. Do you see the wagons and ambulances coming as we talk? A few more hours' delay and it will take double to transport them to army hospitals."

Father did not hear the rest of the two officers' quarrel. He was removed from the wagon and placed in one of the endless rows lying on the ground. He was just one more casualty in a war without end. The trip from the field hospital had made him keenly aware of his pain. He could not stop moaning. He tried, but the sounds were involuntary. He felt ashamed, thinking he was acting like a small child. Although Father was certain everyone heard his whimpers, they were drowned out by the groans of those around him. The sunshine felt good, and Father soon fell asleep, thankful to escape the horrific reality around him.

A shrill distant whistle startled Father awake. He twisted his head so that he could see the locomotive chugging into view. Her Russian iron boiler glistened in the bright sunlight. Steam enveloped the engine as it screeched to a halt. The couplers on a string of slate-blue boxcars clanged together and eradicated the slack between cars. Father could not read the nameplate on the boiler, but the locomotive sported an Indian red livery highlighted with gold and blue stripes. "W.&A.R.R." was painted in gold block lettering on the side of its tender. Gazing at the locomotive, Father's thoughts turned back to the events of the last three weeks, especially the wild train ride that had brought him back to Georgia more than two years after he had left to go to war. He thought of Adeline Knight. The memory of her kiss brought a rare smile to Father's face. He wondered if she would really write him. If she did, he was going to find some way to get back to Chester, South Carolina.

It was after midnight before "Father" Edwin Anderson was loaded into a boxcar for evacuation south. He had a severe headache, and his thigh hurt intensely. Another cold night punctuated his misery. His ripped trousers exposed his bare leg, so he was thankful to be placed inside the railroad car. Its wooden floor was covered with straw. Patients were laid side by side on top of the straw. When the car floor was full, the surgeon Father had heard arguing earlier climbed into the car. A private held up a small lantern so the doctor could survey the arrangement. The warm golden glow enabled Father to examine the car for a short time.

He ascertained numerous boards were missing from the siding on the walls. Obviously, the car had been used to transport healthy troops previously. When the surgeon completed his examination, he handed a sheet of paper to the private and jumped down from the car. The private placed the document on top of a stack of papers sitting by the door. After someone outside closed the door, the private sat down, shifted the papers, and situated himself against a post of the car frame.

Twenty minutes after leaving Catoosa Station, the train reached the Tunnel Hill depot at Chetoogeta Mountain. When it came to a halt, the door opened and several soldiers began unloading the wounded. After he was taken out of the boxcar, Father noticed that a yellow flag was now flying over the new buildings he had seen a week earlier. He was carried inside one of these structures and laid on a crude bed. Its sheets were blood stained and dirty. One of the stretcher-bearers covered him with a dusty blanket. Combined with the heat of a nearby wood stove, the dirty laundry felt cozy to Father.

A doctor pulled a small camp stool beside Father's bed and sat down. "Name?" he asked.

"Private, ah, I mean Corporal Edwin Anderson, sir," Father answered.

The doctor flipped through some papers in his hand, and said, "I am Assistant Surgeon W. J. Burt. This is a shipping and receiving hospital for the Army of Tennessee. Let's see, Anderson…here it is. Bullet wounds to the head and to the right thigh. How are you doing, son?"

"Fine, sir. Well, I guess I'm okay. To be honest, my leg hurts and my head hurts."

"I'll have a nurse change the bandages soon. I'll examine your wounds thoroughly then. But now, let's get you some food. How does hot vegetable soup sound? I've hired four Negro women to cook. Real good cooks, too."

"Bully, sir. I haven't eaten anything except sheet iron crackers since Friday evening."

An hour later, Dr. Burt returned with a convalescent soldier serving as a nurse. "How was the soup?" he asked Father.

"Excellent, sir. Lot better than them sheet iron crackers the quartermaster serves."

"Good. Now, let's remove those bandages and have a look at you."

Dr. Burt finished his examination and said, "Preston's surgeons did a fine job. Barring complications, you should recover completely." Then he moved on to another patient.

The convalescent began to bandage the wounds up. He talked as he worked. "I'm not a real nurse. I've got too many thumbs to do this. Burt is assigning you to Daniel Hospital in Marietta. You'll have real honest-to-goodness nurses there. Some of them are ladies. I hear they is right purty, too."

"That sounds wonderful," Father replied. He thought of Adeline Knight's kiss and smiled again. "I was by here last week and this place was empty," Father added, hoping the nurse would take the hint and clarify why no yellow flag had been up on Thursday.

"Well, with old Rosey taking Chattanooga, Stout, the Director of Hospitals for the Army of Tennessee, orders the hospital here moved to Palmetto, Georgia. Most everything is there now. But with all these casualties from the battle last weekend, we need a shipping and receiving hospital near the field hospitals. There now. I'm finished. You'll be out of here this afternoon."

A plump black woman brought Father another bowl of soup. She was singing "Amazing Grace" very softly.

"Why are you so happy?" Father inquired.

"Cause y'all gen'men fit dem Yankees and plum kicks 'em a-out of de entire state of Georgie."

Father knew she was trying to deceive him, only saying what she thought a white soldier wanted to hear. He recognized that the slaves all favored the Union cause now. Lincoln's Emancipation Proclamation would have set her free if the recent battle had turned out differently.

For a moment, a dreadful thought flashed across his mind. Did the Confederate army lose the battle after he was wounded? Were the Yankees on their way? Father only had seen hospitals since he had been shot. These always continued to function even when behind enemy lines. But railroads didn't, so he concluded that his train ride was sufficient evidence that the Yankees did not defeat his comrades. Besides, this slave would have been less submissive if her potential liberators were nearby.

The song she sang seemed like an innocent expression of her Christian faith. And it surely was. But Father suspected the song expressed a belief that most white Southerners would find heretical, the imminent approach of the Year of Jubilee. In the Old Testament, every fiftieth year was classified a "year of jubilee." Among the laws recorded in Leviticus 25:8-55 was an edict that during the Year of Jubilee, all Israelite slaves were to be set free. Slaves throughout the Confederacy equated the Year of Jubilee with their own freedom and hoped Lincoln's armies would bring the celebration with them.

"Do you know 'How Firm a Foundation'?" Father asked. "It was my wife's favorite hymn. She died last spring."

"Yea suh, I's knows it."

Her rendition was interrupted by a shrill whistle. A short time later, Father was again loaded into one of the Western and Atlantic's pervasive slate-blue boxcars. The precious little straw that once covered its floor had been crushed and obliterated by previous passengers. Lying on the floor, he noticed a small writing desk was attached to the car's bracing. He could not see what, if anything, was on the desk, but he could see the top half of a small improvised shallow cabinet that hung above the desk's surface. A battered wooden stool was pushed under the desk. A dark indigo coat with brass buttons was draped across one of the horizontal wood bumpers nailed to the car's frame.

As Father studied the desk, a man climbed into the car. Although he was bald, the man looked to be of military age. Nevertheless, he wore civilian clothing, checkered pants, a black vest, and a linen shirt with a black tie. The chain for a pocket watch dangled across his vest. His long dark hair was combed back. His mustache and a hint of a goatee were fashionable but failed to give him any distinctive appearance. He reached into his vest and pulled out a gold pocket watch. Flipping open the cover, the man checked the time, leaned out the door, and waved his arm. The car pitched forward and as it did, the man, who obviously was the train's conductor, leaned over and appeared to write at the desk. Father guessed he was noting the departure time. The train slowly picked up speed. Moving along at fifteen miles per hour, Father watched the trees fly by the open door of the boxcar. By now, the conductor was seated at the desk and seemed busy with some paperwork. Eventually, the conductor turned around and caught Father staring at him. He politely asked, "How are you feeling?"

Father wanted to say, "Abysmal," but instead he replied, "Okay." *Okay!* he thought. *I'm tuckered out and hurt like...*

The conductor's voice interrupted his thoughts, "Good. We'll have you in Marietta soon. They'll take good care of you there."

"Thanks," Father said. It was artificial, but it was the only thing that came to mind.

"I'm William Fuller," announced the conductor.

The name surprised Father. The unimposing figure didn't look like a hero, but Father remembered reading about Yankee engine thieves who had tried to wreck the Western and Atlantic mainline during the spring of 1862. They had stolen a locomotive named the General and would have been successful if not for William Fuller. He had chased after them, first on foot, then on a pole car, and finally on three different locomotives. He finally caught up with them near Ringgold, Georgia.

"I'm Edwin Anderson," Father said in time. "Are you still the conductor on the General?"

"Yes," Fuller replied. "How did you know?"

"I read last April about your pursuit of them Yankee train thieves. I've always been interested in the latest technology...well railroads are changing things. I won't be surprised to see locomotives running at sixty miles per hour one day."

"We were pushing seventy on the Texas that day. It was the scariest moment of my life. But I suspect you're right."

"Mr. Fuller, do you suppose I could see the General when we get to Marietta?" Father asked.

"I'll see what I can do. Were you a railroad man before the war?"

"No, believe it or not, I was a Baptist preacher."

Except for his rebuke of Lindsay's profanity, this was the first time Father had admitted he was a minister of the gospel since

Ann's death. His disclosure didn't feel natural, but strangely, just speaking the words aloud had been therapeutic.

When the train reached Marietta, Fuller jumped down from the boxcar, spoke to a team of stretcher-bearers, and pointed at Father. They climbed into the car and began unloading the patients. Father was the last one, but they unloaded him from the opposite side of the car. As they headed toward the front of the train, the man at Father's feet spoke. "Mr. Fuller said that you wanted to see the locomotive."

Father smiled and said, "If it's not too much trouble."

"Glad to oblige. But we need to hurry. If Saunders catches us doing this, he'll pitch a conniption fit for certain."

"Who's Saunders?"

"Dudley D. Saunders is the post surgeon here in Marietta. He's the chief cook and bottle washer around these parts. He's a real hard case. He runs everything by Stout's book."

"Who's Stout? Seems like I've heard his name somewhere before."

"Where are you from? Everybody knows who Dr. Stout is."

"I just came down from Virginia two weeks ago."

"Oh, one of Longstreet's boys?"

"Yes, sir," Father answered with pride. "A member of the Columbus Guards, Company G, Second Georgia Volunteer Infantry Regiment, Benning's Brigade, Hood's Division of Longstreet's Corps, Robert E. Lee's Army of Northern Virginia."

"Samuel H. Stout is medical director of hospitals of the Army of Tennessee. Here she is, the famous General."

Father could not help but admire the locomotive. From its tender to the strap iron cowcatcher on the front, it displayed the technology that was changing the world. The tender's profile was a simple, rectangular shape. Its dark green sides were trimmed in gold leaf and vermillion stripes. "W.&A.R.R." in gold block letters boldly proclaimed its owner's pride in the machine. The Western and Atlantic Railroad was owned and operated by the state of Georgia, and this was one of its premier engines. The locomotive's polished Russian finish reflected the sky, giving the iron horse a blue tint. Three domes and a Radley-Hunter balloon smokestack crowned the top of its silhouette. The wooden cab was painted to match the tender. Beneath the cab, two of the four red drivers were visible. These magnificent wheels were sixty inches in diameter and were connected to each other and to a cylinder at the front by heavy metal driving rods. The boiler was the modern wagon-top design. A polished steel angle beam was suspended from the cab and boiler. It ran the entire length of the locomotive and served as a walkway for the engine's crew. It also revealed the engine's age. Running boards had replaced this feature in more recent railroad designs. Although close observation revealed signs that war shortages were impacting daily maintenance, the locomotive's overall appearance demonstrated the esteem in which its crew held it. Strange, mysterious creaks and hisses made the huge iron beast seem to be a living creature instead of a machine.

Before he could observe more about the locomotive, the stretcher-bearer spoke. "We better move on before the doctor catches us."

CHAPTER ELEVEN
"Better supplied than any hotel"

FATHER TURNED HIS ATTENTION TO HIS NEXT STOP, THE Fletcher House Hotel, a red brick building with four floors. James Andrews and a majority of his raiders had slept here the night before they had stolen the General in their failed raid on the Western and Atlantic Railroad. Father remembered passing the building, now being used as a hospital, a week earlier. The woman who reminded him of Polly had been standing nearby. Memories of her came rushing into Father's head. Since the stop in Chester, South Carolina, Adeline Knight had dominated his yearnings for feminine companionship, but now, this brick building rekindled the strange attraction for Polly that he had suppressed since the day he had seen her in the hallway of the church parsonage. Briefly, he fantasized that she might actually be in Marietta. He began to wonder what their reunion might be like.

The voice of the stretcher-bearer spoiled his fantasy. "Dr. Saunders may be a hard case, but he gets results. He'll have you up and back to your unit in no time. Good luck."

"Same to both of you. And thanks for the tour of the locomotive."

"You're right welcome," replied one of the stretcher-bearers.

By then they had folded their litter and were walking out the door. Father realized that between his fascination with the General and his dream about Polly he had virtually ignored his two benefactors. They had risked disciplinary actions to let him see a locomotive, and he hadn't even asked their names. He tried to recall what they looked like. He couldn't.

Father looked around. Extra beds filled every inch of space. They were set up to accommodate the massive influx of wounded that the railroad constantly was disgorging. Six bunks were tightly fitted into a room that normally contained two beds. Each bunk contained three tiers. Unlike the receiving hospital at Tunnel Hill, the sheets here were clean. However the stench in the room was appalling. Most of the wounded had not bathed in weeks. Their uniforms reeked with the smells of sweat, gunpowder, and blood. Infection in many of the wounds added another dimension to the putrid aroma. A few randomly placed candles supplemented the light from a lone coal oil lamp in one corner of the room.

His two benefactors had laid Father on the bottom tier of one bunk. A black man, probably a slave, removed Father's brogans. It was the first time since he had left Atlanta that he had taken them off. The man placed the shoes under the foot of Father's bed. He also took off Father's canteen, haversack, and jacket and hung them on a peg in the wall. Then he covered Father with the blankets that had been folded on the end of the bed. Father couldn't remember the last time he had slept in a real bed. Even in his pain, it felt good.

A nurse passed among the wounded men, handing each new patient a perfume-laden cloth. She showed each soldier how to place the cloth over his nose and mouth to protect against the foul emanations and poisonous odors in the room.

As the nurse approached Father, she seemed strangely familiar. He tried to concentrate, but his mental resolve surrendered to physical privation. Lack of sleep and loss of blood had taken its toll. Father dozed off. The nurse bent over to awaken him. Instructing him about proper usage of the cloth was deemed vital for his welfare. When her hand touched him, she gasped. It was sufficient to rouse Father. He looked into her face. Even in the dim candlelight, he recognized Polly. Excitement flooded over him. He smiled. Then exhaustion triumphed over passion and Father dropped into a deep sleep.

When Father finally woke, Polly was sitting beside his bed holding his hand. Her diminutive fingers felt so stimulating. Once more a thrill ran down his spine, causing his body to tremble slightly. Polly sensed him shiver and spoke.

"Ed, how are you feeling?"

"Polly, is that really you?"

"Yes, Ed, it's me. Now answer my question. How are you feeling?"

"Well, at the moment I'd say I am as worthless as a Continental," Edwin answered.

"Oh I wouldn't say that. You have improved significantly since your arrival."

"I guess those few hours of sleep helped," Edwin said half-heartedly.

Polly laughed and retorted, "A few hours! Edwin Anderson, you have been asleep for over two days."

"Guess I was plum tuckered out."

"Tuckered out! You were shot twice, once in the leg and once in the head. And I am beginning to think the head injury did more damage than the surgeon says," Polly joked.

"Who's this surgeon who thinks my head is normal?" sneered Edwin.

"Dr. Ferdinand Eugene Daniel of Mississippi. He's quite a character. Back in Chattanooga, he was sparking a local belle named Miss Vannie Vogle. First time he tried to kiss her, she had to run outside to spit out her snuff. But he's a good doctor. When I first arrived in Chattanooga, one surgeon…I don't recall his name…had me melting Minie balls in an iron pot. As soon as the lead liquefied, I poured sulfur powder into the pot and stirred it. When it dried, it was a charcoal color powder. It was used to treat gangrene, but it was ineffective, and Dr. Daniel argued against continued use of the remedy."

Edwin smiled and said, "Bully. I have a good sawbones. I'm sure I will be hunky-dory soon. Now tell me about Mrs. Polly Brenton. What are you doing here?"

"Well, sir, I am the ward master for this section of the hospital. I am responsible for the room's cleanliness and for supervising the nurses. Dr. Saunders has contracted for some slaves to do the cleaning and other chores."

"So I guess that makes you an overseer," said Edwin. He intended the remark to be a joke, but Polly's expression immediately announced she did not find it funny. He regretted saying anything. Edwin assumed the problem lay in the social status of an overseer. Only large plantations employed them. Most were career professionals who boasted of their skill in handling slave labor. Many were notorious for their cruelty to black slaves. As a group, they generally were considered unreliable and of low grade. Edwin assumed his joke insulted Polly's dignity.

In reality, Edwin had irritated something much deeper in Polly. She still could not reconcile a lifetime of indoctrination that Africans were inferior creatures with her experiences while nursing the slaves at Stillwater. Delia may have had less education than white folks, but Polly had discovered she possessed a superb intellect and a delightful personality. The rest of the slaves that she had doctored may have seemed less brilliant, but their reaction to adversity clearly exposed their humanity. Polly had not become an abolitionist, but she had concluded that slaves were human beings, not property.

After a moment of awkward silence Edwin apologized. "Polly, I am sorry. I did not mean to hurt you. I guess years of army life have made me coarse and unfit for polite society," he said, trying in vain to distance himself from the remark with this feeble excuse.

"It's all right," said Polly. She desperately wanted to talk with him about her feelings about slaves, but she was afraid that if Edwin knew her opinion of black people, it would drive him away. She considered Edwin to be her closest friend. Or more accurately, the representation of the Edwin Anderson she had fabricated in her mind after Richard's death had become her best friend. This imagined Edwin was a composite of the real Edwin and Sir Galahad. She could tell him anything because the actual Edwin was not present to hear her. Although she had made some friendships through her army medical service, Polly did not allow anyone, not even Kate Cummings, to develop the intimacy she and Ann had shared. After Ann's death, Polly had subconsciously made Edwin Ann's surrogate. She imagined having the same conversations with him as she had with Ann. However, now that she really was talking to him, she could not say the same things.

"You were telling me about your responsibilities here," said Edwin.

"Yes, I have two matrons working with me. They manage the daily operations and prepare prescribed diets for the patients. I have a couple of civilian nurses, but most nurses are injured soldiers."

"Sounds like you are a busy person," Edwin commented. "But Polly, when I asked what you were doing here, I guess I really meant to ask, 'Why are you here?'"

"Ed, I guess you are responsible for that," she answered.

"Me? I don't understand."

Polly reached into the pocket of her skirt and pulled out Edwin's letter. She handed it to Edwin. He glanced at it and recognized his handwriting. At first he was puzzled. He had written Polly only once in his life, after Sharpsburg, to tell her about Richard's death. It had to be that letter, but he was surprised that she had kept it, even though her letter to him was in the pocket of his jacket, which was hanging on the wall by the bed. But he did not disclose its survival to her.

"Do you recognize this?" she asked.

"My letter about Richard?" he responded.

The conversation had taken an unexpected surreal turn, and he was less than comfortable with its new direction. Although he had fantasized about seeing Polly again, his dreams were more like a medieval knight who galloped up on a white horse and rescued her from the dragon. Her words now were taking him deep into a reality he could not escape or evade.

"Yes. It was the worst correspondence I have ever received in my life."

Edwin felt terribly guilty. He knew that he had no culpability in Richard's death—the Yankees had killed Richard, not him—but he had been the one who had written that letter that hurt Polly.

"I suddenly became one of those widows I witnessed grieving in front of the newspaper office. I had learned a little medicine by doctoring Mr. Lewis's slaves when they were sick or injured. So I decided to use what little I had learned to prevent as many wives as I could from getting a letter like this." Polly's explanation eased some of Edwin's sense of guilt. "I'd best get back to my duties. I'll check on you again later, Ed."

As Polly walked away, Edwin contemplated their conversation. A few weeks earlier, in Chester, South Carolina, Adeline Knight had aroused his animal instincts. The few minutes they had spent together had offered no opportunity to get to know her. The attraction had been purely physical. His earlier visions of reuniting with Ann's best friend had aroused the same emotions, but now he found Polly Brenton, the person, to be extremely appealing. He wondered what Adeline Knight the person was like, too.

Edwin's unexpected arrival in her hospital ward had created an equally troubling quandary for Polly. Polly's romance with Benjamin Larimer had pushed many of her thoughts about Edwin aside. Part of what had made Edwin so appealing was the safety of romanticizing about him across the miles. They shared a common bond of loss, but Edwin had been far away. His letter had made the dream tangible, but a letter was only a piece of paper. Now Edwin was not hundreds of miles away in Virginia. He was in the room where she must be every day. She would be required to see him, to talk with him, and touch him daily. Could she suppress an attraction that she had imagined for almost a year? And where did Benjamin Larimer fit into her life now?

A willowy woman Edwin did not know came and sat on the side of his bunk. She wore a brown homespun dress with a pale yellow apron. Her auburn hair was pulled back and tied with a pink ribbon. Edwin could see that it was turning gray. Her face appeared haggard. The skin was dry, almost like leather. Yet her brown eyes were still bright. In one hand, she carried a tin cup and in the other, a tin plate. She pulled up a small table and placed the cup and plate on it. The strange woman took a knife and fork out of her apron and cut a small bite of meat from the plate's contents. She surprised Edwin when she started to feed him as if he were an infant. Nevertheless, her charming expression disarmed any apprehension, and Edwin opened his mouth. As he chewed, he suddenly realized how famished he was. He had only eaten a couple of hardtack crackers and some soup since Sunday morning. As he ate, his new angel of mercy chattered.

"I-ah am Julia Bilbry and I-ah am yo' nurse. I-ah he'p a-out Doc Daniels and Mrs. Brentons so y'all have ti-ahm to recov-ah.

Doc says you are on a full diet. I-ah have beef and cawn bread. I-ah have snap beans and fresh cawn fo' you too."

The meal was not Ann's home cooking or Frederick Wilhelm's restaurant cuisine, but it was filling. Edwin "ate the dishrag," soldier's slang for wiping a plate clean.

"Miss Bilbry, that was delicious. Those vegetables are right smart better than army crackers."

"Yea-is. I-ah reckon dat they sho-nuff is. Docta' Stouts insists his hospitals are, and I-ah quote, 'to be better supplied than any hotel in the Confederacy'."

Not long after he finished, a lean man in a tailored gray wool officer's uniform entered the room. His frock coat had a double row of brass buttons on the front, black cuffs that were trimmed in the gold braid of a major, and a single star embossing his black collar. Around his waist was a dark green sash, indicating he was a surgeon. A black leather belt was fastened over the sash. Its round brass buckle was embossed with a single five-point star inside a circular wreath. No weapons or accouterments were attached to the belt. His dark hair was parted in the middle, and his only facial hair was a small well-trimmed moustache. The surgeon methodically went to every bunk and talked with each man. In his left hand, he carried a stack of papers. During each conversation, he periodically flipped the pages and read to himself. When he reached Edwin's bunk, the surgeon looked down at him and said, "I'm Doctor Daniel. I'll be treating your case while you are here." Dr. Daniel was silent briefly as he read Edwin's file. Then he said, "Corporal Anderson, you are doing fine. It was rough at the front, wasn't it?"

"You have nary idea, Doc," responded Edwin.

"No, I suppose I don't. I was a private in the Eighteenth Mississippi Infantry and fought at First Manassas. But things have changed since then."

"You were in the infantry?" asked Edwin.

"Yes. I was still in medical school when war broke out. So I enlisted. After President Davis's proclamation releasing medical students from the ranks, I returned to the New Orleans School of Medicine. I graduated just before the Yanks captured the city. I've been a surgeon with this army ever since."

Learning that the physician had fought in a real battle as a foot soldier appealed to Edwin's psyche. He supposed the doctor would be more sympathetic, having once experienced the same tribulations of the infantry. For his part, Edwin decided he must listen to this physician and follow his instructions precisely.

Several days passed without an opportunity for Polly and Edwin to talk much, but she checked on him every day. Both of his wounds were healing nicely. She worried about his diet however. An insufficient supply of beef had been supplemented with salt pork for those on a full diet. Half-diet patients still received toast and soup. Low-diet patients were supposed to have rice and milk, yet milk was all but non-existent. Acquiring fresh vegetables likewise was becoming more difficult. Shortages were crippling Confederate medical treatment as well as its military efforts.

On the Sunday following their initial conversation, Polly arrived at Edwin's bed around six o'clock in the morning. Under one arm, she carried a folded clean uniform. In her hand was a pair of wooden crutches. Slightly behind her right shoulder stood a big burly black man dressed in the course jean wool known as "Negro cloth." Edwin assumed he was one of the slaves under Polly's charge. His physique reminded Edwin of Obadiah at Stillwater. The memory of Obadiah and Stillwater surprised Edwin. In the past, his recollections of the Lewis plantation always were centered around Ann.

"Time for you to get out bed before Dr. Daniel accuses you of being a deadbeat. He does not like malingerers! He will go to great lengths to detect anyone shirking their duty. Now get up and get dressed."

Edwin started to stand but suddenly felt dizzy. He grabbed the bedpost to prevent himself from falling face first onto the wooden floor.

"Careful, Ed," cautioned Polly. "Don't rush. You've been in bed for a week now." Then she turned to the slave and said, "Cuffee, give Corporal Anderson a hand." Edwin stabilized himself before Cuffee could assist. Polly handed Cuffee the clean uniform. Then she said to Edwin, "Go with Cuffee. You need bathing."

After his bath, Edwin put on linen undergarments, a clean checkered pullover cotton shirt, cotton socks, and a wool-cotton jean cloth jacket and trousers. The jacket and trousers were a light warm gray in color. The jacket's cuffs and collar were dark blue kersey wool. Six wood buttons adorned the front. Edwin tied his old brogans while Cuffee hung his old trousers and shirt on the wall with his "blue" jacket.

"The shirt and jacket need cleaning. The pants will have to be thrown away. Until they can be replaced, these will do," explained Polly.

Cuffee helped Edwin stand on the two crutches. Each was a single wooden pole approximately four feet in length. A carved wood cradle was inserted on the top of both poles. Edwin took a few steps. When Polly was satisfied with his ability to walk with the aid of the crutches, she said, "You look nice. I think I will allow you to escort me to church this morning."

"Escort you to church, you say," replied Edwin. "I don't think I can go that distance. Besides, I am not certain I want to go to church." Edwin had not attended a worship service since Ann's death, and the unexpected summons to go to church rekindled his deeply personal battle with God. He could feel the anger growing within and began to wonder if every conversation with Polly was going to end in disaster.

"Don't worry," Polly responded. "Reverend Tichenor is holding chapel down the hall."

"Who is Reverend Tichenor?"

"Isaac Tichenor is pastor of the Baptist Church in Montgomery and chaplain of an Alabama regiment in Mobile. I understand that last month, he delivered a powerful fast day sermon before the Alabama General Assembly."

Not wishing to antagonize Polly any further than he already had, Edwin consented to go with her. Edwin sat quietly and listened to Tichenor. He was a dynamic speaker.

"When shall we have peace?" began Tichenor. "Two weary years of war have wrung this question from the agonized heart of our bleeding country."

Edwin was captivated by the sermon. He listened intently as Tichenor sought to provide an elusive answer.

"The continuance of this war does not depend upon the result of battles, upon the skill of our generals, the valor of our soldiers, the wisdom of our statesmen, the resources of our country, or the mad determination of our foes; but upon the will of our God," continued Tichenor. "He who hath said, 'The wrath of man shall praise him, and the remainder of wrath he will restrain' will give us peace when we are prepared to receive it."

The statement resonated with Edwin and demanded his full consideration. He was not sure what significance it held, but he knew that he must meditate upon it. Edwin tried to remember the Bible reference for "The wrath of man shall praise him, and the remainder of wrath he will restrain." He knew it was a passage out of the Psalms, but he could not remember where in the book it came from. When they returned to his ward, Edwin sat down on the side of his bed and asked Polly to hand him his Bible, which was still in the pocket of his old jacket. She reached inside the jacket and pulled out a small hardback Bible, a tintype of Ann, and the letter she had written Edwin after Ann's death. Edwin's face turned red. He was embarrassed that Polly had discovered his secret preservation of her letter.

Polly sat down on Edwin's bed and said, "I see that I am not the only one clinging to old bad news."

Then she handed Edwin the three items. He hastily inserted Polly's letter into the cover of his Bible, leaving Ann's photograph on top. He looked at Ann's face with desperate desire. Oh how he wanted her back, but she was gone forever. Polly did not press him. The two sat in silence and grieved together.

Finally Edwin said, "Polly, I miss her."

"I know. I miss Richard, too."

Those simple words, "I miss her," opened a flood of emotions Edwin and Polly had been suppressing for so long. For several hours they laughed and cried while recalling memories of their deceased spouses. For the first time, both of them shared their true feelings with someone else. Finally, they described Richard and Ann's deaths to each other. Polly peered intently into Edwin's eyes as he described the panic on the hillside above Rohrbach Bridge. All of her misgivings about Richard's death were erased. He had died just like Ed had written. Listening to him talk was painful but liberating. Tears rolled down Polly's cheeks. Edwin was crying, too. He reached over and put his arm around her. His embrace was comforting, so she snuggled against his shoulder until he finished. Then Polly sat back up so she could look Edwin in the eyes as she talked about Ann and the children.

"Ed, Ann said for me to tell you that God will never forsake you. She said she will see you when you get to heaven. But she said for you not to come too soon. Then she said the strangest thing. I'll never forget her exact words. They were so strange."

Polly paused until she heard Edwin ask, "What did she say, Polly? Tell me, please."

Polly looked at Edwin and continued speaking, "Ed, Ann was talking about you and she said to me, 'Polly, please take care of him. He needs a woman's strong hand.'"

Hearing Ann's admonition encouraged Edwin to disclose his spiritual struggle. Surely Ann knew him too well and foresaw his battle with God even before it erupted. Surprisingly, Polly did not react with horror at his confession. Nor did she shun him as he had expected. In fact, she seemed to become more approachable than ever.

"Ed, I won't go so far as to say God caused Ann's death. But I'm sure He could have kept her from dying. I can't tell you why He didn't. I don't think anyone can do that. But I do know this; Ann is better where she is now than she would be if she were still here."

"I don't understand," said Edwin.

"Well, after Richard was killed, I felt just like you. Then one day I realized how selfish I was being in my thinking."

"What do you mean 'selfish'?" Edwin asked.

"Ed, in our sorrow, we are guided by our pain and only are thinking about how Ann or Richard's death has affected us. But what has it done to them? Yes, their earthly life is over. But I mean what has really happened to them? They're with Jesus. They are so much better off there than here. When I realized what had happened to Richard, that he was finished with this world of pain and suffering and was enjoying the wonderment of heaven, I found peace with myself and with God. I don't mean that it stopped hurting. I suppose I will grieve for him until the day I die and go to be with him. But for now I can cope with my grief."

Although Polly was not on duty, she had spent the entire day in the hospital. Edwin and Polly's conversation had made them oblivious to time. The sun was disappearing over the western horizon. The room was turning dark. One of the convalescing soldiers serving as a nurse came into the room and lit the coal oil lamp. The warm yellow glow softly illuminated the ward. Edwin and Polly remained absorbed in their conversation until the officer of the day interrupted them. He instructed Polly to return to her quarters. She went over to the wall and took Ed's old clothes with her when she left.

Edwin took off his shoes and jacket. He placed the shoes beneath his bunk and spread the jacket across the foot of the bed. He pulled the covers over him and lay there reflecting on the day. He thought about Polly and their discussion. He recalled the sermon. Then it hit him. His mislaid scripture was Psalm 76:10. "Surely the wrath of man shall praise thee: the remainder of wrath shalt thou restrain." He pondered the meaning of these words and their application for his life. Surely the verse taught that even the most rampant evil still was governed by God. In the end, God would override that evil so that humanity would bring praise to Him.

Even Ann's death and the war somehow fit His purposes. Perhaps likewise, the verse indicated that God had allowed Edwin to vent his wrath, but now it was time for him to start praising God. Maybe then God would restrain the wrath that was plaguing him. Although he still did not fully grasp what God was saying, "Father" Edwin Anderson was certain God was trying to tell him something.

CHAPTER TWELVE
"Gangrene"

DURING THE NIGHT, A PATIENT IN THE BUNK ADJACENT to Edwin's bed died. He had been hit in his abdomen with canister and had suffered intensely. Just before dawn, two orderlies removed his body, placed it on a stretcher, and covered it with a blanket. Lifting the stretcher, they carried the corpse out of the ward. A short time later, a convalescent soldier serving as a nurse changed the linens on the bunk. After breakfast, another train stopped in front of the Fletcher House hospital with more wounded from the Chickamauga battlefield. A new patient soon occupied the vacated bed.

Edwin watched as the orderlies situated his new neighbor. He was dressed in a jean cloth uniform typical of the western armies. The new soldier was a mere boy, perhaps sixteen years of age at best. Except for a trace of peach fuzz, his face was adorned with freckles rather than facial hair. His brown eyes were bloodshot, as if he had been crying. Indeed, his expression suggested overwhelming dejection.

"Good morning," Edwin said cheerfully. "Welcome to our humble home."

"Mornin'," replied the recent arrival drily.

"My name is Edwin Anderson, but the boys call me Father."

"Father?" the young boy asked curiously.

"Yes, sir. I reckon I am the oldest soldier in the company, probably in the whole regiment," Edwin answered.

"What's your regiment?" the boy inquired.

"Second Georgia. Who are you with?"

"Forty-third Alabama," boasted the youngster.

"Forty-third Alabama, you say. Y'all part of Bragg's army?" Edwin queried.

"No, sir, Father. I'm part of Gracie's Brigade of Preston's Division. We've been up in east Tennessee until a week or so ago."

"I was up in Virginia myself."

"Virginia?"

"That's right. I'm in the Columbus Guards," Edwin said with pride. "We're part of Benning's Brigade, Hood's Division, Longstreet's Corps, in General Robert E. Lee's Army of Northern Virginia."

Edwin noted with satisfaction that the boy's expression changed from self-pity to admiration when he heard "Robert E. Lee's Army of Northern Virginia." There was silence as the boy soaked in the news of Edwin's unit affiliation. The reputation of Lee's army already had achieved mythical proportions in both North and South. Many in the Army of Tennessee attributed Lee's success to the inferiority of eastern Yankees. But most people spoke of it with reverence. The men of Gracie's Brigade were raw green troops at Chickamauga. On the slopes of Horseshoe Ridge, they had proven to be tough fighters. But their success had not yet had time to completely dispel the venerated image the Army of Northern Virginia still held in the boy's mind.

The boy commented, "Guess you've seen lots of battles."

"Too many," answered Edwin. "Veracruz, Williamsburg, Yorktown, Garnett's Farm, Malvern Hill, Second Manassas, Sharpsburg, Gettysburg, and the one last week. You seen much action?"

"Veracruz?" the boy responded. "I don't think I've heard of that battle."

"Probably not. You likely weren't born when I fought that one. It was in Mexico back in '47 when I fought for the old flag."

"Jumpin' Jehoshaphat! Mexico!" squealed the boy.

"That's right, Mexico. This is my second war," Edwin said with smug composure.

"Last Sunday was my first," the boy said with a grin.

"First war?" teased Edwin.

"My first battle," snapped the boy. Then he whispered, "I guess that makes it my first war, too."

"Where did you get hit?" asked Edwin.

The question obviously struck a nerve. The boy's expression reverted to its previous dejection. He didn't answer Edwin immediately. Finally he said quietly, "Didn't get hit."

"What do you mean you 'didn't get hit'? Why are you here if you are not wounded?" demanded Edwin.

"Dang it!" barked the boy. "I broke my leg."

"Easy, son. What happened?"

"I was on a water detail after the battle. I slip on the crick bank and crack! I break my leg. Fought all afternoon Sunday and didn't get a scratch. Then I fall down and break my leg. Fit my first battle and break my leg. I could have done that on Paw's farm."

"Say you were in the battle Sunday afternoon? I was hit that afternoon. Never have heard what happened. Can you help?" asked Edwin.

"Well, Father, I can tell you about what happened where I was at. But with them deep woods all around us, I guess I missed a lot. We were in reserve most of the day. Orders came down about five o'clock, I guess it was. Anyway, the orders were for us to charge this hill. Someone called it Horseshoe Ridge. Others referred to it as Snodgrass Hill. I'm not sure which is correct. Anyway, we charged up it through this cornfield. Got within about forty yards of the Yankees. They were behind barricades, but we stood there and shot it out with them fo' near on an hour. By that time, we were out of cartridges and pulled back fo' resupply. By then our brigade had driven the Yankees off the hill. You could hear the cheering everywhere. Still sends a chill up my spine when I think of it. Next morning there were nary a Yankee within miles of us, except the dead and wounded ones of course. The rest skedaddled back to Chattanooga."

"'Skedaddled' you say. I knew we would beat 'em. Thanks, son," said Edwin. "You never did tell me your name. Guess maybe I never asked."

"Abner, Private Abner Lanford from Eutaw, Alabama."

"Good to know you, Abner."

"Pleased to know you too, Father."

Both soldiers were drained. Abner had been in a field hospital until the previous day when he was loaded onto the train. He had not slept much in over a week. Edwin was beginning to feel ill. He also started feeling severe pain in his leg.

When Polly came by to check on him that evening, she noticed that Edwin was running a fever. She pulled his blanket back so she could change his bandages. A shocking discovery greeted her when she removed the old dressing on his leg. The tissue around his wound was showing signs of discoloration. The sore also was leaking a foul-smelling discharge. Polly started trembling. She had seen these symptoms before and their appearance did not bode well for Edwin.

The next morning, Polly accompanied Dr. Daniel on his rounds through her ward. The physician did not need to examine Edwin long. Daniel stated flatly, "Miss Brenton, the patient has a scorbutic state that favors foul gangrenous ulcers. His diet has consisted of too much salt pork. The best cure is pharmacological. You must have him eat more vegetables."

The physician's diagnosis stunned Polly. Edwin had scurvy and was developing gangrene. The prognosis for such patients likely was amputation of the infected limb and a strong probability that the injury would be fatal. She already had lost her husband and best friend. In her mind, Edwin was about the only friend she had left. If he died, she surely would be alone in the world. Just the contemplation of his demise left her feeling forlorn and empty. In reality, Polly had forged numerous friendships during her time as a nurse, but Edwin's condition overshadowed them all.

Edwin was moved into a canvas tent set up alongside the Fletcher House. Hospital gangrene was contagious, and infected patients were isolated from the others. Statistics indicated the mortality rate for gangrene patients housed in tents was less than that for patients in buildings, so gangrene wards were set up in tents whenever possible.

Nurses for gangrene patients likewise were restricted. They could not dress the wounds of other patients for fear of spreading the highly contagious infection. After nursing a patient, they rigorously washed their hands with a chlorine solution. Polly immediately volunteered to stay with Edwin. Over the next several days, Edwin's health worsened. He seemed oblivious to Polly's presence. Injections of an antiseptic, oil of terebinth, were given but did not prove effective. Polly tried desperately to improve his health, but she lacked the training and skill he needed. Nursing him totally occupied her thoughts.

As Edwin's condition deteriorated, Polly's gloominess could not be hidden. Dr. Daniel attempted to distract her, to no avail. One morning during his rounds, as Daniel bent over looking at Edwin's infected wound, Polly began weeping uncontrollably. Instinctively, the physician put his arms around the hysterical woman and patted her back.

"Do you think you can save him?" Polly pleaded.

"I have read where Federal surgeons are treating hospital gangrene successfully with savage cautery using pure nitric acid and bromine," said the physician. "Mrs. Brenton, prepare your patient to have etherization, and we will see how effective this new Yankee treatment is."

Edwin was given the general anesthesia, and the new medication was injected into his infected leg. Because syringes were new and lacked a sharp needle, Dr. Daniel had to cut a small incision at the point of injection. After the procedure, Polly dressed the wound with bandages and powdered charcoal.

She continued to follow the doctor's instructions precisely. Polly brought a small glass filled with brandy mixed with tincture of iron. Edwin hesitated to drink it, remembering his embarrassment from his drunkenness before Gettysburg. Nevertheless, Polly's tender persuasion swayed him to accept the glass. Within a few days, he was drinking the medicine willingly. Although the season for fresh vegetables was coming to an end, Polly procured enough through some local farmers she traded with on a regular basis. The price was extortionate but the purchases ensured Edwin ate vegetables at least twice a day. Slowly his wound healed. Both he and Polly were relieved when Dr. Daniel declared amputation would not be necessary.

One afternoon, Polly appeared carrying two crutches. "Okay, lazy, it's time you stopped loafing. Here, let's you and I take a walk. You are going to take your supper at the table today. And there will be no breakfast in bed tomorrow! Now get up."

* * *

Nearly a month later, Edwin was getting around well on his crutches. One Wednesday afternoon, an orderly came through the ward distributing letters. Confederate mail was notoriously inefficient. That some mail had caught up with patients in the hospital was nothing short of a miracle. Edwin was a little surprised when the orderly stopped at his bunk. George Titcomb occupied the middle tier above Edwin. He was from Kentucky. Union control of that state severed all mail connections to the Confederacy, so George had not heard from his family in over a year. The top tier was occupied by a cavalryman named Proctor. He was in bad shape, and Edwin knew nothing about him. Edwin and George watched the orderly place a letter on Proctor's bed. However, Edwin was dumbfounded when the orderly stooped down and said, "Corporal Anderson, I have two letters for you today."

One was crumpled and tinted with dust. It was addressed to him at the hospital. It obviously came from someone in the army. The return address revealed it was from John Lindsay. The other was a slightly smaller white envelope. Two blue stamps bearing the image of Jefferson Davis were affixed to one corner. They were canceled in Columbia, South Carolina. The letter was addressed to *Father Ed Anderson*. Beneath the name, the address was crossed out. The crossing mark was in pencil, but the address was in ink, leaving it very legible. *Father Ed Anderson, Co. G, 2nd Geo Inf., Benings Bgd, Hoods Div, Longstreet Core, ANV*. Beneath the crossed out address, "*Forward to Daniel Hospital, Marietta, Georgia*" was written with the same pencil used to cross out the original address. The envelope did not have a return address, but it did secrete a hint of perfume. Edwin started to open it but restrained himself, deciding to save it for later.

Edwin opened Lindsay's letter. He pulled out a single sheet of paper and chuckled. One side of the page was decorated with a red and blue zouave holding a United States flag in one hand and a rifle in the other. He was reading a sign that said, "on to Richmond."

Outside Chattanooga, Tenn.

Oct. 10, 1863

Dear Father,

We just learned that you are still alive. Thought I would let you know that the company is doing well. Bob Enderman and Lt. Patterson were killed at Chickamauga. The rest of the men are doing fine. However they could use a Baptist preacher. Some of them are using profanity. So you best recover and get back here soon. Otherwise the language in the Columbus Guards might make it impossible for us to return home.

How do you like this paper? I requisitioned it out of a Federal haversack. Its owner won't be needing it any longer. I don't think he is going to make it to Richmond.

Your obedient servant,
John Lindsay

Edwin accepted the deaths of his two comrades with little emotion. Three years of carnage had hardened him to dead soldiers. It was just the natural order of things. Soldiers got killed. One became stoic about their deaths. Only truly close comrades cracked that emotional armor. Edwin also recognized Lindsay's morbid sense of humor. His friend obviously had taken the stationery from a dead Union soldier on the battlefield at Chickamauga. Edwin folded the letter back up, put it in its envelope, and laid it on the bed beside him.

Then Edwin held the other letter under his nostrils and breathed in its sweet scent. Very deliberately, he placed one corner of the envelope between his teeth and peeled one end of the envelope off slowly. Reaching inside, he pulled out two pale blue sheets of lined paper and began to read. The handwriting was bold and legible, but the spelling and grammar were abysmal. It was difficult reading, but as he deciphered its contents, Edwin's interest grew. The message was both shocking and stimulating.

Septemer 10
Dearest soon to bee lover,

I did not fergit yo address. so i tok pen in hand to rite u. i kin stil taste yo lips. U said yo intenjuns wer not honorable. i has ben thinkin bout that and i wont u to know i thin i kinda like that. if u kin get a furlow & come to cee me i kin tak kare of u. u mite lik it enuff to stay & git hitched. i so did lik <u>Kissin</u> u. i hope we kin <u>kiss</u> lots mor soon. i is certin u will like tuchin me. i am so lonelee i mite lets u tuch mi busom. i allways wil rememba that day at the stayshun. U ar the best lookin man i hav seen in a long time. I so wood lik too hold u agin. Kiss U too.

Take good kare of yosef. Don't git shot and killed lik mr. mcdonald did. u wont bee able to kiss me if u do. rite me soon and let me know how u r doin. Let me know when u r comin bac too Chester. i will rite u agin when I Can.

Yo lover always,
Adeline Knight

Adeline's prose might have been difficult to untangle, but she made her point well. Edwin put the letter back into its envelope. He sniffed it one more time and put it under his pillow. He lay in his bunk and thought about that day in Chester, South Carolina. He did enjoy kissing Adeline, and he wondered what might have happened if he had not gotten back on the train. Then he began to contemplate going to see her before he returned to his company. He was sure that he would get a furlough prior to going back to the army. He could go then. His mind was going in a direction that he had previously believed to be immoral, but he could not help himself. He was a man, and something about Adeline Knight really attracted him. And she clearly entertained similar aspirations. He would enjoy sensuous dreams tonight.

The following Sunday morning, Polly made arrangements for an ambulance to transport a few of her patients to Marietta Baptist Church for the morning worship service. The red brick building on Kennesaw Avenue was too far away for them to walk there. She and Edwin sat together on the ride and in the church service. The trip was Edwin's first time outside the hospital since his arrival. The service did not make a big impression on him. He could not recall afterwards who had preached or what had been said. His attitude towards God had improved tremendously as a result of his talks with Polly. Reverend Tichenor's sermon had been a turning point. Since then, Edwin frequently meditated upon Psalm 76:10. "Surely the wrath of man shall praise thee: the remainder of wrath shalt thou restrain." He had not forgotten his commitment to praise God rather than battle Him, but today he was focused more on Polly than on church. No longer having any reason to restrain his attraction for Polly, Edwin had begun to think about the possibility of matrimony. So far, their relationship had remained purely one of friendship. Nevertheless, spending time together was bringing them closer to each other.

Their conversations had become incredibly personal and extraordinarily open. Polly had even told Edwin about Jacob Prescott's beating and her subsequent miscarriage. They had exposed their innermost secrets to each other. Well, most of their secrets. Edwin had not told Polly about Adeline Knight, and she had not told him about Ben Larimer. Edwin had compartmentalized the two women. One offered physical gratification; the other long-term companionship. Edwin was unwilling to admit he might be forced to choose between the two. Polly, however, was so absorbed in her work that romance failed to take permanent root in her life. For the present, Edwin was near. She spent extended periods of time with him and was aware that they were paying attention to each other, but she attributed that to their past friendship. Polly had not considered that subconsciously, something else might be occurring. She had yet to give serious thought to a romantic relationship with Edwin.

The hospital had started receiving wounded from Bragg's siege of Chattanooga. Polly and Julia Bilbry were standing outside the hospital as new patients were being unloaded from the train. Polly caught a glimpse of a one-armed figure getting off the last car. His uniform no longer was quite as dandy, but he moved with the same swagger. She knew immediately that he was Major Benjamin Larimer! Polly's heart raced. A hundred questions flashed through her mind. *Will he remember me? Or was Chattanooga one of them wartime flirtations? Will he notice me? What will I say to him?*

Polly's musing was interrupted by Julia's voice, "Miss Brenton! Miss Brenton, are you listening to me? Where is yo' mind?"

"Sorry," replied Polly. "I was distracted by…" She didn't finish her sentence because she realized Benjamin had seen her and was coming toward them. She could feel the pounding of her heart. The closer he came, the faster it beat.

"By what?" a puzzled Julia asked. She had never seen Polly so oblivious to her duties as a hospital matron.

Benjamin clicked his heels, and Julia was suddenly aware of his presence. She turned to examine the man who has caused such uncharacteristic disruption in her supervisor. His once immaculate gray uniform was soiled with perspiration and dirt. Its once glistening braiding had acquired a patina. His black hair was greasy and matted. And he needed a shave, but he was handsome. Julia thought a woman could drown in his dark brown eyes. He lifted his kepi with his right hand and said, "Polly." Then he turned to Julia and said, "Ma'am." Having completed the formalities, he grabbed Polly by the waist and pulled her against him. Even though he had only one arm, his grip on her was firm. She felt safe and secure there.

"I-ah see yo' not go-wine to have mo' ti-ahm fo' me. I-ah can see the nex' po' man, and you can fin' ti-ahm to he'p the colonel."

Julia's reference to Larimer's rank took Polly by surprise. She was so enthralled by Benjamin that she had not noticed the second star on his collar.

"Ben, you have been promoted!" Polly exclaimed.

"Yes, it goes with field command. I'm currently executive officer for one of our Mississippi brigades. It's a temporary assignment, but until its real executive officer returns to duty, I'm going to be there."

"Why are you in Marietta then?" Polly inquired.

"To see you, my dearest."

"Really?"

"Yes, really. Dr. Saunders wrote and told me that you were here. I need a new mount. Mine was shot at Chickamauga. So I was able to get leave in order to purchase a horse. And what better place to buy an animal than the city where you are? So here I am."

"Chickamauga? I thought you were in Mississippi," Polly said.

"I was. But I escorted Walker's Brigade from Mississippi to join the Army of Tennessee. The reason I was in Chattanooga was to coordinate the transfer. Best assignment I ever had. Without it I never would have met you."

Then squeezing her tightly, Benjamin kissed Polly passionately on her lips. This was the second time they had carried out such a public display of affection, but Polly was too enthralled with Benjamin's caress to care what anyone thought. She didn't even notice the cheers from the less seriously wounded on the platform.

Over the next few weeks, Polly was in the hospital less than usual. She performed her duties adequately but did not stay in the ward during her off-duty time as had been her custom. In the past, her patients' total well-being dominated her existence, but now she seemed only concerned with their physical health. She spent all of her free time with Benjamin Larimer.

Edwin noticed Polly's inattention more than anyone. Her visits to his bedside had decreased noticeably. When she did come by, she concentrated solely on his leg and head wounds. If he attempted to initiate any type of personal conversation, she made some excuse and went somewhere else. Obviously she was shunning him for some reason, but Edwin had no idea why. He racked his brain for some offensive word he had spoken or gesture he had made but came up blank. Her behavior hurt him deeply. His fantasy about marriage vanished, but his yearning for female companionship did not.

Edwin received another letter from Adeline Knight. Its content was similar to the previous one. Between his improved health and Polly's estrangement, he thought of Adeline more often. He wrote her back, and they began mutual correspondence. Although prospective physical intimacy dominated their letters, they began expanding to other topics as well. Edwin learned Adeline had acquired her excellent penmanship by filling out inventory sheets in her uncle's dry goods store. However, copying labels and order forms did not compensate for her lack of education. Nevertheless, Edwin was beginning to grasp her perplexing writing style. He also began to plan a visit to Chester, South Carolina, for Christmas. Adeline lived alone in a small house outside of town. Edwin needed little imagination to envisage what might happen when he got to her home.

* * *

By Thursday, November 26, 1863, panic was everywhere. Word had spread quickly about the Confederate defeat at Chattanooga. On Tuesday, the Yankees had attacked and captured Lookout Mountain. The next day, they attacked and captured Missionary Ridge. The Confederates' retreat from Missionary Ridge turned into a rout. The battered Army of Tennessee fell back all the way to Dalton, Georgia.

Rumors already were circulating that Stout had ordered the hospitals in Marietta to be evacuated. The staff in the hospitals of the Army of Tennessee had learned it was expedient to prepare rather than ignore the rumors, so in anticipation of a possible move, Polly started organizing the staff and packing some of the ward's extra supplies. As she and Julia Bilbry inventoried the items, Dr. Daniel came through the ward.

"Mrs. Brenton, what are you doing?" he asked.

"I'm just making sure we are prepared to move if it becomes necessary."

"I don't think that is likely. Dr. Stout has ordered the hospitals in Dalton and Rome to relocate. But he doubts we will be required to move before spring at the earliest. Winter weather will be setting in soon. Therefore, I doubt we will see much activity before March or April. Then the spring rains will make movement in this Georgia red clay impossible. So unless you hear otherwise from me, carry on as usual."

"Yes, sir."

Daniel made his rounds and left the ward. "I-ah guess we was a-out of ty-une," remarked Julia as Daniel walked away.

"I guess we were," laughed Polly. "Always best to check with the choir director before you sing the tune."

Five minutes after Dr. Daniel left, Lieutenant Colonel Benjamin Larimer entered the ward. He was dressed in a new uniform. The tailored frock coat was cadet gray with two rows of seven brass buttons in each. Its only decorations were the customary sleeve braid and two six-pointed stars on each collar. Around his waist, he wore a crimson officer's sash and a black leather belt. A pistol holster and his foot officer's sword were suspended from the belt. A pair of dark blue trousers completed his ensemble. His appearance was the epitome of what a Confederate officer should look like.

Polly was dressing a patient's wound when he came in, so Larimer waited by the door. As soon as she finished bandaging the patient, she went to him and said softly, "My dear Colonel, may I be of service?"

"Polly darling, can we step outside for a moment?" he replied timidly. "I have orders to be on the afternoon train to Atlanta, and I have something I must ask you before I leave."

They stepped outside just as a northbound freight rumbled by. Its rhythmic *choo, choo, choo* combined with the recurring *click, click* of its wheels across rail joints drowned out any conversation, so Polly and Benjamin stood there holding hands until it passed. Then Larimer turned to face her. For a brief moment they simply looked at each other. Then he spoke. "My darling Polly, I realize that we have had very little time to get to know each other as we would like. But these are extraordinary times, and we must act in accordance with the present situation."

Polly listened and thought to herself, *He sounds like he is giving an army report.*

"I have grown very fond of you since we met," continued Larimer. "Fond? Pardon me but I am right nervous. You are making me behave like a school boy. Polly Brenton, truth is, I love you and want to spend the rest of my life caring for you. Would you consent to becoming my wife?"

"Ben, this is so sudden…and unexpected," Polly responded, pausing between each word so that she would choose just the right one to say next. "I am deeply honored," she continued, "but I am not sure I am ready to…"

Benjamin interrupted her and said, "Polly, I know this is sudden. You do not have to give me an answer today. Darling, I will be back here in a week to ten days. You can answer me then. I love you, and I think that you love me. I know we will be happy together."

Once again Larimer kissed Polly in public. However on this occasion, the kiss lacked some of the previous passion. Instead, Benjamin's lips were stiff and uncertain. His behavior was like a nervous adolescent who had worked himself up to ask a girl to a dance and having asked, needed to escape because he did not know what to do next. Polly had never seen the confident soldier behave so awkwardly.

Benjamin's proposal had caught Polly by surprise. Although they had spent virtually every free second together, she had been too enamored with the moments to consider the future. Her first reaction was to say "Yes," but there were many things to think through. She really enjoyed being with Benjamin, but did she enjoy their togetherness enough to spend the rest of her life with him? Did she truly love him? Then there was the matter of Jacob Prescott. Ben knew about Richard, but she had not mentioned her first husband. How would he respond to her divorce? Would he want to become her third husband? And what was Edwin's role in her life? For the first time in weeks, she thought about Edwin Anderson. Was it possible that she actually loved *him*? Polly Brenton recognized her life had reached a crossroads. Her answer to Benjamin's question would determine his future, her future, and perhaps even Edwin's. As she headed back inside, she thought, *I'm going to spend lots of time on my knees praying. God, you ARE going to have to help me with this one.*

CHAPTER THIRTEEN
"And, lo, I am with you alway"

BENJAMIN LARIMER PROMISED POLLY THAT HE WOULD return for her answer in a week to ten days. It actually was three weeks later. During those three weeks, Polly struggled with her decision. She desperately wanted to talk with someone about her choices, but she didn't know whom to turn to. Certainly she could not discuss Benjamin with Edwin. And she questioned the propriety of talking with her superior, Dr. Daniel, or her subordinate, Julia Bilbry. So Polly remained silent. For two weeks, she unsuccessfully attempted to sort out the confusion churning within her.

Then, in search of sweet milk for the hospital, Polly and Julia drove a buckboard out to rural Cobb County. The trip exposed how the war had transformed societal ideals of women. Before Fort Sumter, southern society had viewed women as needing male protection. Two women traveling alone in a strange community would have been inconceivable. They would have been accompanied by a man. He may have been a slave at the reins driving, but he was a man. Now the vacuum created by so many men going away to war compelled women to do jobs customarily perceived to be a man's domain. Women plowing fields had become a common sight throughout the South.

The two women huddled in their coats as they rode along the dusty red clay roads. At first they chatted about various situations at the hospital. This discussion came to an abrupt end when they approached the first farm. A split-rail fence protected the dead stalks of the previous season's corn crop. Two cows grazed in an unfenced field across the road. An old log cabin served as the residence. Numerous outbuildings surrounded it. Polly was only able to acquire two gallons of fresh milk, but the farmer promised to sell her some turnips if she would come back in a few weeks. Between farms, Polly and Julia continued talking about the hospital. Finally, Julia broached the subject of Polly's quandary. "What's going on between you and that handsome colonel?" she asked innocently.

"Why what do you mean, Julia?" replied Polly.

"I-ah mean that when a certain Colonel Larimer is around, you spend all of yo' ti-ahm with hem. I-ah reckon you are right fond of hem."

"Why yes, I am. He is a wonderful soldier," stated Polly.

"That's not what I-ah mean and you know it," Julia retorted. "When are y'all go-wine to get engaged. I-ah seen y'all kissing, you know."

"Well, since you brought it up, he has already asked me."

"So what did you say? You accepted didn't you?"

"No, but I didn't say 'no' either."

"You didn't say 'yea-is,' but you didn't say 'no.' Miss Brenton, those are yo' only two choices."

"Well, not exactly. He is coming back here in the next few days, and I am to give an answer then."

"What are you go-wine to tell him?"

"I'm not sure."

"Not sure! Polly Brenton, if a rich, handsome colonel asked me to marry hem, well honey child, I-ah reckon I-ah am right sure I-ah would say yea-is. Now I-ah can't make yo' decision fo' you, but if I-ah was you, I-ah would become Misses Polly Larimer in a heartbeat. You don't get these opportunities right often."

"Mrs. Polly Larimer. Sounds good, doesn't it?" Polly said. The words were as much to herself as to Julia.

Julia continued pressing for the marriage and was so skilled at doing so that by the time they had returned to the hospital, she had persuaded Polly to accept Benjamin Larimer's proposal.

Edwin's health continued to improve. Although still on crutches, he was no longer confined to the ward. He enjoyed the privilege of coming and going without supervision. Frequently in the afternoon, he signed out and hobbled the half block into town, but the day after Polly and Julia had traveled to rural Cobb County, the weather turned cold and wet. Since he was unable to leave the building, he rambled through the various wards and rooms. He encountered Julia Bilbry in the dining hall drinking coffee. She invited Edwin to have a cup with her. As usual, the coffee was not the real beverage. The Union blockade had effectively terminated the importation of coffee beans. The common substitute was made from peanuts and chicory. Julia and Edwin passed the time by sharing the latest gossip and rumors. As they were sitting there, Polly walked by the door.

"Did y'all know she is betrothed?" asked Julia.

"Who?" a bewildered Edwin asked.

"Misses Brenton," Julia answered.

Edwin's daydream of marrying Polly had faded, but the news that she was engaged hit him like a cannonball. Though Edwin had inferred that she would not be his wife, he had never thought about her becoming someone else's. He felt sick and was unable to respond.

"Well actually, she is not officially engaged," Julia proceeded to say. "Colonel Larimer has proposed, but he went to Atlanta or somewhere before she could accept. When he gets back, she is gowine to say 'yea-is.'"

The news that Polly had not actually accepted Larimer's proposition suddenly reversed Edwin's gloom. Later that evening he confronted her. "Polly, what is this I hear that you are engaged to be married?"

Edwin's question unexpectedly raised doubts in Polly's mind again about marrying Benjamin. It also rekindled the connection with Edwin. Their talk was like their conversations during the first weeks after Edwin had been admitted to the hospital. Polly didn't share any hint that Edwin might be a factor in her uncertainty, but she confessed her doubts regarding marriage to Benjamin. Edwin seized her opening to debate strongly against the marriage.

"Polly, did you have any doubts before accepting Richard's hand in marriage?"

"Some, I suppose. I had just run away from an evil man, and I wanted nothing to do with marriage," answered Polly.

"But that concerned your circumstances, not Richard," replied Edwin. "How did you feel about Richard?"

"I knew I was in love with him."

"Did you have any doubts about your sentiments for Richard?" Edwin prodded as if he had not heard Polly's answer.

"No, I loved him so much. I couldn't imagine him not being part of my life."

"Well, I'm sure the day will come when you may feel the same way about another man, but if you are having any doubts about marrying this man Larimer, then say, 'No' to his proposal. I'm not saying this because Richard was my friend. I'm saying this because I want you to be happy, Polly. How do you really feel about Colonel Larimer?"

Edwin and Julia became two strong-willed protagonists in Polly's mind as she waited for Benjamin's return. Julia continued to encourage her to marry him. Edwin argued against it. Neither line of reasoning was totally satisfactory in swaying her. However, the hours she spent with Edwin made it impossible for Polly to deny that her feelings for him were not strictly platonic. She did not know what might happen between her and Edwin, but she realized her feelings toward Edwin Anderson made marriage to Benjamin Larimer foolish.

Polly didn't want to break off her relationship with Benjamin completely. However, she realized that if she did not accept his marriage proposal, he might no longer wish to pursue her. Continuation of their courtship would then be Benjamin's decision, not hers.

The last of the patients had just finished lunch when Benjamin strode into the hospital. He and Polly sat in one corner of the hospital dining room to talk privately. Ben wanted to immediately ask Polly for her answer to his matrimonial proposal, but he decided it best to work up to the question. "My darling, I'm sorry I was gone longer than I thought I'd be. Last summer, General Johnston sent me to assist General Wright, commander of the Atlanta district. Colonel Lemuel Grant, the chief engineer for the Department of Georgia, was constructing Atlanta's fortifications. They had requisitioned every available slave in and around the city of Atlanta, but they did not have sufficient darkies to do the work. So they sent me into south Georgia to impress more slaves. We threatened a few plantation owners, you know, saying we would eliminate all exemptions and take every darkie they own. In no time, thousands of darkies were digging furiously and singing away as they worked. They were as happy as a lark."

Polly knew that the slaves were not happy, but many white Southerners, especially some who owned large numbers of slaves, labored under the delusion that the black population was content.

"Grant finished the works around Atlanta on December first," continued Larimer. "That's why I was summoned to Atlanta. I had to return the darkies to their owners. It took longer than I anticipated, but I got every Sambo back to where he belongs."

Polly was puzzled. After a brief moment of uncomfortable silence, she said, "But you told me that you were on leave in Marietta to buy a horse."

"I was. My orders included a leave for that before I reported to Colonel Grant. He didn't know exactly when he would finish, so my leave put me where I would be available whenever he was ready. It also gave time for me to find a horse…and I hope a wife."

Larimer's use of the disparaging terms 'darkie' and 'Sambo' disturbed Polly. They were not uncommon in the deep South, but she never had heard Ben use them. She wondered if Obadiah had been among the slaves Larimer had requisitioned. The image of Obadiah in a column of slaves walking out to dig trenches, with Larimer supervising, may have been emblematic, but it dismissed any lingering doubt about her final decision to decline Larimer's matrimonial proposal. Their world views were too dissimilar.

Even more troubling was Larimer's less than candid attitude about his leave. Polly understood the need for military secrecy. However, returning slaves was hardly a clandestine operation. Besides, he could have stated he was on an assignment without revealing the nature of the task. His demeanor may only have been inadvertent, but Polly felt deceived. She knew that trust was vital for a healthy marriage. She now was certain that she was making the right decision. Too many disparities existed for her and Ben to have a fulfilling relationship.

"Ben, you are a special man, but at the present, I find I cannot consent to become your wife. There are things about me that you do not know and I cannot address currently. I care too much about you to hurt you," said Polly.

"If you don't wish to hurt me, why are you rejecting me?" Larimer responded.

"Ben, don't make this harder than it is."

"Darling, I love you and want to spend the rest of my life with you."

"Perhaps in time that might be possible, but not now."

Hoping to coerce Polly into consenting, Benjamin decided to pursue a now-or-never tactic. "Polly, are you sure about this? I must have your final answer now. I cannot put my life on hold indefinitely. I want to have a family. I want you to be the beginning of that family. But time is of great consequence. There is no end in sight to this war. It is likely to continue another five years or longer. I likely will not survive it if it does, so I must start my family soon. If you are not willing to become engaged now, I must look for someone else."

He wants to breed me the same way he breeds cattle on his plantation. This is not love, Polly thought.

Benjamin regretted his words even before he was finished. He could see in Polly's eyes that their effect was the reverse of what he had solicited. They only succeeded in driving a wedge between Polly and him.

"Ben, I cannot marry you now," Polly answered. Then she added, "Or ever." Suddenly, Polly felt the lifting of a great weight. Having declared aloud that she would not ever marry Benjamin Larimer, she was completely at ease with her decision. She did not know what was in her future, but he was not going to be part of it.

Larimer stood to leave. He looked down into Polly's green eyes and said, "Polly, I will be in Marietta until eight o'clock this evening. If you change your mind, you can find me at the railroad depot."

"Ben," Polly said, "I will always cherish my memories of you and of your proposal. But they must remain memories. It is best we both move on from here."

Larimer yearned to grab and kiss Polly on her moist lips, but he knew he must not. Instead, he bowed and kissed the top of her hand, placed his kepi on his head, and turned to leave. After he vanished through the door, Julia slipped into the dining room. Before she could inquire, Polly spoke.

"It's over, Julia. I am not going to marry Colonel Larimer."

Julia was caught off guard by the abruptness of Polly's announcement. It seemed too final. Before Julia could pursue Polly's reasons, Polly quickly rose and returned to her duties in the hospital. She would erase Ben's attraction by devoting her life afresh to the service of her nation's wounded heroes.

After learning of Polly's potential marriage, Edwin had applied for a Christmas furlough. His health was improving daily, and he believed a trip to Chester, South Carolina, was feasible. His correspondence with Adeline Knight had moved beyond suggestive hints. On occasion, their letters were explicit. Both shared their craving for physical intimacy, and each expressed their willingness to accommodate the other's sexual appetite. Edwin had fantasized about spending the holidays with Adeline even before learning of Larimer's proposal to Polly. Each morning, his excitement grew exponentially. Running parallel with his sensual excitement was a spiritual sense of guilt. Everything he had believed all of his life had taught him that his designs were sinful. Although he couldn't quite shake these troubling thoughts, the more he concentrated on Adeline, the easier it became to cope with them.

While Polly and Larimer were talking in the dining room, Edwin lay in his bed daydreaming about Adeline. His imaginings were interrupted by Dr. Daniel. The surgeon pulled up a chair beside Edwin's bed and sat down. "Corporal Anderson."

"Sir," Edwin said as he sat up.

"You requested a furlough for Christmas. What were you planning to do?"

"Sir, I have a girl I want to visit."

"A girl? If she is your wife, why not have her come visit you?"

"No sir, she's not my wife. I'm a widower."

"Oh, then what is her relationship?" inquired the doctor.

Dr. Daniel's question stupefied Edwin. He didn't know how to answer it. He couldn't divulge his true intentions toward Adeline. After what seemed an eternity of awkward silence he blurted out, "Fiancée." Edwin paused briefly recalling the ribbing he had received from John Lindsay that day in Chester. "Sir, she's my fiancée," he said calmly.

"I see," Daniel said.

Sensing that the doctor knew he was not being entirely truthful, Edwin looked down and spotted a nail in the wooden floor. He concentrated his focus on that nail so as not to look Dr. Daniel in the eye.

"You planning to get married while you're on leave?" asked the doctor.

"No, sir."

"Good. I'm sorry, but I must deny your application."

"But sir, I haven't had furlough since I joined up in 1861, and I've been through the mill since then. I need a furlough. I'm almost ready to take a French leave."

"Now let's show some horse sense. If you take off without leave, the provost is going to catch up with you and you will be in a real fix. Let's not get in a huff. I am denying you leave because you have not recovered sufficiently to travel. That fiancée of yours will need a live groom when the time comes."

"Yes, sir," Edwin said sourly.

Deep inside, Edwin was relieved that his furlough had been denied. Despite his prior excitement over the prospect of seeing Adeline, he had always been troubled by the morality of the intended visit. Adeline had made no secret that she intended to sleep with him. She frequently referenced Dr. Harmon Knox Root's *The Lover's Marriage Lighthouse*. He wondered how such an obscure work came into her sphere of influence since, judging from her letters, Adeline's skills in reading and writing seemed limited. He was not familiar with the 1858 book, but according to Adeline's letters, Root advocated sex before marriage so that a woman might better choose a compatible partner. Edwin was too entrenched in his biblical roots to agree. The former pastor still labeled premarital sex as fornication, and fornication was a sin. Nevertheless, Edwin's infatuation with Adeline Knight had combined with his male sex drive to temporarily muzzle the minister's sense of right and wrong. If not for Dr. Daniel turning down his request for furlough, he would be in Chester, South Carolina, fornicating with Miss Adeline Knight come Christmas. Instead, Edwin spent Christmas with Polly Brenton. Ironically, Polly's red hair reminded him of Adeline.

Edwin's emotions stole some of his Christmas joy. He could not deny his disappointment over not getting a furlough. The memory of Adeline's kiss generated an internal rage over being blocked from uninhibited time with her. Then just as his temper was on the verge of unleashing some hysterical frenzy, his conscience repressed his sensual frustration with pragmatic rationale. Edwin realized that he really did not know much about Adeline, except for her libertine ideas. He reasoned that he surely would have had greater regret if he had gotten his furlough. Probability suggested he might contract some incurable venereal disease from such a promiscuous woman. The state of medical treatment for these ailments remained primitive. The classic pun, "a night with Venus, a lifetime with Mercury," foretold an infected victim's destiny poetically and accurately; mercury was the standard treatment for sexual ailments. Or what if Adeline had gotten pregnant?

As this logic gained ascendency over his thinking, Edwin's attention turned back to Polly. For a brief time he reveled in her presence, but the fact that Polly had even considered marrying someone else created within Edwin an impression that she was unavailable to him. Eventually, Edwin's illusion that Polly was inaccessible brought back dreams of Adeline, and the vicious cycle repeated itself. So rather than celebrating Christ's birth, "Father" Edwin Anderson fought a pointless battle over an episode that had never happened, a battle that was really between good and evil. The winner of this contest still seemed uncertain. Edwin remained unable to negotiate a truce to his war with God. God seemed set on bringing him to unconditional surrender. But Edwin's carnal desire for Adeline was not yet ready to yield.

Edwin's health improved dramatically. In early January, Dr. Daniel elevated him to convalescent status and assigned him to duties. Some days, he and Polly worked directly together. On other days he didn't even see her. Rarely did they have an opportunity to talk. Consequently, he thought more and more about Adeline Knight, or at least about the romanticized image of her that he had formed from his memory of that day in Chester and from the letters she had written to him.

Edwin had not received a letter from Adeline since November. Aware of the Confederate mail's shortcomings, he did not give it much thought. When a letter finally arrived in the middle of February of the new year, he was elated. Hurriedly he opened it and began to read. Adeline's salutation telegraphed the letter did not bring welcome news. There was no "Dearest soon to bee lover" or other provocative greeting.

> *Januwary 11*
> *Dear Father,*
>
> *I am sorry u did not git to come to cee me at Christmas. so i tok pen in hand to rite u and tell u what happen. i war certin i wood bee lonesum cause u war not here. Dr Root sez a woman should tri free luv to bee shur a man is rite fer her befour they is married. U said yo intenjuns wer not honorable. i hoped a few nights with me mite change ur mind & we'uns wood git hitched. Well Elijah Imboden came hom to Chester during Christmas. He ask me fer sum horezontal refreshmint for his Christmas present. Since u war not here I sez to hem that he mite as well go 1st and we'uns could try. We waz a purfect match. So we are gettin hitched next time he is home. If he gits kilt, I will rite u and if u steel is free u kin cum cee me. I will all ways remember ur kiss.*
>
> *With luv,*
> *the future Adeline ~~Knight~~ Imboden*

The letter both hurt and amused Edwin. Adeline had rejected him in favor of some local bumpkin but entertained the notion that if her chosen suitor died, Edwin could audition to become her next husband. Looking up from Adeline's letter, Edwin saw Dr. Daniel approaching.

"Another letter from your fiancée, Anderson?"

"Well, not exactly," Edwin answered.

"Not exactly?" inquired Dr. Daniel.

Edwin knew he no longer could hide the truth, so he confessed to the surgeon the true nature of his relationship with Adeline. Then he explained the contents of the letter.

"Sounds to me like I did you a favor by denying your Christmas furlough," said Daniel.

"Yes sir, I guess you did," acknowledged Edwin. "Say Doc, have you ever heard of this Dr. Harmon Knox Root?"

"Root? What would you know about Root?" asked Dr. Daniel.

"Not much, Doc. Adeline read his book…*Lover's Lighthouse*, no, *Lover's Marriage Lighthouse*, I believe was its name. So do you know anything about him?"

"Yes, he's a Yankee doctor. His *Medical Lighthouse* essays are quite popular in some northern circles. He espouses an odd combination of Bible verses and medical science."

"*Medical Lighthouse*? Adeline called it *Marriage Lighthouse*."

"*Marriage Lighthouse* is one book from his *Medical Lighthouse* series. In it he advocates some radical ideas concerning men and women," answered Daniel.

"Is he one of those free-love Yankees?"

"Well, I'm not sure I would classify him in the same category as Fanny Wright, but he does hold some unorthodox views about marriage."

"Who's Fanny Wright?" asked Edwin.

"She's been dead for over a decade, but she was a radical abolitionist and the leading voice advocating free love."

"A woman?"

"Yes, she gave lots of lectures up North, published some books, and generally agitated respectable people. Why she even promoted miscegenation."

"Miscegenation?"

"Sexual relations between people of different races." The doctor continued, "You were a Southern Baptist preacher before the war, right?"

"Yes, sir."

"I don't reckon then that you and Dr. Root would agree about what the Bible says."

"Doc, I don't agree with a lot of Southern Baptist preachers."

Daniel chuckled and said, "Never knew many preachers to agree with everything another preacher said."

Edwin smiled and continued, "Yes, but sometimes I think we might do a better job of 'rightly dividing the word of truth.' Remember how before the war, preachers said Genesis 9:25 declared that slaves were cursed descendants of Ham? Well Doc, it doesn't say that. The verse clearly indicates Noah was angry about his son Ham's behavior, but I'm pretty sure the verse concerns the ancient Canaanites more than it does our slaves. The passage likely is a prophecy about the Israelite conquest of Canaan."

"Anderson, I'm not a theologian. I will stick to medicine and leave the meaning of Bible verses to you ministers."

"Well, I will acknowledge the corn. I don't always get it right. Sometimes my exegesis of scripture leaves a lot to be desired. I didn't go to college. I'm a self-educated man. But I have learned some Greek and Hebrew. I also have studied the history of ancient and modern times. The folks in the Bible were real people living in a real world. Their words made sense to them. I figure the more I know about what they meant to them, the better I will know what they mean for us. Don't you agree Doc?"

"That makes sense," Daniel said.

"It not only makes sense, sir, it is essential for humanity that we get it right. Suppose those preachers spouting off about the Negroes being cursed, just suppose they stuck to preaching God's truth instead of using Bible verses as proof to justify society's whims? If they had done so, we may have been able to avoid what has happened over the last three years. But they didn't. And so instead of rightly dividing the word of truth, we used it to strengthen our human opinions. Instead of finding out what God actually is saying to us, we pronounce His words mean whatever fits our point of view."

Unexpectedly, Edwin realized he was condemning himself. For too long, he had not genuinely sought guidance from scripture. He had readily seen the Bible's misuse by others, but he had failed to see how his prejudicial inferences colored his own conclusions.

"Corporal Anderson, you have a point there. Perhaps we can discuss this at a later time. I need to make a report for Dr. Stout now," said Daniel.

"Yes, sir."

Daniel turned and headed for his office. Edwin went over to his haversack, which hung from a peg on the wall. Reaching inside, he pulled out a small, brown hardback New Testament. He took a pair of reading glasses from the pocket inside his jacket. While holding the New Testament in his left hand, he set the spectacles on the bridge of his nose with his right. His thumb rested on the front cover of the Bible. Relaxing his hand, the book opened automatically to its endpapers. Inside the front cover in an elegant penmanship was an ink inscription:

PRESENTED TO PVT. EDWIN ANDERSON AFTER THE BATTLE OF FREDERICKSBURG BY THE SUNDAY-SCHOOL AND PUBLICATION BOARD OF THE GENERAL ASSOC. OF THE BAPTIST CHURCHES IN VIRGINIA.

Edwin paused momentarily to recall the white-haired minister and two female companions who had given him the New Testament the previous winter. One, an elderly lady in a black dress, Edwin presumed was the minister's wife. The other, a much younger woman, apparently was a member of his congregation. With the forefinger of his right hand, Edwin flipped the page to the flyleaf and read:

"THE NEW TESTAMENT OF OUR LORD AND SAVIOUR JESUS CHRIST, TRANSLATED OUT OF THE ORIGINAL GREEK; AND WITH THE FORMER TRANSLATIONS DILIGENTLY COMPARED AND REVISED. AUGUST:

CONFEDERATE STATES BIBLE SOCIETY, INSTITUTED IN THE YEAR 1862. PRINTED BY WOOD, HANLETTER RICE & CO. ATLANTA, GA. 1862."

Uncertain as to where he should start reading, Edwin meditated upon what he had said to Dr. Daniel: *Instead of finding out what God actually is saying to us, we pronounce His words mean whatever fits our point of view.* He looked up as if he were peering into heaven and prayed, "Lord, I surrender. I'm listening now. Speak and I'll do my best to hear what You are saying." He flipped the page and began reading, "The Gospel according to St. Matthew, Chapter One. *The genealogy of Christ...*" he sat on the side of his bed and read the entirety of Matthew's Gospel without interruption. He felt as if he were reading it for the very first time. He ended with the final statement from Matthew 28:20, "...and, lo, I am with you alway, *even* unto the end of the world. Amen."

Edwin's war with God was over. He might not know what experiences were in his future or understand why things happened the way they did, but he was certain that whatever had occurred in his past and whatever might occur in his future, Christ was present with him. He may not always be aware of His presence, but nonetheless, Christ at all times was there.

CHAPTER FOURTEEN
"...as his dying request"

POLLY WAS MAKING HER HOSPITAL ROUNDS WHEN THE orderly handed her a letter from Larimer. Ben had returned to Marietta briefly in January to find out if Polly had changed her mind about marriage. However, Polly no longer found him desirable. She had enjoyed his visit, but every ounce of amorous attraction was gone. Polly nonchalantly glanced at his handwriting and slipped the letter into her pocket. Later that afternoon, she took a brief break in the dining hall. She located an empty table and sat down. Reaching into her pocket reminded Polly of keeping Edwin's letter in the same place. For a brief moment she reflected upon the changes in her relationship with Edwin since first reading it. Then she pulled out Larimer's letter. She calmly opened the envelope with her forefinger and took out a single page. She instantly was horrified. The paper was stained with blood. Even though she could foresee its content, Polly painfully read each line. At first, the words were written in a legible script. Then with the last paragraph, the handwriting became scribbled and difficult to read.

Feb 24, 1864 @ Mill Creek Gap
My dearest darling Polly,

I know that you have twice said no to my proposal of marriage. However, I still love you and hope to one day change your decision. Until I have the opportunity to see you again face to face, I hope you will not deny me the privilege of corresponding with you.

The cavalry has been skirmishing to our front all morning. The enemy is now visible in strength. I will finish this letter as soon as we drive the Yankees back.

I take pen in hand once more to write and tell you that I have been wounded. I fear it is mortal. If I never see you again in this world, may we meet in the next.

Your obedient servant,
Benjamin Larimer

Beneath Larimer's signature, in a different handwriting, was a notation:

Mrs. Brenton, Col. Larimer has died. I am forwarding you this letter as his dying request.

Lt. Jn. J. Stephens

She looked at the date again. The letter had been written almost three weeks earlier. Polly slumped across the table and wept. Edwin entered the room, and upon seeing Polly, walked over and asked, "What's wrong?"

"Ben was killed."

"I'm sorry," Edwin answered, trying to sound sympathetic. He really wasn't sorry. The emotional callousness that enabled soldiers to endure the brutality of combat would not permit pity for the removal of a rival. He didn't fancy seeing Polly suffer, but he was not sorry Larimer was dead. He sat down beside Polly and put his arm around her. Eventually, Polly sat up and looked at him. Her eyes were red and puffy. Tracks of tears still were visible on her cheeks.

"Ed, am I some kind of Jonah?" she asked.

"Jonah? I'm not sure I understand what you mean," Edwin responded.

"Am I bad luck? Every relationship I have had ended with the man dying. Jacob Prescott is dead. Richard is dead. Now Ben is dead. Ed, you best stay clear of me, or you'll be dead, too."

"Honestly, it seems to me that Richard was the only one with whom you had a genuine relationship. It was a Yankee bullet that killed him, not being married to you. Remember, I was with him when he died."

"Thank you for being so kind. But I cannot stop thinking that somehow I'm to blame for their deaths. If I stayed with Jacob, he might have changed. If I had insisted Richard not go, maybe he would still be alive. And I broke Ben's heart, causing him to get careless."

"Polly, you mustn't do this. If you stayed with Prescott, he likely would have killed you. Richard and Larimer were soldiers. They died fighting just like thousands of others have died. Don't forget, I have been on those battlefields. Men die. No one knows why one dies and the one next to him lives. When it's your time, there's nothing you can do."

"What about Ann and the children? They were not on a battlefield. But I moved in with them and they died."

"You also moved in with Mr. Lewis, and he's still alive. I still hurt deep inside whenever I think of Ann. And I think of her a lot, but I take comfort in knowing you took care of her until the end."

Polly reached over and hugged Edwin. Then she rested her head on his shoulder. Edwin remained silent for a time and just held Polly. Then he asked, "Polly, do you remember what you said to me that first day here?"

"No, not really," she answered.

"About being selfish?"

"I guess maybe. I forgot about that."

"Well, I never told you, but it really helped a lot. I know Ann is in a better place. I'm glad she's not suffering like us. Who knows how much longer this war will last. I honestly don't see an end anytime soon. Why would we desire for anyone we love to be a part of this mess?"

"Thank you, Ed," Polly said. She could feel the resurgence of the bond they had once shared. Polly felt secure in Edwin's arms and could sense something special was taking place in that moment.

Julia Bilbry interrupted the mood, saying, "Misses Brenton, Eliza needs you in the kitchen."

Polly vainly endeavored to postpone going, but Bilbry was insistent. Polly rose. She took a step, hesitated, and turned to look at Edwin, scrutinizing his uniform jacket. It was the blue-gray jacket he had worn when he had been admitted to the hospital. His pants were the jean wool pair issued by the hospital. Hospital policy mandated patients be discharged wearing their original uniforms unless the uniform was damaged too badly for service, but seeing Edwin in his uniform did not fully register with Polly in her grief.

"Ed, I've got to go now, but we can talk more later," she said.

"Can't be much later. Doc Daniel released me. I'm going back to Virginia tomorrow. That's why I was looking for you," said Edwin.

Edwin's news stunned Polly. Just as she was starting to uncover her true feelings toward him, he was being taken away, perhaps forever. A sad despondency engulfed her. The former premonition of Edwin's death again haunted the corridors of her mind.

"I will see you this evening," Polly replied. Turning to Julia Bilbry, she said, "Please take that filthy jacket and wash it for me. We can't have this soldier going back to Lee's army looking like this. What will they think of us in Virginia?"

She had cleaned the jacket shortly after Edwin's arrival, so her orders came out of her emotions rather than the jacket's condition. Cleaning it was a final gesture of care for someone she loved very much. Subconsciously, the token deed was her way of clinging to Edwin a short time longer. Until the jacket was returned, he could not leave for Virginia.

"Yea-is ma'am," Julia responded. She stepped toward Edwin, and with her hand extended to take his jacket, said, "Now Corporal, you bes' hand me yo' coat so I-ah can clean it fo' you."

It was dark before Edwin and Polly were able to spend time together. They sat outside the hospital and talked for several hours, but their feelings about each other remained unstated. Both were too nervous about the reception their true affections might evoke. Around four o'clock in the morning, Julia Bilbry again interrupted with word that it was time for Polly to go on duty. Bilbry also returned Edwin's cleaned jacket.

Later that day, Polly escorted Edwin over to the railroad depot. Before boarding the train, Edwin leaned over to kiss Polly on her cheek. Instead, she kissed him on his lips. He wasn't sure if she had meant to or if it had been accidental. Polly wasn't sure either. It just happened. But the moment their lips touched, Edwin pulled Polly tightly against him and kissed her back. They were still kissing when the conductor called for all passengers to board. Ascending the car's steps, Edwin halted briefly to turn and speak to Polly.

"Polly Brenton," he hollered, "I'm going to marry you!"

The locomotive's whistle drowned out her response. The train pulled away from the station with Edwin standing on the car platform watching Polly until she disappeared as the train rumbled around a curve in the tracks. Polly stood waving at him. Tears once more ran down her cheeks, only now they were tears of joy.

CHAPTER FIFTEEN
"*Measures necessary for the... defense of the city*

JAMES LEWIS RODE INTO COLUMBUS TO MEET WITH Samuel Stout, Medical Director of Hospitals for the Army of Tennessee. Stout had begun setting up hospitals in the city during the Atlanta campaign. He had initially encountered some local opposition over his use of the Muscogee County courthouse as a hospital. Despite a unanimous resolution by the mayor and city council requesting that all hospitals be relocated outside the city limits, the existing hospitals remained, and new hospitals were still being established in Columbus. Lewis hoped he could negotiate a contract to provide vegetables to one or more of them. His opinion of doctors had not softened much during the more than two years since the death of his beloved daughter and grandchildren, but selling produce might yield him a profit, and in these stark times, a person did whatever was necessary in order to survive.

Lewis spotted John Lindsay untying his horse on Broad Street. Lewis stopped, dismounted, and began tying his horse at the vacant spot. Upon recognizing Lewis, Lindsay awaited the opportunity to speak with Edwin's father-in-law.

"Good day, Mr. Lewis," Lindsay said.

"Good day to you as well, John. What brings you back home?"

"Came home to see Helen and our baby girl. You know, this is the first time I've been back since being wounded around Chattanooga, and the first time I have seen that precious little darling."

"Ah yes, I haven't seen you since before she was born, so congratulations, John. How was Ed when you last saw him?"

"Father, err, I mean Edwin is fine. He's been back with us almost a year and is recovered completely from his wounds. Astounding how an old man like him can keep up with us youngsters."

"Did you get furlough because of the new baby?"

"No, sir. They don't issue furloughs for that. My papers say I was awarded this furlough 'for marked gallantry and dauntless courage in front of the enemy.' You know how I always told everyone I was a hero. Well now I have the papers to prove it," Lindsay replied in jest.

Lewis knew that despite Lindsay's facetious tone, he no doubt was telling the truth about his gallantry. After some more polite conversation, Lindsay mounted his horse to leave, but instead of kicking his spurs into his horse's sides, he sat there looking down Broad Street. At the intersection with Bryan Street, a provost marshal was staring at Lindsay. Unlike the provost guard within a field army, town provost marshals had an extremely bad reputation among combat veterans. Many marshals were amateur thugs. They used provost duty as an excuse to escape active military service and frequently abused their position for personal benefit. Their authority included the power to arrest anyone simply out of suspicion. No evidence of a crime was necessary.

"Anything wrong, John?" Lewis asked.

"Humbug! No, sir. Just them good-for-nothin' provosts. They treat me like I am a jailbird, always demanding I show my papers. I'm no deserter, and I won't bow down to no toy soldier."

"John, perhaps cooperation is the better part of valor."

"Never been for cooperation. I was not a cooperationist in 1861. I was a secessionist. And I'm still not a cooperationist today."

"John, I think you best be careful. He is carrying a rifle."

Lindsay didn't respond. He simply sat upright in his saddle and slowly rode away down Broad Street. The provost marshal took aim and shot him in the head. He died instantly. James was stunned. He rushed to Lindsay's lifeless body and knelt down beside him.

Dr. Colzey also saw what had happened. He yelled at James to stay with the body. Then he ran to inform Lindsay's father. The gunshot alarmed the whole town. A mob quickly assembled at the site of the shooting. Lindsay was well known and very popular in Columbus. The provosts, on the other hand, were strangers and disliked because of their imperious role. The incident provoked a firestorm. Members from Wheeler's Cavalry Corps reinforced the civilians, and the crowd quickly overpowered the provost. They headed for the post headquarters shouting, "Hang him! Hang him!"

Led by Cooper Lindsay, John's brother, and Robert Howard, his brother-in-law, they seized the provost commanding officer, Colonel Von Zinken, too. They were determined to lynch both men. Fortunately, Lindsay's father arrived at the scene and stopped them. He was very persuasive, saying, "Don't harm him; 'Vengeance is mine; I will repay,' saith the Lord!" After much pleading, he convinced the mob to disperse. An uneasy peace settled over the city of Columbus. James Lewis was deeply disturbed by the episode and did not sleep that night.

* * *

More than a year had passed since Edwin had returned to his unit. Polly stayed with Stout's nomadic hospitals. She spent the winter of 1864-1865 with Dr. Daniel at Lauderdale Springs, about twenty miles northeast of Meridian, Mississippi, and approximately fifty miles north of Benjamin Larimer's home. Polly met the colonel's parents. They were a delightful elderly couple who had lost two sons in the war. Benjamin's older brother had been killed at Fort Donelson. His younger brother rode with Nathan Bedford Forrest, and they had not heard from him in six months. Polly made two trips to the Larimer plantation that winter. The Larimers knew their son had proposed marriage to Polly but were not aware of her rejection. They seemed to find a degree of consolation in thinking their son had been engaged. Polly decided that she would not spoil their solace, so she said nothing, and they received her as family. Save for their unaccounted for youngest son, Polly essentially was their only family.

The outings to the Larimer plantation brought back nostalgic memories of Stillwater. Polly and James Lewis exchanged letters periodically, so she kept abreast of him and Delia. Unlike most of the women serving in the Confederate medical service, Polly had not taken any extended leave time. Most went home at least once or twice a year. However Polly had neither family nor a home. Mr. Lewis frequently invited her to come back to Stillwater, but she always felt it would be awkward. But the welcome Mr. and Mrs. Larimer extended to her reminded her of those last few weeks with Mr. Lewis. Perhaps she did have a family after all. At any rate, she was determined to find out.

Spring was in the air when Polly left Lauderdale Springs for Stillwater in late March of 1865. She caught a ride on a hospital train from Lauderdale Spring to Meridian, Mississippi. The trip from Meridian to Selma, Alabama, was approximately 105 miles, but it took four days. The trains barely made ten miles per hour on the worn-out tracks, and she had to transfer trains four times. She reached Selma on Friday, March 31. Selma and Montgomery were not connected by railroad, so she sought passage on a steamboat. A ticket for the trip cost $200, which Polly did not have. When she told the ticket agent that she was an army nurse, he offered her deck passage at government expense. The steamer's captain overheard Polly's exchange with the ticket agent and introduced himself.

Polly thanked the captain for his concern and identified herself as Polly Brenton of the Army of Tennessee Medical Service. When the boat captain learned who she was, he offered Polly free passage. His son had been one of her patients in Chattanooga and had written his parents, telling of her kindness. When the boat reached Montgomery on Saturday afternoon, Polly decided to wait until Monday to go on to Columbus. The only lodging she could find was an empty boxcar that had been placed on a siding for refugees. She had slept in boxcars previously when the hospital had relocated from Chattanooga and during the Atlanta Campaign, so she didn't hesitate to avail herself of the makeshift accommodations.

Three other families already occupied the car, but they happily made room for Polly. Margaret Cross, her daughter, Parthenia, and sons Matthew and Joseph were from New Manchester, Georgia. Margaret and her family had fled from the mill town prior to Sherman's arrival. She had heard that the women who remained in town had been shipped north as prisoners. Her husband had been in the Army of Tennessee, but she had not heard from him in over a year and presumed he was dead. Her children were all small. The oldest, Matthew, was only nine but had been forced to shoulder some adult responsibilities because of their circumstances. Parthenia was six, while Joseph was four. They occupied one end of the box car. Margaret invited Polly to share her family's space, and Polly gladly accepted the offer.

The other end was occupied by two older couples. Dr. John C. Dalton and his wife, Harriet, looked to be in their late sixties. He had been a physician in Nashville before that city had fallen to the Union army. Since that time, he had been displaced from Chattanooga and then Atlanta. The other couple, Henry and Varina Franklin, owned a small plantation in the path of Sherman's destruction on his march to Savannah, Georgia. They were hoping to reach relatives in Mississippi.

The three families shared their meager provisions with each other and cooked on an open fire beside the boxcar. Although she had nothing to put into the pot, the refugees generously shared their meals with Polly. They alleged her portion was their contribution to the war effort. At night, Polly wrapped up in a worn piece of carpet and slept on the floor with her new-found friends.

On Monday morning, Polly took the Montgomery and West Point Railroad east and arrived in Girard that afternoon. Just east of the Summerville Road, a line of fortifications caught her attention. Their discovery cast a somber mood over Polly. She had never considered that the war might come to Columbus. In her mind, the city always had been an unspoken haven. Just as she had fled there to escape Jacob Prescott, she was returning now to escape the war. She was still contemplating what those trenches foretold when the train crossed the Chattahoochee River and pulled into Columbus.

As she stepped down from the car, she spotted a familiar face, that of Julia Bilbry who was counting boxes. Julia had transferred to Columbus after the hospital in Marietta had been relocated. Polly rushed over to her. When Julia saw Polly, she threw out her arms and embraced her former supervisor. The soldier with Julia watched the reunion with complete indifference. Then he started to load the boxes into a nearby army ambulance.

"Misses Brenton, God has sent you to me," Julia said emphatically.

Ignoring the implication of Julia's comment, Polly asked, "What brings you to the train depot today?"

"Pickin' up some medical supplies," she answered. "What are yo' doin' in Columbus? I reckoned yo' were in Mississippi."

"I was all played out. I've taken furlough and came here to visit Mr. Lewis at Stillwater."

"Misses Brenton, I-ah need yo' he'p fo' a patient." Julia's voice softened as she spoke, taking on a grave tenor.

"Julia, I'm on my way to Stillwater for a rest. I'll stop by and check on him in a few days."

"Misses Brenton, please, he's my-ah neph-yu, my oldes' sista's only son. He's got the gangrene. I-ah remembah how fi-ahn you was with that Corporal Anderson. Want you please take ti-amh to ri-ahd and see hem."

A flood of emotions filled Polly's mind when Julia mentioned Edwin's episode with gangrene. She recalled the affection she had felt during his long illness. She also remembered the anxiety. That memory was now compounded by her present trepidation. Edwin's last letter had been dated February 22. In it, he disclosed that he was sick with fever. As a nurse, she was well aware that many more troops died of disease than wounds. When the soldier finished loading the boxes, Polly and Julia climbed upon them, and the vehicle scurried down Randolph Street.

* * *

"Father" Edwin Anderson had rejoined the Columbus Guards a few days before the Battle of the Wilderness. Initially, he was unable to keep up the pace marching, so he straggled a lot, but by the end of the month his body had once again adapted to the rigors of active campaigning. However, the company was changing. Theodore Fogle had been promoted to Lieutenant but was killed in the Wilderness. Lt. Samuel Cleghorn, Lt. Samuel Pitts, and Sgt. Tom Coleman were wounded in the same battle; Harris Johnson had been captured.

Father spent the winter of 1864-1865 in the trenches outside Petersburg. In February, he developed a high fever and chills. When his symptoms grew worse, he was sent to the massive Chimborazo Hospital in Richmond. After three weeks there, his health improved dramatically. Nevertheless, he remained weak, so the doctors finally granted him a thirty-day furlough effective March 18. He decided that he would go see Polly in Mississippi and along the way, stop in Columbus and visit Mr. Lewis.

The trip to Columbus evolved into quite an adventure. Sherman's campaigns in Georgia and the Carolinas disrupted travel far more than Rosencrans's capture of Chattanooga prior to the Battle of Chickamauga. Father took the Richmond and Danville Railroad to Danville, Virginia. There, after an eight-hour delay, he transferred to the Piedmont Railroad. The Piedmont was less than a year old, but even by Confederate wartime standards, it was in horrible shape. The forty-eight mile trip on this decrepit railroad frightened Father more than some battles. He was relieved to reach Greensboro, North Carolina, just before dark. Unable to catch a westbound train until the next morning, Father spent a restless night in the depot. At half past ten in the morning, he finally departed Greensboro on the North Carolina Railroad morning mail train. The North Carolina was among the best railroads in the Confederacy. Father slept most of the trip. Arriving in Charlotte around midnight, he spent another sleepless night in a railroad depot. Taking the Charlotte and South Carolina Railroad, he reached Chester, South Carolina that afternoon. Father pondered visiting Adeline Knight. He wondered if seeing her would revive his attraction for her, and he also was curious if she was married yet, but in the end, Father realized he had changed. He had returned to his core values and was ready to tell Polly that he loved her. He dared not risk damaging his newfound relationship with her.

This time, when the train stopped at the Chester station, no admiring crowd greeted Father. Panic and despair pervaded everyone Father encountered. Sherman's army had come within ten miles of the city a few weeks earlier and destroyed the tracks south of Chester. From here, Father would need to find other transportation. Again, Adeline flashed across his mind. Perhaps she could help him. However Father decided his wisest course was to head west without delay. It had taken almost a week to get this far, and he was only halfway to Columbus. Mississippi was even further.

Looks like I have a long walk ahead of me, Father mused. *Let's see, it's at least 350 miles to Columbus. I can cover twenty-five miles a day. That will take me another two weeks. That only gives me a week to get to Mississippi with no time there and no time to get back. Oh well, I'll worry about getting back after I see Polly. Edwin, let's get going. At the double quick! March!* With that, Edwin stepped out at a brisk pace.

When he asked for directions, a local Methodist pastor offered him a ride to Unionville. A farmer in that village allowed him to sleep in his barn for the night. His gray uniform opened every door. So it was that wherever Father traveled, people gave him food and shelter. Occasionally someone provided transportation. Day after day, Edwin inched his way across South Carolina and then Georgia.

As he trekked westward, he picked up bits of news, mostly hearsay. He heard that Lee had evacuated Petersburg, and Richmond had fallen. That seemed dubious to Father. Despite an obviously deteriorating situation, the fighting spirit of the Army of Northern Virginia remained intact, he thought. An even more unbelievable rumor was that France had declared war on the United States and was sending troops to fight for the Confederacy.

North of Milledgeville, Father entered the zone of Sherman's march to the sea. For three days he walked through scenes of destruction. Contact with people was rare. Most had fled when the Yankees had torched their farms and towns. Lonely chimneys marked the locations of their former homes. Scorched fields were sprouting new green shoots of grass. Sporadically, Edwin saw a freshly plowed field, but he found no food in the desolated landscape. Nights were cold, and he had no choice but to sleep in the open. The lack of provisions and shelter deteriorated his still weak body, and his progress slowed.

Near Griswoldville, Father learned of the horrific battle fought in that community that past November. The Georgia Militia had attacked Sherman in a vain attempt to end his invasion of the state. Comprised mainly of men over the age of sixty and boys under sixteen, the militia fought with fanatical determination. However, they were too few to stop the northern juggernaut. Of the two thousand Georgians engaged, over six hundred were killed or wounded. In one local family, a man, two of his sons, and his brother were dead. Another son was injured severely. Father was appalled by what he heard. *How much longer must this cruel war continue?* he wondered.

As "Father" Edwin Anderson worked his way westward through Georgia to reach Columbus, Federal cavalry under General James H. Wilson simultaneously was racing eastward through Alabama to reach the same destination. On Thursday, April 13, the mayor and city council of Columbus gathered for a special, secret meeting. The official records of the session noted that the purpose was "to adopt some measures necessary for the welfare and defense of the city."

Late Friday afternoon, Edwin reached Macon. He went to the station of the South Western Railroad and took a train to Butler. The next morning he found space on a Muscogee Railroad train to Columbus. Shortly before noon, the train's locomotive eased into the station at Columbus. Four years after leaving to go to war, Edwin Anderson had returned home.

Unfortunately, Edwin had no time to absorb the moment. As he stepped on the station platform, an army captain confronted him and impressed him into the militia forming to defend the city.

"But sir, I'm on my first furlough in four years," Edwin protested.

"Corporal, I don't care if it's your first furlough in forty years; you are needed to defend this city. Army needs supersede personal privileges. Yanks will be here in less than two days. If we don't stop them, there won't be a city for you to take furlough in," the captain remarked.

"Yes, sir," Edwin said grudgingly.

Edwin was handed a rifle and accouterments. He was assigned to an ad hoc company composed of city residents, local militia, and walking wounded from the city hospitals. The company formed up on Randolph Street and then marched toward Broad Street. They passed familiar places that brought back fond memories. Columbus Baptist Church and Frederick Wilhelm's restaurant especially evoked pleasant recollections. At the intersection with Broad Street, the column turned right and continued marching until they reached Franklin Street. There the column turned left and disappeared into the covered bridge that spanned the Chattahoochee River.

CHAPTER SIXTEEN
"Believest thou this?"

LATE SATURDAY AFTERNOON, EDWIN ANDERSON'S NEWLY formed company filed into the fortifications on the hills west of the Chattahoochee River. Once he was inside the entrenchments, Edwin took time to examine his position and appraise his comrades in arms. A few were wounded soldiers from the Army of Tennessee. They had been convalescing in Columbus hospitals until conscripted into the city's defense. However, most of the recruits were civilian volunteers from the city or nearby communities. They mainly were old men and boys. Two of them had fought in the Mexican War, and one elderly man had fought in the Creek Indian conflict three decades earlier. Except for a few previously discharged from the army due to poor health, the rest lacked combat experience and military training. The company commander was a convalescing lieutenant from the Army of Tennessee. It was apparent to Edwin that the company could not fight as a cohesive unit. If the Yankees did show up, the company's only hope was to stay inside the fortifications and just shoot at the enemy in front of them.

After the command "Rest" was given, Edwin climbed out of the breastworks to survey the position. The trench was six feet deep and eight feet wide. A square fort with four bronze howitzers stood to the left of the trench while six rifled Parrott guns were situated in a redoubt on the street behind the dugout. The firing position on the entrenchment's front sloped toward the direction from which the enemy was expected and allowed one to look down into the city of Girard. From Edwin's perspective, although the fortifications were inferior to those around Petersburg, the position was strong. Even the motley force around him should be capable of holding it.

As Edwin scrutinized his company's prospects in an engagement, a bright flash lit the evening sky, followed by a deep rumble. A few moments later, a second flash and rumble announced the commencement of a spring thunderstorm. Heavy rain began falling, filling the trench with water. The way the new recruits scampered out and ran to find shelter amused the veterans in the unit. Notwithstanding their mirth, the novices' behavior also vexed the veterans. If these green troops ran from a few drops of water, what would they do when faced with a barrage of Yankee bullets?

The rain continued into the night, making the soldiers miserable. They crowded into a few tents and canvas shelters that had been erected behind the entrenchment. While the huddled recruits talked about the next day's battle, the veterans provided encouragement to their uninitiated comrades. Eventually, the camp grew silent and nervous citizen-soldiers and hardened veterans dozed off.

The sun had not yet risen when the company first sergeant awakened Edwin and told him to rouse the men. A short time later, roll call was held and a detail was designated to secure rations for the company. The lieutenant announced that some men would be permitted to attend sunrise services in Columbus churches. It was Easter, and the enemy had not yet approached the city. As the sun rose in the east, church bells pealed. Men selected to attend church services walked down the hill toward the Franklin Street Bridge. The clear sky signaled a beautiful spring day.

The rest of the company inspected their weapons and performed any maintenance necessitated by the rain. Edwin examined his rifle carefully. It was a Model 1861 Springfield rifled musket, very similar to his usual Enfield. Inside his cartridge box, he found a dry rag and wiped the moisture off the gun. Taking a cap out of his cap box, he seated it on the rifle's nipple. He pointed the barrel towards the ground; yelled, "Popping a cap!" and pulled the trigger. The small blast caused the grass to undulate. The weapon was functional. Other experienced warriors along the line were performing the same procedure. Once their own weapons were tested, the veterans assisted the novices in checking their rifles.

Having secured his equipment for battle, Edwin prepared himself for whatever his fate might be. Sitting on the back edge of the trench with his feet dangling off its rear wall, he pulled his New Testament from his jacket pocket. Looking at the page to which he arbitrarily opened, he read, "Jesus said unto her, I am the resurrection, and the life: he that believeth in me, though he were dead, yet shall he live: And whosoever liveth and believeth in me shall never die. Believest thou this?" He recognized the passage as John 11:25-26. He soaked in the sunrise and meditated on Jesus's words. He thought them so appropriate for an Easter Sunday.

The impending battle added a whole new dimension to the meaning of these two verses. When the enemy reached Columbus, men would die. Perhaps today he would be killed. He had as much chance of being slain as anyone else. He thought of the recent carnage at Griswoldville. His current comrades were even less adapted to combat than the militia who had died in that massacre. Edwin realized that his odds of surviving the fight were not good. Yet here Jesus said that the person who believed in Him, "though he were dead, yet shall he live: And whosoever liveth and believeth in me shall never die." The words meant that if he did get killed, he would not really die. The hypothesis was ludicrous. And still Jesus's question "Believest thou this?" solicited Edwin to believe it not only was possible, but that it was in fact true.

Edwin recalled one of the ghastly sights he had witnessed in the Battle of the Wilderness. That battle had been fought on the same site as the 1863 Battle of Chancellorsville. The bodies of dead Federal soldiers were buried hastily in shallow graves after the earlier battle. Many of those corpses had been exposed a year later and their bleached bones and skulls littered the ground.

Then Edwin's thoughts turned to Ann and his deceased children. Their memory was as vivid as ever. He still could picture Ann standing at the top of the stairs. He could feel James landing in his arms and hear Charlotte's thrilled scream. As he reminisced, he recalled his conversations with Polly in which they discussed heaven not as a theoretical concept, but as an actual place. "Believest thou this?" Jesus asked.

"Yes, yes I do," Edwin answered inaudibly.

Around two o'clock Sunday afternoon, the serenity ended abruptly. Federal cavalry were sighted approaching Girard from the southwest on the Sanford Road. The guns in the fort and on the road opened fire. On the Sanford Road, a Federal battery of four Napoleons rumbled up a nearby knoll and unlimbered. Quickly, a ferocious artillery duel ensued. Edwin and the rest of the infantry hunkered down inside their trench.

"Well gentlemen, they've opened the ball," muttered Edwin.

"Yea-is, if any of you militia survive this ruckus, you can tell folks that you have seen the elephant," one of the Army of Tennessee veterans added.

"Load!" screamed the lieutenant. The uninitiated civilians hesitated, but those who had "seen the elephant" quickly reached into their cartridge boxes and rammed paper cartridges down the barrels of their rifled muskets. Observing their experienced comrades, the neophytes did likewise.

Edwin could see the fear in the eyes of a young boy. The boy couldn't have been more than thirteen years of age. Edwin looked at him and asked, "Scared?"

"Yes, sir," the kid whimpered.

"Me, too," Edwin said.

"Really?" the young boy asked.

"I'd be crazy not to be afraid," answered Edwin.

"Amen," another veteran added.

The lieutenant ran up to where Edwin and several veterans were waiting. "You men know skirmish tactics?"

"Yes, sir," several voices replied.

"Come with me."

The detachment worked their way to some rifle pits between the fort and the river. Another group of soldiers joined the detachment there, bringing the total number to thirty. The lieutenant calmly briefed the detachment on their mission. "Listen men, between us and the Yankees is Mill Creek. The only way the Yankees can get across this creek is a footbridge. We have to fire it. We must move quickly before they can take it. So fall in. We are all new to each other. So identify your file partner, and don't forget him. When I give the command, deploy as skirmishers and let's do this."

The ad hoc unit climbed over the top of the entrenchment and moved methodically toward the bridge, spacing themselves ten yards apart. As they approached the bridge, they began to advance by firing. Edwin's file partner was ten yards to his left. They dropped to their knees. Edwin squeezed off a round. His partner leaped up and ran forward about ten yards. Edwin rapidly reloaded. As soon as he returned his ramrod to its place in the rifle and seated the cap, Edwin yelled, "Ready!"

His partner fired. Edwin jumped up and ran forward until he was about ten yards beyond his partner. He patiently waited until he heard his partner shout, "Ready!" Then he squeezed the trigger once more. The entire detachment advanced systematically to Mill Creek using this leap-frogging drill. At the creek, designated soldiers set fire to the bridge. Once smoke began to billow upward and flames engulfed the structure, the detachment retreated using the same tactics. After returning to the entrenchments, the group dispersed to their original units.

A short time later, Edwin could see a second column of black smoke rising into the sky. The fort blocked his view, but he guessed that Columbus's defenders had set fire to the City Bridge spanning the Chattahoochee. In order to get into the city, the Federals now had to capture the fortifications. Except for sporadic firing, the fighting died away. As the sun set on that Easter Sunday, the impromptu Confederate force still blocked the Union army from entering Columbus.

Visibility practically was nonexistent in the darkness. Inside their fortifications, Edwin and the rest of Columbus's defenders nervously awaited the Yankees' next move. Around eight thirty, rockets were launched from behind the Confederate lines. Their flaming tails streaked into the sky and burst into brilliant falling stars, illuminating the battlefield. The north end of the Confederate line erupted in heavy firing. The bass voices of cannons punctuated the relentless cadence of musket fire. The infantry maintained a steady rattle as soldiers frantically loaded and fired.

Edwin and the men in his company listened intently and peered warily into the darkness. As the volume of fire grew, they cast anxious glances in the direction of the shooting. A flickering yellow-orange glow lit up the sky. The shooting rapidly increased in strength and then died out. The lull increased the insecurity among the defenders. Had their comrades further north repulsed the Federal attack, or had they been vanquished by the Yankees? The silence did not last long. Heavy gunfire erupted once again. Not long after the shooting resumed, Edwin began hearing human screams added to the din. The volume of gunfire decreased, but the noise level was supplemented with other sounds. Edwin was unable to determine what they were or their significance.

The clatter of galloping horses near the six Parrott rifled artillery pieces caught Edwin's attention. A few minutes later he heard someone scream, "Yanks in the rear!" Gunshots rang out near the Franklin Street Bridge. The shots created havoc. Muzzle flashes lit up Union cavalry at the mouth of the bridge. Edwin leaped out of the trench and fired in the direction of the horses. Some men from the artillery battery on the road set fire to a few nearby houses to provide light for their cannons. They could see the Yankees withdrawing northward. However, not long afterwards, a wave of Confederate soldiers swept down from the direction of the heavy firing. The burning houses exposed the magnitude of the panic. They had dropped their guns and were stripping away accouterments as they raced for the bridge. Their numbers swelled as seconds passed. Mounted Yankee cavalrymen mingled among the fleeing Confederate infantry. The blue-coated riders made no effort to strike down retreating Confederates. They too seemed focused on crossing the bridge.

Edwin was transfixed by the sight. Seeing more and more Union cavalry, he realized the entrenchments were no longer tenable. Unless he got to the bridge soon, he would be captured. He was terrified by thoughts of going to a northern prison camp. Without any further deliberation, he bolted for the bridge. Unlike most in the fleeing mass, Edwin held on to his musket. Reaching the Columbus side of the bridge, he noted a few gray-clad troops attempting to make a stand and stem the tide of battle. Edwin slowed and contemplated taking a stand with them. Hearing a voice shout "Throw down your arms and surrender" ended his deliberation. He raced down Franklin Street and spun right on Jackson Street. He could hear sporadic shots within the city. He knew some Yankees already were in town, but their exact numbers and location remained uncertain.

As he crossed Bryan Street, Edwin glimpsed Yankee cavalry riding down Broad Street. He was breathing heavily, but adrenaline and fear drove him on. Randolph Street was less than twenty yards ahead when a horse and rider whipped around the corner. Everything transpired within seconds, but in Edwin's mind they unfolded in slow motion. The rider wore a standard blue shell jacket trimmed in yellow, sky blue pants tucked in black cavalry boots, and a blue kepi with a brass crossed-saber pin. He was mounted on a dark bay horse with black stockings. Its coat was covered in a lather of sweat. The rider held the reins in his left hand and a Spencer carbine in his right. As he turned on to Jackson, he spotted Edwin. When he jerked the reins back, his horse rose up on its hind legs. Edwin stumbled as he stopped abruptly.

The reins pulled the horse's head to the rider's left, obliquely exposing his right flank to Edwin. The Spencer was leveled and pointing at him. Edwin peered into its barrel muzzle. At that moment, its bore seemed larger than .52 caliber. He clutched his own rifle in his right hand, holding it just behind the rear band. Subconsciously, Edwin began raising the gun as he sought to avert his fall. He heard the rider yell, "Surrender, grayback!" The voice shifted Edwin's attention to the man's face. It was flushed with excitement. A yellow blaze flashed from the Spencer's bore just as Edwin caught sight of the Yankee's blue eyes.

Edwin failed to hear the sound of the shot. Everything went silent. The bullet burned as it ripped through his flesh. He dropped his musket and tumbled to the ground. He rolled over and attempted to spring back to his feet. He made it to his hands and knees. Looking up, he saw the Yankee cavalryman finish cocking the Spencer and aim it at him.

"That's enough, grayback! I said, 'Surrender,'" screamed the cavalryman.

Behind him, Edwin heard the clatter of more hoofs. He turned his head and glimpsed two more Federal cavalrymen standing a few feet to his rear. He dropped his head and muttered, "I give up."

"What did you say, reb? Sing out!"

Edwin again lifted his head and repeated loudly, "I give up. I surrender."

"All right you Secesh. That's hunky-dory. Slowly stand up. Keep your hands out where I can see them."

Edwin stood up and felt a sharp pain in his left arm. The bullet had gashed his upper arm, leaving two bullet holes in his sleeve. Although the wound was superficial, it bled profusely, soaking the wool jacket around both holes. The victorious cavalryman marched Edwin to the home of Randolph Lawler Mott, which was adjacent to the Franklin Street Bridge. Mott, an anti-secessionist, was sympathetic to the Union cause even while his son served in the Confederate army. More cavalrymen warily watched over other captured Confederates in Mott's yard.

The next day, Edwin and the other prisoners watched helplessly as the mills along the Chattahoochee River burned. They could also see numerous fires across the river in Girard. All over town, everything belonging to the Confederate government or used to support the war effort was put to the torch. The massive columns of black smoke that rose into the sky could be seen for miles. The destruction of munitions stored in the city added the sound of repeated explosions to the inferno. Around noon, the Federal guards distributed hardtack to the prisoners. After eating a few bites, Edwin decided to read his New Testament. He took the Bible out of his jacket pocket. With it, he also pulled out a folded paper. He flipped it open and read his furlough papers. His leave was over. He was scheduled to report back to the Columbus Guards in Virginia today. "Guess that won't happen," he mused.

Just before sunset, a Federal surgeon ordered the wounded taken to the hospital. The Union army already had started leaving Columbus, heading towards their next objective, Macon. While they would take the majority of prisoners with them, wounded prisoners could impede the speed of their advance, so all wounded Confederates were paroled and left in the care of the Confederate hospitals in Columbus.

The guards were not screening the wounded closely. Edwin's blood-stained jacket was sufficient to secure his transfer. Along with a dozen other prisoners, he was escorted up Franklin Street to Jackson Street. This was the same route he had taken for flight the previous night. Edwin found it ironic that the army that had stopped him a few hours earlier was now providing him an escort down the same street. As he walked along, he witnessed drunken Yankee soldiers and the city's impoverished inhabitants looting houses. They also passed numerous contrabands roaming the streets celebrating the Year of Jubilee. Thousands of the freed slaves had flocked into the city seeking the safe haven provided by Lincoln's soldiers. The prisoners continued until they reached the Muscogee County Courthouse. They entered through the high brick wall that enclosed the courthouse lawn.

The Muscogee County Courthouse had been rented by the Confederate government. It was part of the fifteen-hundred-bed Walker Hospital. Polly spent most of her time in it after coming to Columbus. During the past week, many of the patients and much of the staff were removed to safer locations. Polly did not wish to leave Columbus, so she volunteered to stay with the patients who could not be moved. She had gone to church Sunday morning and spent the early afternoon checking and double-checking her resources. Like most civilians in the city, Polly was filled with anxiety and trepidation after the opening shots near the City Bridge. She did not leave the hospital once the shooting commenced. During the night, the gunshots seemed to be in the city itself. To her, it seemed as if the sun would never rise that Monday. A pink tint colored the eastern sky when Dr. Francis Ticknor and an army officer entered the room where Polly was mixing blackberry wine with water to give to her patients. Her heart sank when she saw them. The officer's uniform was blue. A shiny saber hung from his belt, showing his status was not that of a prisoner. Ticknor informed her that the city had fallen, and she could expect new patients from the city's defenders. He did not know how soon they would arrive.

Polly had just finished organizing a room for the influx of new patients when Edwin walked through the door. She recognized him immediately. His face was smeared with black powder and dirt. His hair was disheveled and his eyes bloodshot. His uniform was filthy. The blood-stained sleeve was foreboding, but it was Edwin…and he was alive! She made a dash for him.

Edwin's thoughts during the past twenty-four hours had been dominated by circumstance and events. Before his capture, he had pondered the possibility that he might be killed, but the passage from John 14:25, "He that believeth in me, though he were dead, yet shall he live," had provided him solace. He no longer wanted to die. Though he very much wished to live, he was not afraid of dying and was at peace with whatever his fate might be. Or so he presumed until the encounter on Jackson Street. He was certainly not at peace with becoming a prisoner of war. The hours in the Mott yard were spent alternating between awe of the conflagration and anxieties about his future as a prisoner.

Yet beneath his fascination with the fires and his consternation over prison, a stronger thought permeated everything, Polly Brenton. She was the reason that he kept traveling towards Columbus even though he knew his leave time would expire before he could return to the Army of Northern Virginia. He was determined to see her even if it meant going A.W.O.L. In one sense, his consternation over capture was more about her than about treatment of prisoners. Imprisonment postponed that moment when he would see Polly again. She was the profounder reason for his despair.

While incarcerated in the Mott yard, Edwin had met a fellow prisoner named James Howard. Howard was from Arkansas. He had been wounded in the Atlanta campaign the previous spring and hospitalized in Columbus. Howard reasoned that going to the hospital might prevent direct captivity and offer better opportunities to escape. Howard used a fake sling to be included in those taken to the hospital so he would not miss such an opportunity. Edwin agreed with his reasoning. As Edwin walked down Jackson Street, he prayed for God to give him the opportunity to escape so that he might go see Polly sooner. The sight of her dashing toward him stunned Edwin. In his wildest dreams, he never imagined that she might be in Columbus. Her most recent letters had all come from Mississippi.

Edwin hardly had time to process his thoughts before Polly grabbed him around the neck and planted her lips against his. He put his arms around her waist, pulled her tightly against his body, and kissed her back. Their kiss was protracted and passionate. Both had desired to express this affection for the other for a long time but had cautiously suppressed it. Both had attempted to divert it towards someone else but discovered that object of their affection to be inadequate. During the past year, they had discovered their attraction was more than superficial. Edwin and Polly had begun revealing its depth, but physical separation curbed some potential means of expressing it. The moment their lips touched, all of their emotions and inhibitions were released. Their love for each other was articulated by that kiss in ways words could not. Their destiny with each other now was sealed.

The reunion was interrupted by Dr. Ticknor. "I take it that you two know each other. Your sparking is blocking the door and impeding my medical practice," he said impishly.

The Union army evacuated Columbus immediately after the city's destruction. The last troops pulled out the morning after Edwin's hospitalization. No one knew how far they had gone, so even though Edwin's minor wound had been treated, he did not leave the hospital until Thursday morning. Polly was determined not to leave him, so she too stayed safeguarded in the courthouse. She had not been to her room in over four days when the two of them ventured out together after breakfast. As they walked through the city, they were horrified by what they encountered. Rubble and wreckage were everywhere. The house where Polly boarded had been ransacked. Its owners apparently had abandoned it when the Union army appeared in Girard. Most of Polly's possessions were gone. She found a few items in the hall and recovered a dress in the yard. It was ripped but could be stitched up. Polly and Edwin picked things up from the yard and the front room of the house. Then they straightened her room up. Apparently the owners had left in such haste that they failed to lock the doors, so the front door was not damaged and the house could still be secured.

Edwin and Polly searched for food without much success. During their hunt, they heard a voice hollering, "Misses Polly." They turned and saw a barefoot adolescent black girl in an old homespun dress. She looked strangely familiar to Polly, but she wasn't sure why.

"Misses Polly," said the girl as she rushed up and hugged Polly.

"Why it is Misses Brenton."

Although Polly had not been able to get away from the hospital to visit Stillwater, she immediately recognized the second voice as Obadiah's. When she looked up, he and Delia were approaching. Instantly, Polly realized the girl was Sarah. She had grown significantly since Polly had seen her last.

"We be free, Misses Polly," Delia said excitedly. "De Lincoln sojurs come and de gen'l say we be free. De Year of Jubilee finally come and we dance de juba."

"We be just walking wherever we please fo' a couple of days," added Obadiah. Then he looked at Edwin and said, "Why glory be, dis here be Marse Anda'son. He be a true gen'man."

Uniforms were among the items burned by the Yankees, so Edwin had been unable to replace his jacket. Delia was staring at its bloody sleeve. "Marse Anda'son, dat be a bullet hole?" she asked.

"Just a minor flesh wound. It's nothing," Edwin responded.

"Missess Polly, we be hungry. Does you have some food?" Sarah inquired. "We not find even a goober to eat."

"When did you last eat?" Polly asked.

"We eat sum hoe cakes at Stillwaters," answered Delia.

Edwin reached into his haversack and handed them a charred husk of corn he had pulled from the ashes of a burned house. It had been all they could find.

The five individuals exchanged news of recent events. Delia and Obadiah also told them about the impoverished conditions at Stillwater. Edwin and Polly warned about anarchy in certain areas of the city. Whites and blacks passing by threw disapproving glances at this spontaneous reunion; they viewed an affable conversation between two white people and three former slaves as annoying fraternization, so after a brief chat, fearing the risks they were imposing upon each other, the two parties went their separate ways. Edwin and Polly ran into John Lindsay's father later, and he gave them some bread for an evening meal.

Polly insisted upon staying in her room at night. Edwin was unwilling to allow her to stay in the house alone, so he slept in the hallway outside her room. They shared numerous jokes about the gossip they surely were starting, but Edwin was truly concerned that the arrangement might cause problems for Polly in the future. So that Sunday, they attended worship service at Columbus Baptist Church, and after everyone had left, they approached Reverend DeVotie at the front door.

"Reverend DeVotie," Edwin said.

DeVotie stared at Edwin momentarily before recognizing who it was that addressed him. He clasped Edwin's hand and asked, "Reverend Anderson, is that really you?" Then glancing at Edwin's blood-stained sleeve he asked, "Ed, are you all right?"

"Yes, it's me. I'm fine. A Yankee bullet grazed me last Sunday, and I have been unable to obtain a replacement jacket," answered Edwin. "I plan to visit Mr. Lewis and see if he still has any of my clothing."

"Fine. If he doesn't, let me know and I'll see what can be done. Now who is this lovely young lady?"

"This is Mrs. Polly Brenton. She was Ann's best friend."

"Oh yes, now I remember. Mrs. Brenton, I'm delighted to see you again. I thought you had gone to Tennessee."

"Reverend, it's good to see you as well. I did. I've been an army nurse since '63."

"Reverend DeVotie," Edwin said. "We want to get married. Would you do us the honor of performing the ceremony?"

"When?" asked DeVotie tentatively.

"Right now," answered Edwin.

"Ed, let's not be too hasty." Then seeing the disappointment in the couple's expressions, he added, "I tell you what. Let's go back inside and talk about it. Ed, you know I need to satisfy my conscience before I consent to performing the ceremony."

The three of them walked down the aisle. Edwin and Polly sat on the front pew. Reverend DeVotie placed a chair facing them. Polly told him everything about her past while Edwin shared the course of events that led to their decision to get married.

Finally, Reverend DeVotie said, "Ed, Polly, from what you have told me, I don't see any impediment to uniting the two of you in holy matrimony. However, I do think you owe James Lewis the privilege of attending the service. Let's wait until next Sunday. I will marry the two of you immediately after worship. That will give you time to contact James. What do you say?"

Edwin and Polly looked at each other. Both were somewhat disappointed, but they knew that Reverend DeVotie was right. So they agreed to his proposition.

On Monday, they borrowed DeVotie's carriage and drove out to Stillwater. With bands of bandits and lowlifes roaming the countryside, the trip was not without potential danger. Happily, the journey was without incident. James Lewis was thrilled to see both of them. When they shared the purpose of their visit, he was even more excited. The three of them spent the entire day getting reacquainted and sharing their experiences since last seeing each other.

When they were ready to leave, James walked the engaged couple out to the carriage. Just before they pulled away, he said, "I'll see you on Sunday. Ed, Polly, I want you to come reside at Stillwater. I have missed both of you more than you can ever know. I regret the way I treated the two of you. Ed, you know that I did not think you were good enough for Ann. Polly, it wasn't until Ann's illness that I permitted myself to be open to you. Can you both forgive me?"

They both had forgiven James's prejudice long ago, but his request gave real closure to the past discord. As for moving in at Stillwater, they promised to consider his invitation.

The following week, on Sunday, April 30, 1865, at the close of the regular worship service, Reverend DeVotie asked the congregation to be seated. Then he called for Edwin and Polly to come to the front. There, before the assembled congregation, he united Edwin Anderson and Polly Brenton in marriage. James Lewis was present. So was Delia, although she sat in the balcony. She and Sarah had returned to Stillwater. Obadiah had decided to go up north and find employment. Their merriment of emancipation had been subdued by the despair of hunger. Delia and Lewis bartered an agreement in which she could live at Stillwater in exchange for cooking meals; Sarah would take care of housekeeping.

Roswell Ellis was present also. He had been in Columbus recovering from wounds when the city had fallen. Although his injuries had prevented his participation in the battle, he had escaped in the darkness when the Union army entered the city. He and his horse had fallen into a ditch in the effort.

Edwin and Polly had planned to remain in the vacant boarding house, but the evening before their nuptials, the owners returned. They invited the engaged couple to stay with them. However, Edwin and Polly decided to accept Mr. Lewis's offer, so after the wedding on Sunday, Reverend DeVotie drove them to Stillwater.

* * *

Columbus had been the last significant battle of the war. By June, the newlyweds were settled in comfortably as Stillwater. Edwin was replacing some rotted boards on Mr. Lewis's front porch when a solitary figure rode up on a gaunt mare. The rider appeared equally emaciated. Edwin was shocked to realize it was Deacon Archibald. His expression was even sourer than Edwin remembered. And his uneasiness was apparent.

"Good morning, Deacon Archibald. This is a pleasant surprise."

"Good day, Pastor."

"Just call me Ed, Deacon. I'm a farmer now, not a pastor."

"Well, Reverend Anderson, that is why I am here. Our deacon board called a special meeting of the church last night, and the congregation has voted to extend you a call to become our pastor."

The front door opened and Polly came out with a refreshment for her husband. "Darling, I brought you a glass of milk. Oh excuse me. I didn't realize that you had a visitor."

"Deacon, you know my wife, Polly, I believe."

"Good day, Mrs. Anderson," Archibald said.

Edwin was unable to restrain a mischievous grin. He could still see the old man calling her a redheaded Jezebel. The deacon missed this smirk, but Polly didn't. Although she was ignorant of Deacon Archibald's insulting label, she was keenly aware of his attitude towards her.

"Deacon, could I get you a glass of milk?" she asked. "I'm afraid milk and water are all we have. Now that the war is over, maybe we can have coffee again soon."

"Yes, ma'am, water will be fine. Thank you so very much."

Edwin knew that Archibald's attitude had not changed. But the world had. He suspected the church had as well. When Polly went back inside, Edwin asked, "Deacon, when you came out here this morning, did you know that Polly and I were married?"

"Yes."

"No congratulations?"

"Of course, Pastor. How remiss of me. I should have congratulated you before I mentioned our call for you to come as pastor."

Edwin could observe Deacon Archibald's irritation as he spoke. He was saying words that he did not mean, but protocol forced them out of his mouth. Edwin thought of Richard's delight in his encounters with Archibald. His empathy for Richard was greater than ever. Then Edwin said, "Don't be upset. It's not a big matter. By the way, Polly is expecting our first child in February."

Polly stood before the marble headstone. She thought about the strange twists her life had taken. Then she spoke, "Ann, you were right. He does need a woman's hand. I've done what you asked. I've made it my purpose for life." Edwin walked up and put his arm around Polly. They stood there quietly and meditated.

Polly remembered the pain she had endured in her marriage to Jacob Prescott and the sorrow Richard's death had inflicted. She thought about how fortunate her choice of rejecting Benjamin Larimer's proposal had been. Mostly she rejoiced in Edwin's love.

Edwin thought about the two wounds he had received in the dark woods of Chickamauga. He would never know who the two Yanks were who had fired the two shots that left him unconscious in a ditch, but if he could find them, he would shake their hands. No, he would hug them. He would tell them how indebted he was to them. Their Minie balls had brought him and Polly together.

Edwin realized God had spared his life at Sharpsburg, at Gettysburg, at Chickamauga, at Columbus, and numerous other battles. He was alive by the grace of God. Why he had survived while over 618,000 others had died, he did not know. He only could acknowledge that he was alive.

In that moment, Edwin savored life, God's gift, a tapestry of both good and bad. His once tranquil life had been washed away by the shifting tides of war. But those same tides had brought him a new future. Tragedy and joy had forged in Edwin an unpretentious, deep-seated faith in God. "Father" Edwin Anderson knew He would be with him whatever happened. *It is so good to be alive,* he thought.

ACKNOWLEDGMENTS

I AM GRATEFUL FOR THE LOVING SUPPORT AND ASSIStance of my family as I wrote this book. My wife, Pamela, proofread the rough draft of the manuscript and provided keen insight for the story's development. A conversation between her and Kristi Pennington sparked the initial idea for this story. My daughters, Anessia, Andrea, and Audrey each contributed their individual professional and personal skills to the final work. My son, Andrew, joined my mess at numerous Civil War reenactments.

In writing this novel, I wanted the fictional storyline to conform to the history of the Civil War. The imaginary characters needed to respond to actual events as well as to the fictitious narrative. Maintaining historical accuracy required the assistance of many people. Therefore, I wish to thank the members of the Columbus Guards and the First Georgia Volunteer Infantry reenactment companies for everything they taught me about soldiering in the Civil War. In addition, I want to thank the members of the American Civil War Railroads Historical Society for their unique knowledge of railroads of the period. I am also grateful to the staff of the Columbus Public Library, the Columbus State University Library, and the Emory University Library for giving me access to historical documents in their possession.

We all should appreciate the work of the National Park Service in preserving battlefields such as Antietam, Gettysburg, and Chickamauga. Touring the actual locations where the Columbus Guards fought was invaluable in describing their combat of 1862-1863.

Finally, I am grateful to Michelle Hutchinson of Wordhelper for her priceless assistance in preparing the final manuscript. Without her probing questions and literary knowledge, this book would have been less readable.

ABOUT THE AUTHOR

LeBron Matthews has been writing for biblical and theological publications for over twenty-five years. *Tides of War: A Novel of the American Civil War* is his first work of historical fiction. LeBron grew up near Chickamauga National Battlefield. As a child he listened intently as his grandmother told him about the family's experiences in "the war." These experiences created a lifelong interest in the Civil War. He became an avid student of the era and a hard-core reenactor for many years. A childhood fantasy was fulfilled when he portrayed a Confederate soldier in a living history demonstration commemorating the 140th anniversary of the Battle of Chickamauga.

LeBron served in Vietnam as an infantry soldier with the 4th Infantry Division and the 101st Airborne Division. He is a graduate of Georgia Tech and New Orleans Baptist Theological Seminary. He is a retired pastor and lives in Columbus, Georgia, with his wife Pamela.

www.ingramcontent.com/pod-product-compliance
Lightning Source LLC
Chambersburg PA
CBHW020403080526
44584CB00014B/1145